TALES FROM THE
FAST
TRAINS

EUROPE AT 186 MPH

TOM CHESSHYRE

TALES FROM THE FAST TRAINS

Summersdale Publishers Ltd
46 West Street
Chichester
West Sussex
PO19 1RP
UK

www.summersdale.com

Printed and bound in Great Britain

ISBN: 978-1-84953-151-1

Substantial discounts on bulk quantities of Summersdale books are available to corporations, professional associations and other organisations. For details contact Summersdale Publishers by telephone: +44 (0) 1243 771107, fax: +44 (0) 1243 786300 or email: nicky@summersdale.com.

p.11, extract from 'Cornish Cliffs' by John Betjeman

p.104, extract from *The Ministry of Fear* by Graham Greene

Disclaimer
Every effort has been made to obtain the necessary permissions with reference to copyright material; should there be any omissions in this respect we apologise and shall be pleased to make the appropriate acknowledgements in any future edition.

*In memory of my grandparents, Neville & Alison, and
John & Dora, train travellers from a bygone age*

ABOUT THE AUTHOR

Tom Chesshyre is staff travel writer on *The Times* and the author of *How Low Can You Go?: Round Europe for 1p Each Way (Plus Tax)* and *To Hull and Back: On Holiday in Unsung Britain*. He lives in London.

Tales from the Fast Trains

'Chesshyre… is an interesting, knowledgeable, discerning tour guide and a most genial companion'
Alexander Frater, author of *Tales from the Torrid Zone*

'transforms seemingly unsurprising familiar territory – whether the Eurostar terminal at St Pancras or the cities of Frankfurt and Antwerp – into the stage for insights and adventures'
Dea Birkett, author of *Serpent in Paradise*

To Hull and Back

'Tom Chesshyre celebrates the UK… discovering pleasure in the unregarded wonders of the "unfashionable underbelly" of Britain'
THE MAIL ON SUNDAY

'You warm to Chesshyre, whose cultural references intelligently inform his postcards from locations less travelled'
THE TIMES

CONTENTS

'People don't take trains – trains take people.'
(after John Steinbeck)

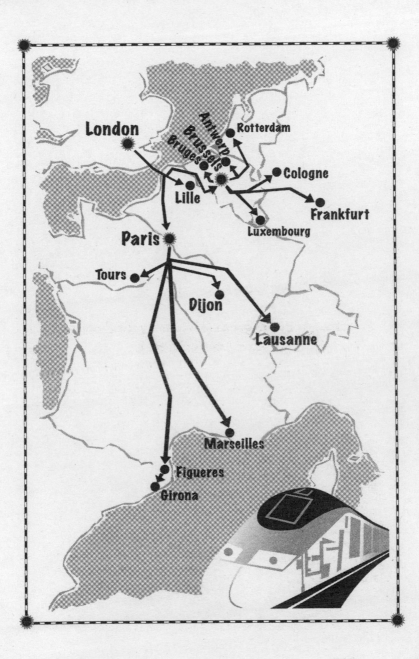

London

Antwerp
Brussels
Bruges
Rotterdam
Cologne
Lille
Frankfurt
Luxembourg

Paris

Tours
Dijon
Lausanne

Marseilles

Figueres
Girona

CHAPTER ONE

ST PANCRAS AND AWAY: 'MEET ME BY BETJEMAN'

It's a hot August morning at a bus depot in south London. There's no bus in sight; not a single vehicle, not even a driver lurking in a corner smoking a fag. Minutes tick by as the sun bakes down on a forlorn concourse dotted with blackened pieces of bubblegum and strewn with fast-food wrappers. A sign informs us (I have been joined by a kindly elderly woman with a tartan shopping trolley) that the service runs 'about every 6–10 minutes'. We wait at least a quarter of an hour before a bus arrives, driven at a rate of knots by a bald, expressionless man, his copy of the *Daily Star* wedged on the dashboard. The bus skids to a stop. We board. Then it zooms away, flashing past suburban houses, as though there's some sort of emergency. The kindly elderly woman, gripping a rail tightly, glances at me and raises her eyebrows, seeming to suggest: 'Par for the course.' Which, we know only too well, it definitely is.

And so I make it to my local Tube station, where a humid carriage full of tourists awaits. An enormous American sitting next to me is flicking through a London guidebook. She says to her companion: 'We godda go see Lee-ces-ter Square.' An unshaven fellow opposite is wearing a 'Prague Pub Crawl'

T-shirt. He looks queasy, as though he's been up all night; perhaps he's just come back from Heathrow after a stag do. A woman with a child who has been crying slaps her, inducing yet more tears (and glances of disapproval from fellow passengers). It's becoming stiflingly hot as the carriage fills and the train rolls onwards to South Kensington – as though there's not enough air to go round. Football supporters with Chelsea and Manchester United shirts join us, bringing an aroma of lager to the mix: it's the morning of their Community Shield match. Is there going to be some kind of brawl? There isn't. They're too interested in studying the Tube map, discussing which pubs to visit next.

A typical London journey: delays, discomforts, dirt, overcrowding, with a bit of tension thrown in. But then the escalator rises into St Pancras International station, and everything changes. On the way to the ticket office, I pass a stylish 'Sourced Market', all gleaming tiles, spotlights and shiny display cabinets, with baskets piled high with cucumbers, plum tomatoes, apricots and organic potatoes. There are stacks of fresh loaves, salmon fillets, couscous lunches and pesto salads, and counters filled with tubs of cheeses, salamis and chutneys. Beyond this, on a corner turning into the main run of shops, whitewashed wooden tables are waiting for customers to try out a selection of organic wines lined on neat shelves. Even though we're inside, it's light and airy. Sophisticated-looking folk in sunglasses are sipping espressos at a cafe across the way; possibly French or Italian, judging by their casual espresso-drinking ways. I walk on by, taking in an expensive chocolate shop, a Thomas Pink store (shirts £59), Rituals (purveyors of 'upmarket body toiletries'), and a florist selling £20 bunches of flowers. Everything seems well-to-do, smart and far removed from the rest of London. No 'Prague Pub Crawl' T-shirts, football supporters, piles of litter or sense of slumming it here.

I collect our tickets from a machine without a queue opposite a Body Shop, and then take another escalator to the level of the platforms.

It's quieter up by the trains. I don't venture into the champagne and oyster bar, where a couple of women are happily enjoying midday flutes of bubbly. Instead, I make my way further along to the statue of John Betjeman, who is captured gazing upwards, holding on to his hat, with his jacket flying out behind him. He's wearing rolled trousers with his feet sticking out comically. A sign gives the years of his life (1906–1984) and describes him simply as 'POET, who saved this glorious station' – Betjeman campaigned to stop St Pancras from being bulldozed in the 1960s. I look up at the pale-blue criss-crosses of the semicircular roof, completed in 1868 by the brilliant Victorian engineer William Henry Barlow. What an overwhelming sense of space; it seems impossible that the structure came so close to being destroyed. Lines from a Betjeman poem are etched in a circle on the concourse: 'And in the shadowless unclouded glare/ Deep blue above us fades to whiteness where/ A misty sea-line meets the wash of air.' It captures the feeling of the station above perfectly. And as I ponder how the lines seem to describe the scene so precisely, an American family walks by.

The child points at the statue and asks: 'What's that?'

The mother replies: 'A statue.'

The father steps forward to look more closely. 'John Betjeman,' he says.

They scratch their heads and stare at the amusing statue of the station's patron saint.

'He sure looks funny,' says the mother.

And with that they make their way towards the trains.

I'm meeting my girlfriend E by Betjeman at noon but there's no sign of her. Has she got caught up in traffic on her bus? (She lives quite close by in Shoreditch.) Did I give her the wrong time? (I can't get hold of her as her mobile seems to be switched off or out of reception.) Minutes tick by and I begin to wonder if we're going to make our train; it leaves at 1 p.m. and you've got to check in half an hour beforehand. Then I look towards the huge bronze statue depicting lovers embracing near the station clock. The statue is called The Meeting Place, and I can see E standing beneath it. I walk across.

'I just went to the big statue,' she says. 'The big romantic statue!'

'It's the wrong statue,' I point out.

She looks at me nonplussed. 'But I like this statue better,' she replies, with logic that's difficult to crack.

We take a few pictures by The Meeting Place to mark the start of our adventures: it would, admittedly, have been more romantic to meet here. Then we rush through security (no hassles, no queues, no taking off shoes or belts, no confiscated bottles of water or peculiar body scans), up a travelator, and along the platform to carriage number 12.

Soon, we're off. The train pulls away, bang on time, drawing out of Barlow's beautiful station into the August sunshine. It's a lovely day to be heading south. And the feeling of 'being on holiday', of getting away from it all, hits us immediately. Psychotic bus drivers, overheated underground carriages, crowds and London in general seem somehow distant, as though by boarding the train we've stepped into another country. North London may be outside, with its graffiti and traffic jams, but we are on our way to the Continent... already anticipating the weekend ahead.

There's a strong sense of happily not quite knowing what's coming next, as well as a realisation that these weekends have crept up on us out of the blue. You see, it's not as though we're train obsessives, or that we refuse to fly for 'green reasons'. Quite the opposite: I've always enjoyed catching flights and the sense of excitement of airports, even when departing from the dreariest terminals at Heathrow. In fact, I've always been a bit ambivalent about train travel. Yes, I quite like chugging along and watching through the window as the world passes by, but with all these cheap flights to obscure spots in Eastern Europe, sunny reaches of the Mediterranean and exotic locations halfway round the globe, I never got round to trying Eurostar.

Until, that is, I was sent to Paris on a last-minute work assignment. Eurostar had been running for almost a decade by then, and I found the experience a revelation. In just over two hours (2 hrs 15 min. to be precise) I was in the French capital, having woken up that morning expecting a run-of-the-mill day in the office. Instead, I was walking past Notre Dame and through the Latin Quarter, poking my head in patisseries and stopping at lovely old cafes that I imagined George Orwell visiting in *Down and Out in Paris and London*, one of my favourite books.

It was all so quick; so easy to get out of London and enter a totally different culture. And it made me wonder whether the hassle of airport security and catching annoying connecting shuttles into city centres at the other end was worth it. I loved the sensation of being catapulted out of Britain straight into the heart of an interesting European city. On that first trip, strolling along the Seine and visiting the serene and sprawling Père-Lachaise cemetery, seeing the graves of Oscar Wilde, Chopin, Edith Piaf and Jim Morrison between work appointments, I was totally won over. What better way to travel? The seats were much bigger on Eurostar than on easyJet or Ryanair. You could stroll about without risking the wrath of cabin crews.

You only had to arrive half an hour before departure. It just seemed so *civilised*.

Since that first experience, we've visited Ghent (a quaint Flemish city with lovely canals and a sleepy feel), Brussels (staying in a charming hotel by the Grand Place) and Amsterdam (to see the art galleries). All on speedy, lively and highly memorable weekend breaks.

But why stop there? I began to look at the high-speed map... and a plan of sorts soon formed. It was a simple plan, but I couldn't wait to get it started. I was going to explore Europe on its fast trains. Why not? The tickets were not too expensive, just £69 return to Paris or Brussels. I've paid more for journeys to Birmingham, taking about the same time as reaching Paris. And the map was full of intriguing possibilities: Dijon, Luxembourg, Bruges, Antwerp, Frankfurt, Rotterdam, Tours, Lausanne, Marseilles. Why not try a few of those?

Fast trains to Paris, Lille and Brussels began on 14 November 1994. But now you can go at 186 mph to all sorts of places, with high-speed tracks being laid down across Europe constantly. The link through the Netherlands to Amsterdam (journey from St Pancras 4 hrs 16 min.) was completed not so long ago. There are plans for connections to Italy and Spain; a link between Paris and Figueres in northern Spain recently opened, reducing the journey time by ninety minutes. You can already reach dozens of places throughout France. Not only is there the excitement and fun of catching all these new rides – there's also the sense that high-speed rail travel will be everywhere soon; that Europe will be linked by faster and faster services (200 mph trains are on their way), and that the nature of Europe itself, and how we see it and travel around it, is about to change.

It's as if Europe is shrinking by the day. The day I write this, a story in *The Sunday Times* news section declares: 'TRAINS

TO BEAT PLANES ACROSS EUROPE. IT WILL SOON BE QUICKER TO REACH MANY CITIES BY NEW HIGH-SPEED RAIL LINKS THAN BY JET: AIRPORT DELAYS AND RISING TAXES BOOST THE APPEAL OF RAIL TRAVEL.' The fast tracks seem to be conquering the Continent – we can zip about at vast speeds to places that would have been days away a century ago, major journeys, without taking to the skies. A few hours in a comfortable carriage can get you a very long way. Climb on board at St Pancras and vast swathes of land have opened up: so many places for a new type of weekend break.

So with a quiet six months ahead and a part-time job that makes long weekends for travel possible, I've decided to give it a go. I'll head off on a series of adventures: a trip every fortnight or so. It'll be an insight into places I might never have otherwise visited. It'll also – at least I hope so – turn out to be *fun*. Isn't that what a weekend break should be all about, after all?

'You're hurtling towards forty, this could be your last chance for years,' says E, seeming to relish the word 'hurtling', as the train squeals along north London tunnels in the direction of Kent.

I give her a look. E's a few years younger – a fact she loves to remind me of. 'Give me a break, love,' I reply.

'You couldn't do this with kids,' she says baldly.

I pause to take this in. I know what she's driving at, but I'm not quite sure how to answer. 'I think you could with a small child,' I say, after a bit. You could, I reckon, easily travel with a baby for a high-speed weekend – it would probably be easier than travelling by plane.

But E continues to twist the knife, enjoying her 'you'll soon be past it' line of conversation. 'This could be your last footloose summer,' she continues, warming to her theme in the strange orange light of our carriage as it passes beneath the City.

'Hmmm,' I reply.

'I mean that in a good way: let's make the most of it,' she says.

And with that she flags down a steward in a charcoal-grey uniform: we're travelling in Premium Leisure for a first-trip treat. Soon a mini bottle of Sauvignon Blanc (for E) and a burgundy (for me) are delivered.

'Here's to high-speed Europe,' says E, raising her glass.

We drink to the trip ahead, papers and guidebooks spread out on our neat table with its cute little lamp. So much better, so much more comfortable, so much more the way it should be, than on a budget plane. No sticky seats, no stag groups, no jammed knees or crunched limbs. Just a decent drop of *vin*, a fast train, and two hours to go till Paris.

The hills, haystacks, vineyards, electricity pylons and motorways of Kent soon flash past. Britain seems better when it's a bit of a blur, I'm thinking, as we cross a delightful expanse of the Medway and pass alongside the M20, watching traffic heading slowly for the ferries and the Channel Tunnel. Apple groves and cornfields spread out across the gently undulating landscape before we reach the Folkestone White Horse – a striking limestone figure of a horse with a flowing main and tail carved into a hill overlooking the tunnel's terminal. Apparently there was a great fuss when this was created by the local artist Charlie Newington in 2003 as the hill is a Site of Special Scientific Interest and nature groups opposed this Millennium project. But it looks inspiring, to me, from the train; a sort of goodbye wave to tunnel-goers, or a hello welcome to people coming in the other direction.

And then we plunge into the calming darkness, the lights flicker orange again, we level out, and I imagine all the water, all the ferries and cargo ships (and fish) up above. In a half-hour dash from St Pancras we have left Britain behind. Now we've got cod and mackerel and wrecks of old ships and many millions of gallons of water on top of carriage number 12. The train drops to 100 m below sea level at its deepest point – I know this because a 'Tunnel Trivia' section of Eurostar's *Metropolitan* magazine says so – running through the gritty chalk that stretches across the Channel.

We may have been able to do this for a decade and a half or so, since the tunnel opened, but it still feels somehow impossible. Each time I go, I can't help getting the same sensation. Are we really riding trains under the sea?

Our destination is Dijon, the capital of Burgundy; we're changing in Paris for a TGV connection onwards: TGV stands for Trains à Grande Vitesse and is the high-speed part of SNCF (French railways), which we're soon about to get to know very well. I've never been to Dijon and am curious. We read up on the city, which has a 'slick prosperity' and is an 'affluent university town: smart, modern and young', according to the *Rough Guide*. There's also a section about the golden age of the Dukes of Burgundy during the fourteenth and fifteenth centuries. 'He looks like a rum fellow,' says E, examining a picture of Philip the Bold – who appears to be wearing make-up. Our hotel is named after the first of the great dukes, Philip the Good. The *Rough Guide*'s verdict is 'some rooms stunning, others a little bland' – which sounds a bit hit or miss; the hotel had looked pretty good on the Internet.

We shoot back up above the ground into the light, settled in our grey leather seats with their purple leather headrests as French fields and flatlands that have been fought over in so many bloody battles come into view. There's an ugly plastics factory and several large pyramid-shaped piles of gravel in the approach to Lille. Feeling a little sleepy after the wine, we have a snooze and wake to find ourselves travelling through a corridor of graffiti in the *banlieue* of Paris. Bright swirls declare the names of the graffiti artists: 'YOKOK, 'BANKO' and 'DIAL'. Then we look at our watches. And something dawns on us. We've got just thirty-five minutes to reach Gare de Lyon from Gare du Nord for the onward train to Dijon. Is that enough time?

This is how we find ourselves in a taxi driven by a man who looks like a funeral director, listening to France's version of Jazz FM and speeding along Boulevard de Magenta, scattering pedestrians at every intersection. E has asked the pale-faced driver, who is dressed in a black suit and has heavy black rings under his eyes, to go *vite*. And he is not messing about. A haunting blues number is surreally playing as we make our dramatic progress. E looks at me as if I should somehow take matters in hand (what can I do? anyway, he's making good time) as we take an impressive swerve to miss a bollard, passing a bench where a kissing couple glances up, looking at the driver as though he's mad.

He clearly is. He seems to be going even faster as the music switches to a soulful rendition of a song with the line 'Every time we say goodbye, I die a little' near Place de la République. He takes the Place about as quickly as is physically possibly in an old Renault. We slide about in the back seat, seeing the world *ÉGALITÉ* inscribed at the foot of a statue of a famous figure – it's too fast to tell who. And so we reach the station, with seven minutes to spare before the TGV to Dijon. I pay the nine-euro fare. The funeral director smiles thinly, with just a hint of a twinkle in his eyes. Then we race to a distant platform in a far-off annex and board the first TGV of our trip. The doors close almost immediately behind us. 'If there'd been a queue for the taxi we would have been staying in Paris tonight,' E accurately declares. 'Don't they have a policy or something on how long you should have between trains? I mean, that was skin of the teeth stuff.'

The TGV is a smart affair with black and grey stripy seats and a wine-red carpet. We are in a silent carriage and a sign on the seat in front says: '*Merci de régler votre téléphone portable en mode vibreur*.' We slump in our seats and catch our breath for a bit. We're sitting next to a woman who quickly falls asleep with her mouth wide open like a human goldfish, and a father who is playing cards with two well-behaved children. The flick and occasional slap of a game of twist is all we can hear in the carriage as we quickly leave Paris behind. The TGV holds the world record speed for a wheeled train at 357.2 mph (achieved by a lunatic test driver in 2007), and average speeds on journeys can reach above 170 mph. This compares to the Eurostar's record speed of 208 mph, with a top speed of 186 mph and an average that varies depending on how many stops it makes.

We're soon well out of the French capital, shooting through forests with a royal blue sky above, and breaking into rolling countryside covered in a patchwork of fields. Brown cows munch grass. Villages with green-shuttered houses come and go. We stop at the town of Montbard, where there are three tattered EU flags and a French tricolour on poles by the quiet station. It looks deadly dull, and the *Rough Guide*'s verdict is of the 'pretty but otherwise unexciting hillside town of Montbard'.

E concurs: 'It doesn't look like we're missing much.'

'No, I don't think we are,' I reply – the place looks half asleep.

'Let's not add Montbard to the list,' says E. The 'list', which we're making up as we go along, is where we plan to go on our fast-train weekends. It's a moveable feast: we'll go where we fancy, always aiming for somewhere a bit different – somewhere we haven't been that sounds worth investigating (normally a little bigger than Montbard, mind you).

'OK, Montbard's out,' I say, as we pull away, soon passing wind farms and travelling along a glimmering brown river.

'Actually, love, anywhere's good with me. I just like the adventure. I'll just pack my PJs and passport: you tell me where next!' says E. In reality, though, we're planning the journeys together, poring over maps and plotting routes in pubs after work, and on our weekends 'off' our fast-train jaunts. It's that slightly random feeling of zooming away from Britain and seeing what the fast trains throw at us that I'm hoping to capture.

And with those thoughts in mind, we pull up at our first destination. *'Bienvenu à Gare de Dijon,'* says a big sign.

'I can't believe we're here, it was so quick,' says E.

It's been 1 hr 37 min. from Paris, and we are only a short taxi ride to the Philippe Le Bon hotel. It really does not feel as though we were (almost) meeting by the Betjeman statue just four and a half hours ago. We cross a modern plaza to a taxi rank, avoid a tramp reeking of one too many *vins*, and head for the hotel.

Our fast-train weekends have begun.

CHAPTER TWO

DIJON: 'KIR ROYALES WITH THE DUKES'

The streets of Dijon are quiet. Our taxi driver does not look like a funeral director this time, but he's a lover of jazz and blues too, and he zips around the narrow labyrinthine *rues* towards the Philippe Le Bon hotel at just about the same breakneck speed. As we rush along, the afternoon sun lights up the entrance to Jardin Darcy – a pretty, well-kept park with a fountain at its centre and nobody around. We skirt the park and delve southwards among magnolia-coloured buildings. The city centre seems compact, old and just the right sort of place for a weekend break. There is no traffic and soon we are on a quiet side street at the entrance to the hotel.

First impressions of the Philippe Le Bon hotel are not all that *bon*. Not *bon* at all. We cross a filthy pavement and enter an arched doorway to a drab grey building. A red sign alerts us that the hotel has three stars, though I wonder what that means in Dijon. A poster on the door, of the sort you might expect in a *tabac*, advertises a local fête. Inside, it is dimly lit and no one is about. There are a couple of red leather armchairs in a lounge, and a picture of two ballet dancers on the wall opposite the reception desk. A leaflet grandly promotes the Bar de L'Hôtel, showing a 1980s-style pink and purple room with stools and rows of bottles; but another note informs us that the bar is closed at the moment.

We wait for a while, and then a dark-haired woman arrives. She is wearing black and we can hear a TV or radio jabbering away in a back room.

'Bonjour,' I say, and ask in my schoolboy French if we can check in.

'Bonjour,' she replies, raising an eyebrow and asking for our reservation name.

Civilities complete, she is soon, in no-nonsense style, marching us back over the dirty pavement and across the tiny street to our room in a building opposite. We ascend a winding stone staircase and enter the Jean Le Bon room, named after another of Burgundy's famous dukes. There's a reproduction of an old oil painting depicting Jean Le Bon on the door, showing him with long ginger hair, a ginger beard and a big satisfied grin.

'He's a rum-looking chap as well,' comments E.

All the Burgundy dukes seem to have been characters, judging from the pictures we've seen of them so far.

'Looks like a bit of a laugh though,' she adds.

Inside, the dark-haired woman shows us a surprisingly stylish and comfortable room, which has a high ceiling with exposed beams, cream-coloured walls, a little minibar and a tiny flat-screen TV. There's a decent-sized bed, traditional French shutters on the windows and a neat bathroom. It may not be 'stunning' but nor is it 'bland', as the *Rough Guide* predicted. It feels secluded and private, like our own small apartment in the city centre. The dark-haired woman, in no-nonsense style, departs.

Then, so do we. We drop off our bags and do what you're meant to do coming up to 7 p.m. on a weekend break in the heart of one of France's most famous vineyard regions: we go in search of a wine bar. It does not take us long to find one. But along the way we quickly get a sense of Dijon city life that the tourist brochures don't tell you about. After passing an immaculate little park with benches and the grand copper-domed, sandstone building of the Museum of Burgundy Life, we come to a corner at which a boisterous group of down-at-heel drunks are putting away bottles of wine and cans of beer, gesticulating wildly in animated conversation on the steps of an old building. There is about a dozen of them, and this is obviously a favourite meeting spot: we've seen others tottering by along the side streets nearby, as well as the chap by the station's taxi rank. The shadowy pavements in this part of the town are dirty in ways better not described; it's best to walk down the middle of the roads. One man with scraggly, ginger hair (not dissimilar in appearance to Jean Le Bon on a particularly bad day) lurches our way in trousers that seem several sizes too big. He's wearing a streaky grey shirt that might once have been white, with rips and missing buttons, and saying something in an elaborate, pontificating style that sounds a bit like: 'C'est arrgh-gar: arhhh?'

We do not stop for a chat. Instead, not far along, we find ourselves turning into a beautiful little square named after one of France's most renowned nineteenth-century writers – Émile Zola, best known for his *J'Accuse* polemic defending the falsely imprisoned army officer Alfred Dreyfus. There's a fair bit of modern-day debate, and general chatter, in the square. It's buzzing with life, with chairs and tables spread out under sycamore trees and smart locals gossiping away. There's a restaurant named Les Moules Zola, where elegant diners are piling into great mounds of mussels at tables with neat white tablecloths, a fun-looking Pizz' Zola, a Sushi King and a bar called Les Aviateurs, outside which folk in leather are drinking beers from little glasses, with rock music filtering out into the square. Place Émile Zola – the writer never in fact lived in Dijon – feels lively and very very French (as I suppose it would do in the centre of France). There do not appear to be many tourists around: we don't spot any guidebooks or maps. It's a balmy evening and we stroll to the far side of the square, where we find Le Chabrot. This pitches itself as a '*bar à vin*'; which sounds just about right.

Having polished off huge baguettes not so long ago on the train, our priority is wine. '*À toute vitesse*', as E says – which I take to mean quickly (her French is much better than mine). We sit down at a table with a pink tablecloth. At the next table, a middle-aged man with a goatee, who looks as though he could be a poet or a philosopher, is very thoughtfully sipping a soup. The bar and restaurant is named after the practice of '*faire chabrot, mettre le vin dans la soupe*'; i.e. mixing wine into soup. The poet-philosopher seems to be intently enjoying his soup with wine. I've never seen a soup of any sort so thoughtfully and lovingly consumed. But we order something a little different.

The waitress delivers two glasses of Kir, the cocktail of nine parts white wine and one part blackcurrant liqueur that can be served with champagne instead of wine, when it's known as Kir Royal. It's one of E's favourite drinks, and I'd read on the train that it was invented in Dijon, where it was named after a local post-World War Two mayor named Felix Kir. He had been a great pioneer of the twinning of towns and he used the cocktail to show off both the local wine and crème de cassis at the same time when foreign dignitaries visited. The drink is said to have been invented during the war when the Nazis confiscated almost all of Burgundy's red wine. Locals tired of white wine alone, experimented and created the new mix, which was later popularised thanks to Felix Kir, with his foreign visitors taking the drink's fame around the world.

Seldom can a tipple have had such an unusual past. We raise our glasses and try our cocktails. They taste great, and it's wonderful just to relax after the day's travelling; not that it's been an especially testing day, other than the crazy dash across Paris.

'Steady on, it's strong stuff, love,' says E, noticing me knock back my glass a little swiftly. The poet-philosopher, who seems to be a kind of ghost of Zola, glances over and smiles our way (he obviously understands English). Kir does taste a bit like a grown-up version of Ribena and it's easy to swig it down.

'Are you sure?' I reply, finding it hard to believe that a drink that reminds me of school lunches and childhood can be too potent.

'It's something like forty per cent,' she says vaguely, though I'm pretty sure she's just making that up, and I can't tell if she's being serious or not.

'Just wait till you stand up,' she says, smiling. And as she says this she mimics me gulping down a glass and wobbling about.

Nevertheless, we both finish our glasses of Kir pretty quickly: it's not really a drink that lasts long, whatever E says. We ask for the wine list, and a substantial tome in a red leather cover, as big as a reasonably sized phone directory, is brought over and almost lovingly presented to us. 'Now that's what I call a wine list,' says E, as we flick through the many pages, settling on glasses of Bourgogne Hautes-Côtes de Beaune 2003, a white wine. This costs seven euros each but we might as well push the boat out in Burgundy. The stuff would probably be £10 a glass in a fancy bar back in London.

Time slips by pleasantly looking across a narrow cobbled street with a bus stop, towards the crowds at the tables under the sycamore trees in the centre of the square. We make a plan for tomorrow, using the guidebook and the map. Then we have our first, and we hope last, near-death experience on our fast-trains adventure.

A bus has stopped to pick up passengers, blocking the street. E is in the middle of an involved second glass of Bourgogne Hautes-Côtes de Beaune 2003 discussion about the wine. 'It's complex,' she says, swilling the wine about. 'It talks to you afterwards.'

'Really,' I say, examining my glass.

'I'm not drunk,' she continues. 'Not at all. What you can really taste is the sunshine. The sunshine in the wine!'

As she says this her eyes widen, and get wider, and just as she is trying to say something a moped speeds by on the pavement from behind me – fast – the air brushing my shoulder. An inch or so closer and it would not have been a pretty sight outside Le Chabrot on Place Émile Zola. Tables would have tumbled, delicious wine-soups and wines would have spilled. European Health Insurance Cards, ours at least, would have been called into action.

'Good lord! It was coming straight at us,' says E.

The Ghost of Zola, who is in the middle of an elaborate fish dish, raises both bushy eyebrows, mutters 'ooh la la', and whistles faintly; though he doesn't seem all that surprised. The moped rider, who was helmet-less and about sixteen years old, disappears in a cloud of exhaust fumes around a corner.

It's getting dark; the sun seems to go down fast round here (as does the wine, we're beginning to notice). We finish our glasses 'to steady our nerves', and order a couple more: why not, we're on holiday in Burgundy after all? Anyway it's good research, all this wine-tasting.

'It's good research,' I say, speaking my thoughts.

'Very good,' says E, selecting a Viognier.

The beaming waitress brings our wines. Zola gives us a smile, and orders another glass of red for himself while the waitress is about.

A half hour or so passes by as we discuss the state of the world. 'Another?' I ask, flicking through the pages of the huge red list.

'It would be rude not to,' replies E.

'It's excellent research,' I say.

'Yes, excellent,' E agrees.

Time slides by once more, without further near-death experiences, looking out across the sycamores of Dijon's Place Émile Zola, drinking our fine Burgundy wine. Then we settle the bill, wave goodbye to Zola (with whom we seem to have made friends), and walk along the lanes that don't seem so dirty any more, and past the down-and-outs who don't seem as noisy as they were earlier, to the Philippe Le Bon hotel. We've got a day and a half of discovering Dijon ahead and already we're happily in the fast-train weekend groove.

'Everything is only a dream,' Zola once wrote, and it feels a bit like that when we wake in the unfamiliar surroundings of our pitch-black shuttered room, with its high ceiling and purple curtains in the backstreets of the capital of Burgundy. We eat a breakfast of croissants and wedges of fresh baguette with jam in a basement dining room decorated with strange pieces of multicoloured art made from bamboo. From here, we walk towards the cathedral along cobbled streets; the city is compact and really quite small for an administrative centre of a *département*: in this case, the Côte d'Or. The city limits have a population of about 151,000 people, while the greater Dijon area is more like 240,000. The result is a sleepy feel, especially as it's quite early on a Saturday morning during the French holiday season. There are one or two dog walkers and a few folk returning from *boulangeries* with baguettes in paper wrappers tucked under their arms. 'The rule in France is you've got to get your bread early,' comments E, who worked for a few summers at a chateau in France when she was a teenager. 'If you wait till after midday, it's hopeless.'

We pause at an *immobilier*, which is offering four-bedroom houses for €483,000 and two-bedroom flats for €230,000 – not steep by London standards, but still pretty pricey. We stroll up Rue Monge, passing the fine cream-stone church of St Jean, with its mini-spires and dome. The road takes us up an incline to the grand façade of the Palais des Ducs, where the Dukes of Burgundy had their headquarters in medieval times. It's another perfect, cloudless day. The blue of the sky almost matches the blue of the tricolours hanging at the front of the palace, which these days acts as the town hall and also houses the Musée des Beaux-Arts. We take in a *Produits Régionaux* gift shop near the entrance, where 'I LOVE DIJON' T-shirts are on sale for €16 and little pots of the famous local mustard for one euro. There are also extraordinarily complicated-looking wine-tasting kits retailing for €290, *pain d'épices* gingerbreads flavoured with fig and apricot (a local speciality, six euros), and boxes for making Kir and Kir Royal, consisting of crème de cassis, champagne and Bourgogne Aligoté, considered the best wine to use in making Kir (€35). It feels like a tourist trap... yet there are only a couple of other tourists about.

Which is perfect. On these high-speed weekends, we're not intending to have high-speed dashes about the places at the end of the lines. The whole point seems to me to go fast out of Britain, so you can go slow when you arrive. Along the way, we're hoping to stumble across places of interest; we're not planning heavy itineraries or fixing appointments in advance. The point is simply to 'be a tourist' and see what happens. And when it's quiet, that just makes everything easier. These tales from the fast trains will – I hope – form a series of serendipitous discoveries. I want us to have chance encounters and finds: the good and the not-so-good, whatever comes our way.

So 'being tourists' in Dijon, we buy tickets for the Musée des Beaux-Arts. We know next to nothing about the museum as we cross a cobbled courtyard with an old well in a corner and enter; maybe it's going to be one of those places you walk swiftly round in twenty minutes. We quickly establish it isn't.

There are rooms packed with delicate white marble figurines of ethereal angels and saints. There are rooms full of ancient Egyptian artefacts – mummies, funeral masks, pieces of hieroglyphics – collected by the local Egyptologist Albert Gaget (1856–1916). There are rooms devoted to the works of another local, the sculptor François Pompon (1855–1933), who made a name for himself with his works depicting the animal kingdom: funny little wild boars, sleek panthers, peculiar pelicans, oxen, owls, polar bears, and much else. Most of the works are in white stone and the effect is of entering some sort of weird white motionless zoo, with delightful finds at every turn.

The museum is a warren of curious corridors and side rooms. It's not on the scale of a Louvre or a National Gallery – which gives it charm. We enter a room with oil paintings including a superb work entitled '*Paysage*' by Charles-François Daubigny (1817–1878), a Parisian painter who I have to admit I've never heard of before. It shows a rolling French landscape of the type we saw out of the window of the TGV, dark greens and deep browns beneath a pearly grey sky.

'Every stroke is amazing,' says E, peering close to the frame. 'It must have taken him months.'

There's an arresting picture by another artist I didn't know of, the Swiss painter Félix Vallotton (1865–1925), capturing a young woman wearing pink and brushing her hair in a bedroom with clothes scattered on an armchair and a double bed with a ruffled blanket in a corner. You cannot see the woman's face as her hands are held to her head. Light blazes across her bedroom and it feels as though there is a mystery at the heart of the painting. The title is 'Doing Own's Hair Woman' – at least that's what the display caption says.

There are works by Cézanne showing vibrant country scenes, mesmerising pictures by Monet depicting the cliffs by sun-dappled seas in Normandy, and paintings of women in twisty poses by Edouard Manet. What's so nice about the place is a) we're among only a handful of people looking around, b) it's not grand and pretentious in the way so many art galleries can be, and c) there are amazing works just about everywhere you look, even in hidden away corners.

Not far from a lift shaft in a narrow corridor leading downwards on a slope to another level, we stop to try to get our bearings (we have no idea where we are). As we look at our museum map, trying to make sense of things, we notice a small bronze sculpture on a funny little shelf. It depicts a nude woman on a rock, holding her hands behind her neck, through tumbling hair – looking as though she is lazily and happily stretching upwards. E examines the panel. 'Oh my God, it's a Rodin!' she says. The display reads: 'Auguste Rodin (1840–1917), La Toilette de Venus, 1885.' It really is beautiful. Here we are in a funny passageway in an obscure corner of the museum and there are masterpieces tucked away on dusty shelves – almost looking as though they've been forgotten. In some galleries this would surely be the star attraction, carefully positioned in pride of place for all visitors to see; but not in the delightfully quirky Musée des Beaux-Arts in Dijon.

The best is yet to come. After stopping at an eye-catching picture of a Flemish landscape painted by Jan Breughel the Elder in the early seventeenth century – the detail of tiny countryside figures in the foreground strangely reminds me of the works of industrial scenes by L. S. Lowry, with his matchstick characters walking about the gritty streets of Manchester and Salford – we reach a grand room containing the tombs of the Dukes of Burgundy.

There are tourists here, mainly French, peering at the ornate tombs of two of the great dukes who ruled during the medieval heyday of Burgundy from the 1360s to 1477, when the dukes' influence was important across the Low Countries of Belgium and the Netherlands as well as this part of France. The tombs are fabulously decorated, made out of marble sculpted into lions and angels, with side panels showing monks lurking in carved hollows. The first belongs to Philip the Bold, who, we learn from a museum display, married Margaret of Flanders, soon to become the richest heiress in Europe after the death of her father, the Count of Flanders. It was this marriage that united the region and led to a golden age for Burgundy, during which Dijon, Philip the Bold's favourite town, was built up, creating the pretty historic centre that remains today. The fortune of Burgundy at the time was also aided by money from France, as Philip (clearly a smooth operator) acted as regent for the mad French king Charles VI, who was his nephew, and who had taken the throne at the age of eleven.

He was succeeded by John the Fearless – the second tomb. John the Fearless seems to have been a thoroughly unpleasant chap, known for his fits of anger and for his scheming in the court of France, where he also exerted influence while Charles VI remained incapable of running the country. He made contact with the court of Henry V in the run-up to the French defeat at the Battle of Agincourt, and it was not quite known where his allegiances lay. His life came to an end after fifteen years in charge with an axe to the back of his head, delivered by one of the French king's advisers.

It's difficult not to get caught up in the intrigue of the time, standing amid the tombs, with portraits of the dukes gazing down from the walls. It's not dry and boring – the stories from the time seem to come alive in the echoing chamber, as though medieval phantoms are among us. You get a real sense of history just being in the room. If one place can be said to be the spiritual centre of Dijon, we definitely feel we've found it here.

There were four principal dukes during the glory days of Burgundy. Nasty John (with his nasty end) was succeeded by Philip the Good. Perhaps he was chosen by our hotel owner because he was the most libertine and flamboyant of the dukes – marrying three times, having many mistresses (and at least seventeen illegitimate children), enjoying banquets, music and generally having a fine old life. The Burgundy dukes of the period were great patrons of the arts and, as a museum display says: 'The four dukes, especially Philip the Bold and Philip the Good, lavishly displayed their wealth, attracted artists, musicians and men of letters, built palaces, founded religious institutions and amazed their contemporaries by staging extravagant festivities… in the late Middle Ages the Court of Burgundy became the court of courts.'

Philip the Good was another canny operator, choosing to recognise England's Henry V as the future king of France, and handing over Joan of Arc, who had been stirring up French nationalist opinion, to the English. For this, he received 10,000 gold crowns. Later, he cunningly returned his sympathies to the French, while doing so establishing the Duchy of Burgundy, with Dijon as the capital.

The result was that by the time he was succeeded in 1467 by his son Charles the Bold, things were looking very rosy indeed in Burgundy. But they weren't for long. Charles was a pugnacious character, who had inherited his father's love of the good life but ran the dukedom, which had become probably the wealthiest state in Europe, in the spirit of machismo. He rubbed up the wrong way against Louis XI of France. There were pointless wars. Money began to run out. Eventually, Charles was killed on the battlefield in 1477, and Burgundy was carved up between the French and the Hapsburgs.

The glory days of Burgundy were over, just over 500 years ago. Now the former dukedom is just part of another French *département*. But the pride in that time is still clearly strong in its capital – if all the hotels, cafes and bars named after the four grand dukes are anything to go by.

E and I inspect the dukes' portraits. These hang on a far wall. They certainly were a curious-looking lot. E has a field day with Philip the Bold, who sits in profile with his bulbous nose poking out and his raised eyebrows. He's wearing a bejewelled tunic and looking quite smug.

'He sure likes his lippy, this one,' says E. Indeed, he does appear to be wearing lipstick. 'And look at those eyebrows. Don't tell me those are natural. Look at those arches.'

I take a closer look at Philip the Bold's eyebrows, and say: 'Hmmm,' as I've no idea what else to say.

'What's going on there?' she wonders out loud, referring to Philip the Bold, before switching her attention to John the Fearless: 'Look at this one: he's a right little dandy!'

'Here we have Fearless John with his jewels and his pearls,' she continues. 'Don't you think that's a funny dress he's wearing?'

We move on to Philip the Good, who seems relatively normal, with limited jewellery and not a hint of lipstick, and to Charles the Bold, who has ragged red hair and is solemnly holding a sword... the source of the Burgundy downfall.

After this burst of culture, we step out into the narrow streets of Dijon at the back of the Palais des Ducs. It's a scorcher of a day now – the temperature must be up to 30°C. We potter about and stop by a group of people staring at a stone carved in the shape of an owl. It's attached to the cream-coloured north wall of the church of Notre Dame, and tourists are reaching up and rubbing the owl, which looks a bit worn down by all the attention. There's an English-speaking guide, who we overhear saying: 'You must rub with your left hand. Not your right!' Someone had been attempting to rub with his right hand. 'You must rub with your left hand as it is closest to your heart. That will bring you luck. That is our tradition in Dijon, dating back from the fifteenth century.' The old dukes, in their dresses, jewels and lipstick, probably had a go themselves.

E and I rub the owl with our left hands, catching a bit more of the tour guide's spiel: 'Somebody destroyed the owl in 2001. This is now an almost perfect replica. We were very sad it was destroyed. Perhaps, it was done by someone whose wish didn't work out.' The tour guide crosses the street in the direction we are going and we find ourselves in front of a building marked in our guidebook as being the Hôtel de Vogue, dating from the Renaissance. The building has an ornate roof made out of shiny gold, green, brown and black tiles aligned in symmetrical shapes. It's a very unusual roof, and we overhear the tour guide say: 'Such roofs are a speciality of our region. In the past they showed the prestige of the family living there. The designs are said to come from inspiration picked up from the Middle East – Lebanon, Syria and Israel – during the Crusades. Such tiles are really expensive. If you look at them at the right angle, they glint like gold.'

We copy the group of tourists and look at the tiles at the right angle. They do indeed glint like gold.

'Now I'm an expert on the roofs of Burgundy,' says E, deadpan. 'How about a coffee?'

We do, but first we pass by the church of Notre Dame, with its columns, vaulted ceiling and rows of seats that look more like dinner table chairs than pews. E puts a fifty-cent piece in a tin and lights a little *cierge* (candle) near the altar. It's a peaceful spot and it's strange to think that yesterday around this time we were on our way to St Pancras.

Sitting at a table in the sunshine outside a cafe called Le Jacquemart, we look around. There's still a slow, soporific feel to Dijon; even though it's midday now there are not really many people about. We drink good coffees bought from a waiter who seems pleased to have tourists (not just locals) as customers, and consult a brochure we picked up at the church entitled *Dijon, The Owl's Trail: Let The Owl Show You The Town!* This slender publication highlights the main sights, which you can see by following metal owl symbols bolted to the pavements. There is a page on the church of Notre Dame, which is from the twelfth century, predating the most famous dukes. Philip the Bold left his mark on the structure, we read, by adding a clock known as the Jacquemart to the top of the church tower. The clock was 'a war spoil' taken from Coutrai, now in north-west Belgium, and it depicts a man, known as Jacquemart, smoking a pipe, and his wife Jacqueline. These bronze figures strike the bell on the hour, sending a distinctive echoing clang across the sandstone buildings of the city centre.

The booklet also tells the sad story – possibly a legend – of an unlucky man who went to get married at the church in the thirteenth century. As he stepped up to the entrance, a stone gargoyle crumbled and fell from an awning, killing him instantly.

There was an outcry and all the gargoyles were removed, replaced many centuries later by a sculptor whose masonry was better trusted.

'The poor guy,' says E, looking up at the new gargoyles.

'Not the best way to go,' I agree.

And then we find out about mustard. It's impossible to visit Dijon without learning about its world famous creamy mustard. Our guidebook explains that Burgundy produces '80 per cent of all condiments in France' (a useful stat to add sparkle to any dinner party), and that there are six factories producing mustard, although 90 per cent of the mustard seed used comes from Canada (another sparkling mustard fact).

'Fascinating,' says E, when I read this out. 'Truly fascinating.'

Apparently the 'high temple' of mustard is just round the corner on Rue de la Liberté at a shop called Maille, which we walk over to, discovering the first genuinely busy tourist sight in the city. A sign on the outside explains that Antoine Maille opened his first mustard shop in 1747. The façade of the shop is decorated in gold and black lettering and the shiny window reveals a collection of ceramic antique mustard pots as well as modern versions you can buy.

It quickly becomes clear that there is more to Dijon mustard than, well, just mustard. For a start, there appears to be no end to different flavours. Great shelves are stacked with pots of blackcurrant, parsley, basil, green pepper, honey, cognac, fig and coriander varieties. There are even curry-and-coconut and seaweed-and-rose-petal flavours (if you fancy trying something more outlandish). A display explains that for each season of the year four different types of mustard are tried out on the public as part of an *édition limitée*. The latest concoctions include lemon and alfalfa, tomato and garlic, fennel, and violet and rose petals. Apparently the best selling of the four mustards tested is then kept on, extending the wild and wonderful shelves full of flavours. I buy a pot of 'Dijon Vin Blanc' mustard (€12), which is poured into a ceramic pot from a tap that looks a bit like a beer pump, from a woman who tells me: 'This is the most popular.'

'Why is it pumped out like this?' I ask.

'Because in the old days you would have your ceramic pot, and you would have it refilled. One pot per family,' she explains, before adding: 'We sell about 40,000 kilos of mustard every year.'

Which sounds like a whole lot of mustard.

She explains a bit about the history of the company, which dominates the Dijon mustard market along with Amora, another brand. 'Antoine Maille discovered the secrets of vinegar distillation and mustard making,' she says, handing over my pot. 'And he gained the trust of the public. Soon he was named vinegar maker and distiller to their imperial majesties in Austria and Hungary. Later, he supplied the King of France and Empress Catherine II of Russia.'

His reputation was sealed, and subsequent generations of Mailles kept up the family tradition, though it's now owned by Unilever. Unfortunately for Dijon, there is no European Union law protecting the use of the term 'Dijon mustard', as there is protecting champagne and Parma ham, the friendly assistant tells me. So most of the production takes place outside of Dijon; though there are several local factories.

'Now I'm an expert on mustard!' says E, as we leave. 'That and the dukes and the roofs of Dijon, all in one day!'

The things you discover on a high-speed weekend break.

Afterwards, we wander about the streets, taking in the distinguished façade of Hôtel de la Cloche, a fine old building dating from 1884, near the station. We go inside and find a grand lobby with a huge chandelier and reproductions of the portraits of the Golden Age dukes on the walls (there's no escaping them). It's now part of the Sofitel chain and it was originally opened for train passengers travelling from Paris to the French Riviera – when trains weren't so fast and the journey was best broken up with a stop along the way. We learn this from a hotel brochure in the stylish bar, where we consider having a lunchtime Kir Royal (until we see the price: €18 a glass).

Each of the rooms at Hôtel de la Cloche is named after a local wine, and many of its guests are on wine tours of the region – so says a receptionist. She hands us a list of room rates: €200 a night for the cheapest double. It's twice the price of the Philippe Le Bon (which we've grown very fond of, in our funny apartment-room), but you can understand why people will pay extra for here. There's a real sense of the excitement and grandeur of the early days of train travel in the hotel, which appears to have been given a modern makeover, while retaining all the old touches. Grace Kelly, Maurice Chevalier, Auguste Rodin and Napoleon III, among many other famous people, have all stayed, according to the receptionist.

'Next time here, eh?' says E, raising an eyebrow.

The hotel feels almost frozen in time… and it gives pause for thought. Catching trains around France used to be an extremely glamorous affair and station hotels like this are living proof of what that time must have been like (if all the glitz of Hôtel de la Cloche is anything to go by). Looking around the lobby, it's hard not to imagine what might happen if fast-train travel really does pick up across the Continent. Are we on the verge of a return to those glitzier times? Will we all soon be zooming around Europe on faster and faster trains, stopping off at modern-day versions of the Hôtel de la Cloche along the way? Is a whole new world of travel about to open up?

Perhaps. But we've got a city to explore. We exit down the grand steps of the hotel and stroll along to the Jardin Darcy, passing a sculpture of a polar bear we recognise as being created by François Pompon, whose collection we'd seen earlier at the art gallery. We're becoming experts on Dijon art! We continue along to the eighteenth-century Porte Guillaume, an arch with a plaque with a bust of Thomas Jefferson at its base, celebrating the 220th anniversary of the French Revolution and bearing the words: '*Symbole de l'Amité Franco-Américaine.*' We look into the Romanesque stone church of Saint Philibert, which was used a storage room for salt during the French Revolution. And then we catch a TGV train twenty minutes southwards to Beaune, otherwise known as the 'wine capital' of Burgundy.

We're going for an impromptu afternoon trip (why not, we'd thought, when passing the station and seeing a train was about to depart?). Tourism may be going slowly in Dijon, but it's booming in Beaune. The speedy train ride is through landscapes covered in neat green strips of vineyards, and we are soon amid pleasant squares with agreeable cafes and restaurants in an ancient walled town full of shops selling wine and streets packed with holidaymakers. After the quiet atmosphere of Dijon – which we've both loved – it's almost a shock to the system. Americans pass by saying: 'Gee, I think the wine museum must be that way, I'm not sure.' Well-to-do Brits head to shops with '*visite gratuite dégustation*' advertised outside. Local women walk poodles in the shade of plane trees in the squares. Queues stretch out of *boulangeries*. People pull cases towards the Hôtel des Ducs de Bourgogne. E says: 'Oh no, they're after us again!' She's referring to the dukes, not the tourists.

The main attraction, other than the wine, is the Hôtel-Dieu de Beaune, a charitable almshouse dating from the time of the rule of Philip the Good. We enter and find ourselves in a courtyard surrounded by buildings with familiar multicoloured roofs.

'It's the roofs again!' says E, who clearly has a thing about the roofs of Burgundy.

Inside, we see the rows of tiny beds that elderly folk in need of help used to sleep in, and we slightly wonder whether the entry fee was a touch steep (six euros each). But then we step into a crowded, darkened room with a picture on the far wall. It is a version of 'The Last Judgement' by the fifteenth-century Dutch painter Rogier van der Weyden. It's absolutely beautiful, painted in vivid golds, pinks, greens and reds, with Christ at the top, the Archangel Michael in the centre, making his decisions with the help of scales he's holding, and little naked human figures either heading to the right to a fiery hell, or to the left to a golden door leading to heaven. There is something captivating about the picture, which runs over nine panels: a style of religious painting known as a polyptych. We stand amid the bustle (the room is totally packed), looking at the lovely work of art and almost feeling as though the characters are coming alive; the expressions look so real, the agony of those condemned and the ecstasy of those 'saved'. It's quite a painting.

Feeling as though that picture alone has made coming to Beaune worthwhile, we go out into the main square. One of the great pleasures of Beaune is its many upmarket wine merchants; all of which offer free tastings. It's not the wine capital of Burgundy for nothing. We find a posh place on a corner of the square, in which sparkling bell-shaped glasses are placed on old barrels. Almost before we know what's going on, a bald *sommelier* presents us with a red wine from the nearby Nuits St Georges vineyard, smiles and says: *'A votre santé!'*

We sip our drinks, looking out at the baking streets. But it's cool in here, with air conditioning softly whirring and the bald shop-owner poised to offer us another sample. If you played the game, you could make a good afternoon of trying all the *visite gratuite dégustations* of Beaune – and probably not even have to put your hand in your pocket once.

We stay for another. From his demeanour, the *sommelier* really doesn't seem to mind if we sit around here all afternoon. It's really rather splendid, sitting by the barrels with our glasses and watching the world go by.

After buying three bottles of red, neatly boxed up by our friend, we zoom back on the TGV to Dijon for an evening in Place Émile Zola, where it's another busy, sultry night on the square. I eat delicious *beef bourguignon,* a regional dish, while E has a salad, at a restaurant with crisp white tablecloths. And, of course, we sample some more wine.

'This is definitely a cheeky place to knock back a vino,' says E, sipping a crisp white Bourgogne Aligoté.

'Very cheeky indeed,' I reply, enjoying a delightfully smooth Mâcon red. Without really intending to, but with a sense of inevitability after our first night, we've learnt plenty about the wines of Burgundy. Well, I suppose it would be churlish not to.

'Have you enjoyed Dijon?' I ask E.

'I've loved it,' she says, taking another sip. 'I expected it to be industrial and full of factories. I don't know why: I just did. I like it because it's normal. It's just French people going about their lives.'

As she says this, as if to prove it, a group of children rushes by. Place Émile Zola certainly feels very laid back and normal.

'That's what I like,' she adds. 'It's not terribly trendy like Paris. It's just a nice place to come for a couple of days.'

I agree. There's been plenty to see and do, it's relaxed, there are lots of nice things to eat and drink. But almost more than all of that, the sensation of arriving by train – of speeding in on the fast tracks, without seeing an airport waiting lounge – has made the trip feel like a proper break from the moment we met at St Pancras. From the off, it's been totally different to flying somewhere. Somehow, and it's difficult to quite know exactly how or why, it feels as though we've got to know Dijon much better than if we'd arrived by plane. It just does.

In the morning, before catching our midday train home, we do one thing we could not fit in yesterday: an early morning dip in Lac Kir... named after the cocktail-loving mayor.

The lake is not far from the station, a few minutes by taxi, and soon we find ourselves by a sandy artificial beach with a handful of sunbathers already reclining on towels. There's a row of white changing huts with little A-shaped roofs painted blue – free to use and spotlessly clean. It's a superb morning. Across the still, green water weeping willows line the far bank, where there's a small park and a hill dotted with houses between trees. No one is in the water, and the early morning sun is just the right temperature. A few brown ducks paddle across the middle of the lake, beyond buoys marking the safe swimming limit. Kids are bouncing basketballs at a nearby court. Joggers have stopped by a set of climbing frames and are doing various vigorous stretches and pull-ups. A couple cycles by on a tandem bike. It seems amazing that such a peaceful spot could be so close to the centre of town, and it makes us think the quality of life in these parts is really very good indeed.

It's got wines. It's got history (we'll never forget the Dukes of Burgundy). It's got stunning galleries and sleepy cafes and lovely old squares. It's got terrific lakes that feel as though they're deep in the countryside, even though they're right by the centre of town and the station.

We swim out through the fresh cool water to a platform and lie in the sunshine. What a perfect way to relax before the journey ahead. This afternoon we'll be back in the heart of London, after watching the French landscape zoom by... and we're looking forward to the ride.

CHAPTER THREE

ANTWERP: 'DIAMOND DESTINATION'

We're on our way to Antwerp, and we're stuck. After a screech of metal and a judder, our train has drawn to a halt in the middle of the Channel Tunnel. The lights have dimmed so we can't read our papers, and there is complete silence (other than the gentle tapping of a keyboard somewhere close by).

It has been a grey day back in Britain. The lorries driving along the M20 towards the ferry port had looked forlorn under a low-hanging sky. There seemed to be more electricity pylons than usual in Kent. It was drizzly, damp and generally depressing. It's funny how the weather in Britain can have such an effect on your outlook, we'd been thinking, as the train sped downwards to the tunnel. Even the security staff back at St Pancras had been grumpy. A stony-faced woman in a charcoal-grey uniform had for no good reason barked: 'ARE YOU WEARING A BELT?' The tone of voice and general body language seeming to suggest: 'Move along you idiots. I hate this job, I hate my life and, more than any of that right now: I hate you!' At least that was the way it seemed to us.

And now this. After a long pause, a voice comes on over the scratchy speaker system: 'Please do not attempt to exit any doors!' There's another pause. And the voice continues: 'We apologise for this stop. We are trying to find out the reasons.'

A few minutes tick by in the feeble light, with all those thousands of fish and gallons of water above. It's the end of August, just a fortnight after we last passed through this way, coming back from Dijon.

'Unfortunately there is now a power supply problem in the Channel Tunnel. That explains why the lights have been dimmed,' says a gravelly voice. The speaker clicks off, and there is quiet under the Channel.

More minutes pass by. E gives me a quizzical look. During a very cold spell last winter, trains broke down in the tunnel, leaving more than 2,000 passengers stuck inside for several hours. The problem was blamed on the chilly weather causing an electrical failure. Some of the journeys between Paris and London lasted fifteen hours.

It had definitely not been fast trains then. Are we about to go through something terrible like that now? No. After ten minutes, the lights flicker back on. The gravelly voice says: 'As you can see, we now have power back up. Apologies for the stop.' The train creaks forwards to Brussels, where we are to catch a short connecting service to Antwerp. We soon pick up pace though, zooming out of the tunnel into the familiar French countryside, which looks somehow reassuring, even if it is grey and flat and misty.

I settle back, reading a copy of *The Independent* that I found on a seat back in St Pancras. I can't recall ever actually buying a copy of *The Independent*. But perhaps I should, as there's an interesting interview with Michael O'Leary, the outspoken chief executive of Europe's largest airline, headlined: 'GLOBAL WARMING? IT DOESN'T EXIST, SAYS RYANAIR BOSS O'LEARY.'

In this interview – 'littered with expletives', we are warned at the beginning (making us want to read on) – the motor-mouthed chief executive describes the scientific consensus that man-made pollution is contributing to global warming that could cause major problems as 'horseshit'. He continues: 'Nobody can argue that there isn't climate change. The climate's been changing since time immemorial. Do I believe there is global warming? No, I believe it's all a load of bullshit.' The horses being dropped for bulls all of a sudden. 'But it's amazing the way the whole ****ing eco-warriors and the media have changed. It used to be global warming, but now, when global temperatures haven't risen in the past twelve years, they say "climate change".' He goes on to claim that scientists predict global warming simply to secure funding, and that 'The scientific community has always been wrong in history anyway. In the Middle Ages, they were going to excommunicate Galileo because the entire scientific community said the Earth was flat... I mean, it is absolutely bizarre that the people who can't tell us what the ****ing weather is next Tuesday can predict with absolute precision what the ****ing global temperatures will be in a hundred years' time. It's horseshit.' The horses making their triumphant return.

We're reading this in the suburbs of Brussels, as rows of tall, narrow buildings with terracotta roofs come into view and we pass an Erotic Discotheque with a lurid purple façade covered with pictures of dancers and graffiti on a wall that says 'STOP EXPULSIONS'. What expulsions is not clear, although perhaps it's a message aimed at French bureaucrats working at the city's European Commission HQ – France having controversially begun expelling Roma gypsies not so long ago.

'What a ranter,' says E, glancing at the newspaper. 'O'Leary sure knows how to rant.'

'He sure does,' I reply, flicking through the article, in which he goes on to criticise increases on flight taxes, saying that aviation gets a 'crap deal'. A Greenpeace spokeswoman is quoted as saying: 'Personally, I wouldn't trust 'O'Really' to tell me the price of a seat on his own airline.'

We slide into Brussels Midi station. On a wall near the connections escalator that we're about to take, there's a Eurostar sign boasting of 'ten eco efforts' it has been making, including measures such as recycling waste on trains and 'recycling staff uniforms'.

'Is that the best idea?' asks E. 'It sounds a bit like laundry dodging.'

Travelling into Europe by train does feel 'green' and ecologically sensible... not that that's the point of these journeys. Eurostar says that its trains are 90 per cent cleaner regarding carbon emissions than planes, and the company is committed to cutting its overall emissions beyond tight targets that have already been met – there are all sorts of statistics proving the brilliant eco credentials of trains in the free magazine in the seat pocket. Reading O'Leary's defence of planes, while rolling into a station covered in loud claims that rail travel is the way forward to save the planet, it almost feels as though we are in the middle of a debate. Planes versus high-speed trains: where does the future lie? In terms of eco considerations, it would appear with the latter: not only does research show that planes are 90 per cent dirtier, they also pump out gases directly into the upper atmosphere, where scientists say it is 2.7 times more damaging. A train journey from London to Paris emits 6.6 kg of carbon dioxide per passenger, according to Eurostar, while each passenger on a plane on this route is responsible for 103 kg, and this is without the 2.7 multiplying factor taken into consideration.

Should we care about being green? If we do, are the current excessive levels of flights and emissions, no matter what O'Leary says, going to be a thing of the past? Will we look back on this period of history, with our seemingly constant air-bound trips to distant shores, with a sense of shame? Are we the Selfish Generation (with all the flying about I've done, I'm certainly among the most guilty of this)? Or do we really not care about all this 'greenery'? Is 'being green' just a trend?

'I don't think so,' says E. 'I think it's a good thing – even if we don't really mean to be green, it's good.' E is a great recycler as well as being a cyclist, hardly ever taking public transport and not owning a car.

I'm not that eco-minded myself, though it's nice to feel the warm glow of greenery on the fast trains... whether Michael O'Leary likes it or not.

But enough of all that. We have another train to catch. A short man with a grey moustache and a possibly recycled uniform directs us to Platform 19. In two minutes we are there, and two minutes after that, a pink and grey SNCB double-decker train arrives, looking like a long sleek slug. Very soon we are away, sitting on the upper deck, taking in the huge gold dome of the Palais de Justice, a block of flats with a painting of a snake attached to a politician's head, and a terrace of buildings with sculptures of angels on the roofs. The countryside appears; flat and dotted with villages. We pass a pretty wood of silver birches. We pass a field of sleepy cows. The train pauses at Mechelen, which doesn't appear to be the most distinguished place, but where we see a curious church with a square-topped tower with yellow flags fluttering on top. Next up is Kontich, where the station has weird red, striped platforms, and there's an MTV office block as well as enormous piles of neatly stacked timber. And then we pull in at Antwerp Central. The journey from Brussels has taken just under an hour – the SNCB wasn't the fastest of fast trains – but it's less than three hours since we left St Pancras. Despite our unscheduled stop in the middle of the Channel, we've made good time.

Antwerp Central is breathtaking. 'Wow, it's cool round here,' says E, as we head up escalators from the deep innards of the station into a cavernous space with a huge ceiling with glass panels. Neon blue lights cast odd pools of colour onto elaborate stucco stone walls. We reach the top and find ourselves facing a neo-classical structure with columns, balustrades and arched windows with frames painted aquamarine. A sign painted in gold leaf says 'ANTWERPEN', next to a gold display showing baskets of fruit and wheat defended by swords wrapped with serpents, plus a fine Roman-numeral clock.

It *is* pretty cool. And it's pretty cool for a reason. The first trains between Brussels and Antwerp began in 1836, just six years after Belgium became a country in its own right, independent from the Netherlands. The government wanted to unify the nation, and do it quickly. Having good transport links would bring the Flemish-speaking north together with the mainly French-speaking Walloons in the south, the fledgling government reasoned; helping Belgium feel bound together at a crucial moment. The result was one of the first major train lines in Europe, and the stations in Belgium from those days onwards took on a symbolic importance in the country. When Antwerp's station was rebuilt in 1905, little expense was spared.

From a grand concourse, we catch a taxi to our hotel, passing a row of diamond shops named Luxe Diamonds, Rosy Diamonds, Jemma, Infinity, and Royalty Jewellery. We'd read on the train that more than 70 per cent of the world's diamonds are believed to pass through Antwerp, which has a rich tradition of diamond cutting and polishing dating back many centuries.

'There must be a dozen shops in a row,' says E. 'Look at them!' I do. There are an awful lot of diamond shops. There are also a lot of cobbled streets and tall elegant buildings. We pass a 'QUICK' restaurant and the Terminus Budget Hotel: 'Big service. Nice prices'. There are seemingly endless inviting bars – 'cosy little vino places', as E describes them. The taxi turns a corner and we pull up at a street near the River Schelde.

It's a mild early evening. Our driver has to look up the address of Hotel Matelote, and finally drops us off. It's 'somewhere near here', he says unconvincingly, pointing down a side alley. But soon, after a bit of confusion in the alleys, we find ourselves in a trendy minimalist lobby, with low-slung sofas, spaghetti-like rugs, pieces of wood standing starkly as decoration, and pictures of Jimi Hendrix. We collect our key and walk up a stairway (there is no lift) to a trendy minimalist room.

I don't mind trendy minimalism; I usually quite like it. And as Antwerp is meant to be cutting edge and generally cool, according to the guidebooks we read on the train, we thought we'd try and stay somewhere that fits the style of the city. But this is something else. The room is almost totally white: white blinds, white bedspread, white walls, white floor, white bathroom. This colour scheme is interrupted by an ugly piece of modern art, scuff marks on the white floor, and a damp patch in a corner. The overall effect is not exactly brilliant: it's like being in some kind of hospital ward. On the hotel website, we'd seen pictures of lovely rooms with exposed beams and *colour*. Instead, we're stuck in a small white box.

To try and find out if there is another room available, perhaps one with the slightest hint of ambience, I go back to the reception. On the way, I pass a doorway that is propped open by a cleaner's bucket. It looks as though this one might be empty. I knock on the door and hear nothing, so I nip in to take a look, climbing a few stairs. It's a lovely room with a tucked away feel, with all the exposed beams and character I'd seen on the website. In the reception, I ask if we can move to another room, perhaps the one I'd seen.

'There are no others,' the receptionist replies, matter-of-factly. 'We are fully booked.'

She smiles thinly.

'Oh, what about Room Five,' I venture, suggesting the room I'd just seen.

'That room is for staff when they stay overnight,' she answers, as though this is the most normal response in the world. She smiles thinly once more.

'Oh, is it free for guests tonight?' I ask.

'No,' she replies. 'It is not.'

And with that, E and I go for a walk, leaving our white shoebox behind. The hotel is right in the city centre close to the Cathedral of Our Lady and the Grote Markt. This is the city's main square, which we reach by walking down a cobbled lane with a sushi bar, an Argentine steak house, a pizzeria, a Thai restaurant, and a place serving '140 Belgian beers'. It's busy out and about, with well-dressed folk heading for evening meals. We take in Grote Markt, with its elegant sixteenth-century guildhalls: some in white stone, others in red brick. The façades have high windows and pointed roofs in step-shapes with gilded figurines gleaming at the top. We stop by the famous Brabo fountain. This depicts a legendary Roman figure, Silvius Brabo, who is said to have taken on a mythical creature known as the Druoon Antigoon, a giant who demanded money from ships passing on the River Schelde. He defeated the creature and cut off his hand in defiance, throwing it into the river. The bronze statue shows Brabo in the act of hurling the giant's hand into the water –

looking a little like a quarterback in American football about to send off a touchdown pass.

One of the theories of the name of Antwerp is that it comes from this tale: 'hand-werpen' translates as hand-throw. The name is believed to have slowly altered from this over the years. It's a nice folk story, and it's hard to visit Antwerp without learning the tale of Brabo and the Druoon Antigoon (it's in every tourist brochure and guide).

The cathedral is just off the square: a towering Gothic rocket of a building dating from the sixteenth century. The streets are so narrow that we almost stumble upon the entrance to the vast steeple; I have to admit, if I'm being totally honest, we had been looking around for one of the many 'cosy little vino places'. Instead we find ourselves entering a huge space with a smell of candles and incense, and the deep surge of an organ playing in the background. There's a charge to enter deeper into the cathedral, so as we're just passing by, we step up to a glass divide that separates paying churchgoers from non-paying ones.

Beyond an ornate wooden pulpit and beautiful stained-glass windows, we can see works by Rubens, who lived for many years in Antwerp, adorning the far walls. The highlight is to the right of the nave and is known as *The Descent of Christ from the Cross*. The rich, dramatic painting shows just that: Christ being taken from the cross after his crucifixion, pallid and covered in blood, his head drooping to one side with expressionless eyes. It's an incredibly powerful image. As we stare across, we try to imagine the impact the painting must have had when it was completed in 1611; as well as how many hundreds of thousands, if not millions, of sets of eyes have taken in the image over the centuries. 'It's stunning,' says E – summing up both our feelings.

Behind the cathedral, we find the cosy La Douce wine bar, run by a friendly woman in jeans, who serves crisp glasses of Pinot Blanc and meltingly delicious *croque-monsieurs*. The place has an intimate, chic, laid-back feel with scuffed wooden tables, wooden floors, painted brick walls and gilded mirrors. A couple is smooching by candlelight at the bar. An older woman in black – a dead ringer for the novelist Hilary Mantel – is eating a solitary meal and drinking wine at the table next to us. There's gentle background music with a chanteuse singing about *amore*. We could not have found a nicer spot.

'There is an excess of classy, refined bars in the centre of Antwerp,' says E, messing about and pretending she's some sort of 'city reviewer'. 'It's all very us,' she adds, sipping from her glass of white wine.

I agree, looking about, and it feels good to have arrived so quickly with no waits in the lounge, boarding shenanigans, safety briefings, pilot's welcomes, taxiing to the runway, uptight cabin staff, tight seats, circling before landing, slow shuffling out, waits at the carousel or tedious and expensive transfers. We're suddenly in a historic city centre, without any of the usual bother and stress.

'I definitely didn't miss Stansted or Gatwick,' I say, catching the proprietor's eye for another round of drinks. 'Yes we got stuck for a bit in the tunnel, and yes we had to switch trains – but that was hardly difficult.'

'It was excellent,' E replies, adopting her city reviewer voice once again. 'The train service from St Pancras to Brussels and onwards ran very smoothly: it is to be recommended.'

Then we talk about our trendy minimalist hotel. 'It's a little lacking in atmosphere,' I comment, trying to make light of a Big Mistake on my part: I booked the place, after all.

'Atmosphere?' E responds. 'That is not a word I would use in reference to that hotel!'

And so I switch the subject, and order another round of drinks. But then we go back to the hotel, passing along the echoing side streets and alleyways, with tiny candlelit bars tucked away everywhere. And it gets worse.

It's not that the room or the hotel has changed. It's what's outside that has altered, in the form of what sounds like every well-oiled (or perhaps it's better to say 'steaming drunk and virtually rolling in the gutter while singing and gabbling after 140 Belgian beers') inhabitant of the city of Antwerp passing by through the night.

A typical conversation from our first-floor front-facing room – which enjoys a kind of front row seat to alleyway life – went something like this:

'ADAM! ADAM!' (or Jean, or Bruno, or Jan).

'EHHHH?'

Loud sound of laughter and shrieks from a large group of lads, with perhaps a couple of female laughs mixed in.

'ADAM! ADAM!'

'EHHHH?'

More hilarity followed by the sound of something like a dustbin lid being slammed on the cobblestones. More shrieks.

'WAH-ZEE-WAH-ZEE-ADAM!'

Laughter, and scrape of metal objects along railings. Shrieks. Screams. Broken glass. More laughter.

'EHHHH?'

Sound of clattering footsteps, and diminishing voices echoing down the alleys.

And this is one of the more interesting exchanges. It feels something like living under a flight path right next to a busy airport: lots of noise, and you know it's coming soon. In between the Adams, Jeans and Jans, there are occasional periods of silence in which the sound of someone snoring loudly can be heard through our white minimalist walls. The snore has a deep baritone, almost metronomic quality; keeping time to the slow passage of the night.

Another shrieking group of partying Antwerpians comes past. 'I know they're groovers and we're probably just over the hill,' says E. 'But I can't take this! Does this city ever shut up!'

She puts a pillow over her head.

Revelry comes to an end around 5 a.m., and dawn is heralded by a period of clattering bottles and the sound of street-cleaning machines.

What a (long) night. In the morning, we eat breakfast in a room with a picture of a woman in a bikini eating grapes against a pink background. The painting is gaudy in a way that seems meant to be gaudy. The woman grins at us as we eat our toast, feeling like zombies. It's almost as though the picture sums up what this hotel and so many other places like it are all about: being trendy in a way that's somehow designed to get on your nerves. So minimal there's nothing there; so tasteless it's tasteful. It's almost as though it's a test: are you cool enough to accept our lack of cool? Not right now, we're not. Not after an almost sleepless night.

I go to the reception to ask if there is another, slightly quieter, room.

'What about the one with the bucket propping open the door?' I ask. The bucket had still been there in the morning, and the room had not been used.

'It is not really a room,' says the receptionist, with a cloudy look in his eye, as though what he's saying is self-evident to any human being with a functioning brain.

I look at him; I'm too tired for this. 'What do you mean?'

'The room is not really a room,' he replies, with the faintest hint of a grin.

'The room is not a room?' I ask. It feels as though Kafka or perhaps Lewis Carroll sets the rules around here.

'It cannot be used because of the fire brigade,' he replies, deadpan.

'But staff can stay in the room?'

'Yes,' he replies – looking very sleepy indeed; perhaps he's been up all night, too.

I give up. E and I check out, take a cab to a Radisson Blu hotel overlooking a quiet park, where we get an eighth-floor room that is not in the slightest way trendy or minimalist or bright white or noisy. It's just a nice corporate-style place to stay, with a comfy carpet, a big bed, warm colours, nice art and a decent view. The type of place that American businessmen would (and do) feel right at home in: it's bland, it's quiet and it's just right.

With a spring in our step and a sense of 'what next?' we head forth into Antwerp. It's a bright morning with a handful of people in the happily cluttered, untrendy lobby. We cross a busy street and walk through Stadtpark, stopping to take a picture on a bridge over a pretty olive-green lake. We're just south-east of Grote Markt here, not far from Antwerp Central, but it feels like an oasis of quiet early on a Saturday morning. We're close to an area of the city that's home to an Orthodox Jewish community, and we see many women dressed in black and wearing traditional wigs. Hunched men in large black hats and shoulder-length side curls amble past. We head along the gravel paths enjoying the morning, and stop to look at a moving stone war memorial with a statue of a ghostly, faceless figure wearing a helmet and a long coat, next to a gold inscription that says: '*Aux héros tombés en braves pour la défense des foyers et l'honneur du peuple Belge.*' Then we cross a street and pass beautiful Art Nouveau buildings with elegant figures carved into the façades, before arriving at Theaterplein, a square where there's a bustling market in full swing.

This is an eclectic, bountiful, happy place. Stalls run by smiley folk sell great piles of raspberries, cranberries, blueberries, strawberries (every berry you could possibly desire), figs, peaches, plums, grapes, tangerines, walnuts, cherries, avocados, green peppers, runner beans, pineapples and grapefruits: a veritable vegetarian's dream. In between there are fresh fish counters with slimy creatures with bulbous shiny eyes, butchers with huge slabs of meat dangling heavily from hooks, stalls festooned with cut-price underwear and socks, kiosks offering retsina and champagne, racks of cheap winter fleeces, a section with smelly cheeses lined up on wooden shelves, another offering row upon row of sausages, a stall offering 'Versace' designer clothing, and a trestle table covered with slices of chocolate and walnut cake.

The market leads down a side alley beyond Theaterplein, and a bar named Antigoon, outside which a few crumpled fellows are smoking roll-ups and drinking glasses of beer. The consumption of lager seems never very far away in Antwerp, and they look as though they're having a jolly old time. The alley is busier, with people examining racks of hooky-looking 'Calvin Klein' underwear (it can't be real at a couple of euros) and pricey pots of olives and chutneys, while a busker plays a whimsical tune on a violin. A short way along, the alley opens onto a wide pedestrian-only street known as the Wapper filled with cafes with scarlet chairs and sunshades. Beyond these, we come to a bright Sportsdirect.com with a half price sale on Nike trainers, opposite which we stop by a row of park benches. On one of these benches a man who must weigh about 300 lb is sitting with demurely crossed legs wearing a denim miniskirt, a pink blouse and earrings. He has short grey hair and looks like a trucker.

'That woman is definitely a man,' whispers E.

'Yes, she is,' I reply. Nobody could be in any doubt of that.

The 300 lb transvestite angles his face as though to catch the morning sun rays. His denim miniskirt has enough material to make several pairs of average-sized jeans. He gives us a coy smile and a wink. Antwerp, we're beginning to discover, is full of surprises: it's a singular, spiky sort of place, and you're never quite sure what's coming next: 300 lb transvestites in denim miniskirts and all. And with that we buy tickets to visit the home of one of the city's most famous residents.

Peter Paul Rubens lived in Antwerp from 1608 until his death in 1640. He was born in Siegen in Germany in 1577 and discovered a passion and talent for art early on. After the death of his father (a legal advisor who had been imprisoned for an affair with the second wife of William I of Orange), he moved with his mother to Antwerp, where he received training from two leading local painters. He then spent several years in Italy studying the classical masterworks of the likes of Titian and Caravaggio, before moving to the Low Countries and settling again in Antwerp, where he built a fabulous Italian palazzo-style residence, somewhat to the surprise of his Flemish neighbours.

This is now a museum to his life and works. We'd realised we were on the right track for Rubenshuis by all the 'Rubens Cafes' we'd seen on the Wapper along the way. We enter a darkened room and soon find ourselves walking through oak-panelled rooms with still-life paintings of dead birds (Rubens was a big art collector), an old purple and blue painted kitchen recreated as it would have been in his time, and a hall in which we find one of only four self-portraits he painted. He was not vain when it came to painting pictures of himself, unlike his Dutch colleague Rembrandt, who left about forty such images.

But it's a very familiar picture. Rubens' black almost sombrero-sized hat is slanted to one side and he gazes steadily out of hazel eyes as a pool of tourists gathers around. He has a pale complexion and a gingery beard. We read from a museum booklet that he had eight children from two wives. He married his sixteen-year-old second wife, Helena Fourment, when he was fifty-three. 'Wow, that's quite a difference,' says E, as we walk on to see a portrait of Helena wearing a string of pearls, arching her eyebrows and looking quite happy with matters in a room a little further on. Rubens regularly painted Helena, who is curvaceous and a long way from the size-zero look of models today. It is pictures such as this one that led to the term 'Rubenesque figure', meaning a woman with a voluptuous figure. The couple had five children, one of whom was born after his death (from gout).

We meander along the corridors, taking in the fine art and surroundings. Forget minimalism: Rubens liked to do things with flair, and his house is proof of that extravagant streak. There are ornate chandeliers, walls filled with his art collections (including masterpieces by Titian and Sir Anthony van Dyck), checked black and white marble floors, grand staircases, galleries full of sketches modelled on the Pantheon in Rome, antique busts from the Roman period, Baroque stuccos, and a general air of living life in style.

'That bed is *very* small, by the way,' comments E, as we enter his bedroom. The bed is indeed tiny: you could fit about four of them into the space of our (admittedly enormous) double at the Radisson Blu.

Our little booklet has an explanation: 'At that time people slept in a half-seated position. This was felt to promote good digestion and circulation.'

'Poor them,' says E, as we turn to a painting entitled *Young Boy on His Death Bed*. This picture, by a contemporary of Rubens, shows a boy whose portrait was commissioned after his death. Passing away in childhood was common in the seventeenth century and parents would often pay for such pictures as memories; Rubens himself lost a twelve-year-old daughter named Clara.

It's one of those museums pitched just right: enough to keep your interest, without the kind of overload that makes you lose the will to live and wonder what you are doing *paying* for the pleasure of losing the will to live on a weekend break. First of all, of course, it informs you of the life of one of the greatest painters of all time, about whom I never knew properly before, and whose flamboyant sense of style seems to have lived on in the city ever since. I never knew that he had been a diplomat and travelled across Europe to Spain to present gifts to the Spanish court. I never knew that he was so in love with all things Italian that he wrote much of his correspondence in Italian and signed many letters 'Pietro Paulo Rubens'. I had no idea that he had married a woman a third of his age and had quite so many children. I didn't really know much about him at all... and perhaps never would have if I hadn't caught the fast trains to Antwerp.

But the museum does more than just tell you about Rubens himself. It also conjures up the atmosphere of a time when Antwerp was an incredibly important place of commerce in Europe, said by some to be the richest city on the Continent. From the end of the fifteenth century, when the river Zwin silted up causing the decline of Bruges, Antwerp enjoyed a period of great wealth, becoming a hugely important stop for traders in northern Europe; hence all the grand guildhalls in Grote Markt. It was still a key port during Rubens' lifetime, even after Spanish soldiers had sacked the city, causing the death of 7,000 people in the year before his birth. This act of colonial vandalism – known as the Spanish Fury – was prompted by a delay in payment to the soldiers by the bankrupt Phillip II of Spain. This acted both to strengthen local resistance to the Spanish, but also to scare away English cloth merchants. By the middle of the seventeenth century, when the River Schelde was closed to navigation as part of regional politicking – coinciding almost exactly with Rubens' death – Antwerp's fortunes were on the turn and Amsterdam to the north was about to rise as the powerhouse in this part of Europe.

This ancient competition between the north and the south of the Low Countries, after many historical twists and turns, led to the creation of The Netherlands in the north and Belgium in the south. The division eventually came in 1830, in the wake of the collapse of the Napoleonic Empire. Being in this old house, with its ancient stories and grandeur, you can't help but get an idea about the physical layout of the region... a sense of how the different countries fit into place.

So Rubens lived through the city's last glory days. We walk through his suitably glorious house to his immense, double-height studio. This feels like the centre of the home, and it is where he, along with his many helpers, is believed to have painted many of his finest works including *The Descent from the Cross* (which we saw last night at the cathedral). It's a beautiful space, now thronged with Japanese and Chinese tourists. There are tall hoop-shaped windows, a stone slab floor, and rows of portraits of distinguished gentlemen with red-rimmed eyes. There's a striking picture of Adam and Eve painted by Rubens showing Adam in the process of wooing Eve (he appears to be convincing her of the size of his manhood). Then there is his *Annunciation*, which 'depicts the moment when the Virgin Mary is visited by the Archangel Gabriel with the joyous news that she will be the mother of the Messiah', according to a panel.

'Imagine that,' says E.

'What?' I reply – not sure what she's driving at.

'Well, there she is, Mary, and then this angel comes down and says: "You will have a baby and he will be the saviour of the world",' E says.

'And?' I say – still not sure what has brought this on.

'Well, wouldn't Mary be thinking: "Hold on a minute: what do you mean I'm pregnant? I haven't had sex."'

'Perhaps she might,' I concede.

'It's no wonder she looks as though she's freaking out. I guess it's a different way of finding out you're preggers: no blue line on a pregnancy test, jumping about and mad celebrations.'

'Perhaps not how an art historian would put it,' I suggest, adopting my very best impersonation of Jeeves.

But she's absolutely right, and you do get a strong feeling that Rubens – as is clear from his almost cheeky Adam and Eve – had a sense of the comic side of life. Yes, there are his grand, Baroque pictures of Christ on the cross, and his many depictions of classical scenes. But there are also his very human touches. The characters look real, as though they have a life of their own – that Mary could indeed be thinking to herself: 'Hold on a minute!'

Maybe that's why his art has so well endured the test of time.

After checking out the lovely back garden with its box hedges and classical columns – it feels as though you've stepped into a courtyard in Florence or Rome – we make our way to perhaps the trendiest part of trendy Antwerp.

The fashion district is just to the south of the cathedral and it is full of just about every upmarket brand name you could imagine. I'd expected Antwerp to be a bit of a rough-and-ready port full of beer halls and down-to-earth good times: the type of place that's just made for a letting-your-hair-down weekend break. And it definitely is that, if last night's performance outside the hotel is anything to go by. But it's also described by many as the 'Milan of the north' due to its endless stylish fashion shops. The local tourist board even provides an 'Antwerp Fashion Map' declaring that the city is 'now one of the trendiest destinations and offers a historical framework for avant-garde fashion by Belgian and international designers alike. That is unique, that is luxury!' And a story I'd read on the Internet on the Eurostar on the way over had described the fashion shops in the city as being less sterile than in Milan, with designers who care about making affordable clothes, without the snootiness and aloofness of Italy.

We walk along narrow streets passing the gleaming windows of Louis Vuitton, Hugo Boss, Hermès, Diesel and Armani. There's a shop called 7 For All Mankind that I've never heard of before. It looks a bit more welcoming than the rest, and I suggest taking a look inside.

'Do you want to remortgage your flat?!' warns E, who is less clueless about labels than I am. 'Affordable' in smart fashion districts seems to translate as 'very expensive indeed'.

We go inside anyway to check out racks of €200 and €300 jeans, dodging keen sales assistants and wondering how the ripped-and-worn look could be so incredibly expensive. Why do we buy jeans like this? I can't remember ever seeing deliberately scuffed and battered shoes for sale (though I admit I haven't exactly done market research into this area and could well have missed a battered shoe trend). You wouldn't buy roughed up pairs of underpants or socks with designer holes in them. Would you shell out your hard-earned cash for a new car with designer scratches along the side? Or dented bumpers?

Perhaps a windscreen crack and a few ripped seats? What is it about jeans that makes us want to look like down-and-outs?

I say as much to E and realise I have lost her attention. She's examining a pair of navy-blue skinny jeans that come only partially destroyed. 'These are lurrvly,' she says, in a honeyed tone of voice that hints: 'A present for me, after last night's hotel?'

I look at the price tag: €229.

The jeans stay on the rack of 7 For All Mankind. Outside, we arrive at a shop named Dries van Noten.

'Oh, Dries van Noten!' says E as we are coming up to it.

'Excuse me?' I reply, as I haven't seen the shop's sign and haven't got a clue what she's saying.

'A very good designer. Beautiful, beautiful,' she says, looking at the window display. 'Very expensive, too: your crumpled euros won't get very far in there.'

This is true. In the window a mannequin is dressed in a purple jacket decorated with flowers, a grey T-shirt, shiny black trousers and black high heels. The price tag for this ensemble is €2,788. Yet it doesn't (to my eye at least) look all that different to the type of outfits we'd seen women wearing in the bars and restaurants last night. Is Antwerp full of folk dressed up in €2,788 worth of clothing? It seems hard to believe. But who knows how people in the Low Countries like to spend their money?

The Antwerp Fashion Map tells us that Dries van Noten is one of the Antwerp Six. While this may sound like some sort of group wrongly convicted for terrorism, the Antwerp Six is in fact a set of six fashion designers who rose to fame in the city in the 1980s, when they created a distinctive pushing-the-boundaries look that brought the city to the attention of the world's fashionistas. Ever since, fashion has been big business in the city; as the price tags reflect. After consulting our map and trying to assess which Antwerpians might be decked out for €2,788, we walk on to the flagship store of Walter van Beirendonck.

This is on a side street and Walter was, we are reliably informed, a key member of the fabled six. We entered a large warehouse-like space painted white. In this huge room, lemon-yellow platforms are dotted about, with racks of clothes hung almost as though they are exhibits in an art gallery. A woman wearing heavy-framed glasses and a large blue tunic (a distinctly odd look) invites us to examine the exhibits. A plain black T-shirt at the first platform bears the slogan: 'LOVE WAR ON HATE.' The price? €150. A woollen dress is €580. A hoodie with a 'W' on it comes to €200. 'I know style is an individual thing, but honestly, you wouldn't take that cardigan to Oxfam,' says E, feeling the thin wool on a €270 cardigan.

Outside we pass a Fashion Museum with an exhibition of hats shaped like plates of bacon and eggs, little houses, or sandals. 'A hat can be a veil or an alibi, a head turner or a friend,' says a sign. But that's enough fashion for a while, we're thinking, as we wander about streets with little antique shops, passing pleasant cafes (we stop for espressos in a cute place named Juices and Jazz), bars selling Stella Artois and genever (the sharp local gin), waffle shops, more designer clothes boutiques, and *patisseries*. The roads are narrow and busy with folk going about their business. There are little parks, shops with windows full of well-polished musical instruments, and attractive art galleries. It's a vibrant, friendly, well-to-do place. Looking about and thinking back to Rubens and his slightly mad Italianate palazzo, it almost feels as though the 'golden' days of Antwerp have returned. While the rest of Europe seems to be in terminal decline (with currency and bank collapses and so on), there are folk round here strolling about in €150 T-shirts.

Near the cathedral we go to Restaurant Het Kathedraalcafe. It's an extraordinary place, almost totally covered in ivy on the outside and filled with religious icons on the inside. The icons, we learn from the cheery waiter Eric, were 'collected over thirty years, there are 426 altogether, we started as a small art-cafe, and have expanded'. Amid the gloom and the glare of monks, saints and angels, E has a chunky vegetable soup and I eat an excellent and huge Flemish beer stew. We order glasses of Trappist La Trappe Quadrupel, lovely strong stuff, while watching the early evening crowds arrive and begin to chatter conspiratorially in the candlelight, beneath an old arched red-brick roof. It's an almost eerie place; as though we're drinking our ales in some kind of very unusual church. Bluesy funk music plays in subdued tones in the background. What a great spot to spend an evening... just a few hours down the line from St Pancras, in Belgium.

The nature of a flying visit (or, I should say, high-speed train visit) is that you don't hang around for long. You roll in and you roll out and you see what you can see along the way. Glimpses of local life catch your eye. You miss things. You get lost. Hotel receptionists tell you 'rooms are not rooms'. You discover the delights of Trappist beers. You chance upon winking 300 lb transvestites in miniskirts. You learn about histories you might never have otherwise discovered in a lifetime.

You also get into scraps with diamond dealers (well, almost). In the morning, while E is swimming in the Radisson Blu's cool downstairs 'chromatherapy pool', in which lights flicker between colours in a low-ceilinged room with sun loungers, I check out the diamond shops near the station, a short walk away. There are several within the concourse, but I take a look at a few on the street outside, near a McDonald's and a kebab shop with a huge Turkish flag flying outside. E has a birthday coming up (as she likes to remind me) and where better to buy diamond jewellery than in Antwerp? Shiny Diamonds is offering 'Fifty per cent off, special prices', Rosy Diamonds says it is a 'tax free certified diamond trader', Gold Art seems to specialise in dart player-style gold chains, while a shop called Prestige offers diamond reports by the International Geological Institute. It's all a bit bedazzling and confusing, but I go to the window of one shop (not named), whereupon a short, sharp-eyed woman with orange-tinted hair is soon at my side.

'You want diamonds?' she asks.

'Maybe,' I reply hesitantly. 'How much are they?'

'We have many diamonds,' she replies, taking my arm and leading me into a small very bright, sparkly room. I point to a ring in the window, just to get a vague idea of prices.

She looks at the back of the box, on which there is no price tag, and says: 'This one! Fifteen hundred euros. White gold. Diamond size twenty-nine and sixteen. Ring size fifty-two.'

Then she says: 'Hold on.'

She leaves the room and returns with the owner, a man with olive skin, a pressed pink shirt and a wide inscrutable face. I decide to ask him a few questions: I'm curious about whether there's a boom in diamond trade at the moment, or if business is slow. I show him my journalist's ID.

'I don't really have time for this,' he says; his smile vanishing in an instant when he realises I'm not about to buy his €1,500 ring.

'I just have a couple of questions, it won't take a moment,' I reply.

'Sorry, are you trying to conduct an interview?' he asks in a highly sarcastic voice.

'Yes, I suppose I am,' I reply.

'Are you serious?' he answers, turning very stony indeed.

'Yes, I suppose so.'

'Have a nice day,' he says, glaring at me threateningly. For a moment, I just stare back at him. Then he makes a move as though to open the counter and approach me, repeating in a tone of menace: 'No, I really mean it: have a nice day.'

With that, before I can be manhandled out, and not understanding what this diamond dealer has to hide, I leave. As I walk down the street, I see the owner and the woman with the orange-tinted hair keeping a close eye on me. Half an hour away from E, and I've almost got myself mixed up with the mob.

So much for diamond buying; at least I tried, though I don't mention it to E. After checking out of the hotel, we go to see the fabulous art at the Koninklijk museum, with its many Rubens and other masterworks, and take a stroll along the milky gleam of the Schelde River. We pass the cone-towered medieval castle near Grote Markt and continue into the docks. These are the second largest in Europe, after Rotterdam's, but we don't venture as far as where the ships come in. Instead we turn back for the station, and find ourselves in the midst of the red light district.

Here we're in for a surprise. As well as the obvious things you might expect in a red light district – women in windows, shifty fellows shuffling along pavements eyeing up the women, sex shops and 'anti-stress relaxation massage' parlours – we also find tourists. Not just individual tourists like us: holidaymakers led by a guide holding a flag and taking them past windows full of women in suspenders and high-heel boots. There are children in these groups, even mothers pushing prams. It's really very odd.

I ask a mother with a pram at the back of the group what's going on. She's Dutch but speaks English.

'We're on a tour organised by the city,' she replies.

'By the tourist office?' I reply.

'Yes. By them.'

'Don't you think that's strange?'

'Yes. We find so.'

And with that they catch up with the rest of the group, passing a sign for 'Sexyworld'.

We potter on to the grand station, in time for a Starbucks and our train back. Antwerp is a small city (population about 460,000) but it packs a punch. As we disappear down the escalators into the depths of a station that in itself tells you something about the history of Belgium, we realise it's been a fun-packed couple of days. The next stop on our journey is not so far away in another fortnight's time... where a different kind of entertainment lies in store.

CHAPTER FOUR

LILLE: 'SHORTER THAN MY COMMUTE'

We're speeding through Kent on a sunny mid-September Saturday afternoon with golden light spreading across emerald fields and cotton wool clouds on the horizon. The concourse had been busy back at St Pancras, but it's calm on the train, though we know we haven't got long to go. Our destination – Lille – is just eighty minutes away and we almost feel as though we're cheating: as though this isn't a proper weekend break in Europe. After all, this is shorter than my commute from south-west London to my newspaper's office in east London. If we were travelling north right now, we wouldn't make it much past Leicester. If we were going west, we'd be heading somewhere near Swindon.

But Lille sounds much more fun and there's something incredibly appealing about arriving at our destination so quickly. This is travelling on the fast trains in speed-up mode. E and I don't bother settling into the journey. What's the point? It'll be over almost before it begins. We're soon through the tunnel and listening to the cricket-like bleeps of mobile phones as they adjust to their new surroundings. 'WELCOME TO FRANCE,' says mine. 'CALLS WILL COST 38P TO MAKE AND 14P TO

RECEIVE; 10P A TEXT.' No border controls actually at the borders of Europe these days – just the welcoming buzz and blip of telecommunications.

The weather has turned somewhere under La Manche. There's a tinny rattle of rain on the roof. White cows in a sodden green field look despondent and pay no attention to us whatsoever as we zoom by. A cluster of starlings above a village church banks and forms the shape of an inky comma in the pencil-grey sky. Then there's a break in the clouds and the sun shines through. Amid all the bleakness, a rainbow appears above a copse.

'Isn't that lovely,' says E, switching the conversation from our newspaper-inspired state of Britain rant that's flitted from the number of millionaires in David Cameron's cabinet (eighteen out of twenty-three including sixteen who went to public school) to student debt, bankers' bonuses (£6 million for one very lucky fat cat), Cheryl Cole's latest outfit and David Beckham's new haircut. 'Phooaar' is all E will say on the latter (when it comes to football, E seems to support a one-man team, even though I've red-carded her a few times on the subject). In between all this we've managed to squeeze in 'plans for the future': buying a place together, publishing E's novel (which she's just completed), children. We're finding that high-speed train travel, much more so than flying, seems to lend itself to chatting, chivvying and contemplation. Perhaps it's the scenery flicking by... allowing your mind to relax and wander. Perhaps it's the bigger seats and freedom to move around more easily... the feeling of being less confined than in the sky. Perhaps it's just... leaving the country behind.

Thinking about things in general, I stare through the window admiring the rainbow and totally ignoring a muffled announcement over the speaker system.

'Let's get our bags, it's only a quickie stop at Lille,' says E, breaking my reverie. The announcement was that we are soon arriving. On a flying weekend we might just have made the departure lounge. On our fast train, we're already right in the thick of the action.

Out in the station, we walk past a row of arty, oversized purple flowerpots and find the taxi rank, next to a zinc-coloured glass building housing a Crowne Plaza. There are no taxis, just a bedraggled row of British passengers from the train.

'Why do they have a taxi rank if they have no taxis?' asks E, extremely logically.

'Good question,' replies a man wearing a fleece. He turns out to be on a weekend break to see Leonard Cohen, the septuagenarian Canadian musician, play at the local stadium. To say that my girlfriend is a fan of Cohen would be something of an understatement. She's a lifelong devotee, an acolyte... in E's own words: 'I would follow that man anywhere.' Like the others, we've planned this trip to coincide with the concert. The tickets had been much easier to buy than for shows back in the UK, and we thought it would give a focus to our sprint across the Channel. People travel between London and Manchester or Liverpool to watch concerts, why not Lille? It's a faster journey.

We grumble about erratic French taxis, but eventually one arrives, taking us to our B&B, passing the flying saucer shape of Zenith Stadium where the concert is to be held, a concrete jungle of supermarkets and the grand façade of l'Institut Pasteur de Lille. I'd read up about this before coming and hadn't realised we'd be staying close by. The great microbiologist and chemist Louis Pasteur was appointed dean of the local university's science department in 1854, where he made many of his most important discoveries. It was a fortunate posting as Lille was, and still is, an industrial city. When he received a query from a brewery about beer going sour after fermentation, his investigations set in motion a series of revelations that led to the process of pasteurisation – the heating of drinks such as beer, wine and milk to kill bacteria within them. His name was thus sealed in common language, though he didn't stop there: he also worked on groundbreaking early vaccines for cholera, anthrax, smallpox and rabies.

All just round the corner from our B&B, which our taxi driver cannot find. 'Zere is nothing in zis street, nothing,' he says dismissively, as we arrive outside 6 Boulevard Jean-Baptiste Lebas.

E jumps out and finds there is in fact something: our B&B, a tiny two-bedroom place in a tall stone building on a terrace, with no sign outside. Moments later, we're meeting Chantal, the charming middle-aged owner of La Maison Théodore. She's dressed in black and doesn't speak much English, though E gleans that she's an interior designer who turned her home into a B&B three weeks ago (no wonder the driver was confused).

Everything is very stylish in the downstairs lounge: white leather chairs, lime-green coffee tables, a wicker mannequin 'sculpture', more slightly mad abstract modern art, and a general feeling that each object has been placed just so. Talking at a hundred miles an hour, Chantal leads us up a creaking staircase to our room, which stretches across the entire second floor of the old building. This is pretty chic as well, with a bright purple carpet and a red sofa leading through a sliding door to a large low-slung bed and a posh, shiny bathroom with a vase of beautiful white lilies. There's also a Nespresso machine and a large TV. Through the front window we overlook a pretty park, and, through the back, a collection of happily ramshackle gardens. We've definitely landed on our feet with La Maison Théodore.

'I am not sure about zis,' says Chantal in faltering English, looking at the TV and waving the remote control in my direction, somewhat threateningly.

'What about it?' I ask in faltering French.

'I am not sure,' she replies. 'Programme. It needs zee programme.'

E takes over and discovers that the television is new and Chantal has not programmed in the channels yet. She rabbits away rapidly in French for a while and then turns to me and says: 'That's your job now.'

She hands me the remote control.

Chantal smiles a broad smile. E and she exchange a few more quick-fire words. They turn to me as though there is some doubt about whether I'll be able to programme the TV. But Chantal seems to think it's worth a try. She departs, seeming most pleased by the turn of events.

It's a drizzly Saturday afternoon. Our train left at 1 p.m., we arrived at 3.20 p.m. and now it's after 4 p.m. After the TV programming discussion, E is suddenly not feeling well. She occasionally suffers from migraines and one has just struck. 'It's like red-hot pokers in the eyes,' she says, drawing the curtains and lying on the bed. I fetch paracetamol from my bag and ask if she thinks she can make it to the concert in four hours' time: it doesn't seem likely. She moans in reply, a muffled moan from under a pile of pillows. I ask if there's anything else I can do. She moans once again. I ask if it would be better if I left her in peace and went to get the tickets from Zenith Stadium (you have to collect them from the ticket office, which is being opened early to avoid massive queues).

She moans and the duvet and pillows tremble at the same time.

I take this as a 'yes'. So I head downstairs, worrying about E. I meet Chantal in the corridor and try to explain the situation in French. This involves me pointing at my head and saying something like '*Elle est maladie à la tête*'– which I don't think is quite right. But she gets the gist, as she says '*C'est terrible*' and offers me some aspirins.

I explain that E has taken pills already and is resting; at least I try to. Then I say I'm off to the stadium.

Chantal nods sagely, and says slowly in English: 'In Lille you are better on zee feet than zee car.'

It doesn't take long to realise she's right. The city centre is compact and we needn't have bothered with a taxi from the station. Under a heavy grey sky, I cross Boulevard de la Liberté and soon find myself in a square with a huge stone arch with imposing columns, classical figurines and a drawbridge. This is Place Simon Vollant, named after a seventeenth-century engineer from Lille. He constructed the victory 'gate' in honour of Louis XIV's capture of the city in 1667 from the United Provinces, at a time when the Netherlands and Belgium were one, with an influence that spread beyond current borders. It's a beautiful structure that you almost stumble upon after the dreary boulevard. I circle the gate, taking in its elegant, well-maintained public gardens. Bells chime across the square, which is next to a Gothic-looking Hôtel de Ville. European Union and tricolour flags flutter on long poles, while street performers dance below on the steps of the town hall. I walk past the building, decorated with thousands of *fleur-de-lis* emblems and beside a tiny park full of box hedges and purple flowers. Opposite this is a tower dating from the fifteenth century and originally built as a defence watch by Phillip the Bold (the dukes again) during the golden age of Burgundy. Now, it has been converted into a Resistance memorial.

It's all very pretty and it's all very French. Just a couple of hours ago I was squashed on the Piccadilly line, cursing London Underground while being (uselessly) informed that delays were caused 'by red signals'. Now I'm in an interesting French city wondering why I've never come here before.

Using a map from the Eurostar ticket office in St Pancras – quite a few destinations have tourist pamphlets and maps stacked in racks by the ticket machines – I turn left onto Boulevard du Président Hoover. Across the road, there are giant adverts on the side of the curved walls of the Zenith Stadium for eco-awareness and psychology conferences as well as an event entitled '*Les hommes viennent de Mars et les femmes de Vénus*'. I join a long queue waiting to collect tickets for the concert, listening to an Englishwoman wearing pink discussing her brother with friends.

'He does Internet dating and he's got a spreadsheet so he can remember what each of them does for a living,' she says loudly. 'He's nothing if not organised, so when he cancelled meeting me the other day I was furious. He said he had a festival to go to, and he'd forgotten about it. A festival! He wouldn't have forgotten a festival. It would have been on his spreadsheet.'

The woman continues in a similar vein for several minutes as the queue inches forwards, concluding with: 'We've got to stop making excuses for him!'

And then one of her group, a man in a blue windbreaker, turns to me. 'British?' he asks; he must have seen me looking at the map, which has tourist information in English.

I confirm my nationality.

'How much did you pay for your tickets?'

I tell him how much.

'That's good. I'd have been very upset if you'd got them cheaper.'

A black man who has just exited a tent pitched below a walkway into the stadium approaches us and holds out a piece of cardboard that says: '*Cherche deux billets.*' We shake our heads and he tries a few others before returning to his tent.

'We saw him in Madrid,' says the man in the blue windbreaker, as rain begins to pour. He's referring to Leonard Cohen, the singer known for his introspective lyrics and penchant for the darker side of life, not the fellow sleeping beneath the stadium. 'And Weybridge too.'

He pauses for a bit. 'I love "Gypsy Woman",' he says thoughtfully. 'I think his best poetry is in his song lyrics not in his written poetry.'

They ask me what I'm doing here. I tell them we've come for a quick weekend to see the concert and the sights of Lille, whatever they may be. The woman in pink, who describes herself as a 'high-class call girl' when I ask her (though I get the impression she's joking and she soon admits 'alright, I'm a teacher'), says: 'We love the trains. They make Lille very do-able. Except for the loos in Ebbsfleet. The loos are rubbish.' The group had boarded their Eurostar train at Ebbsfleet in Kent.

'The bacon sandwiches at Ebbsfleet are no good either,' says her companion, a doctor named Jim, who tells me his favourite Cohen song is 'Secret Life'.

They seem generally down on Ebbsfleet.

Next I'm talking to their friend Nigel, who turns out to be the deputy chief inspector of prisons in Britain. 'Staff said to me: "You're not going to go and see that miserable bastard, are you?" But actually I think his cheerfulness keeps breaking through. He's full of optimism and he recognises beauty in life.'

'He's very sexy as well,' says the woman in pink.

And before we know it, after more chat and discussion of favourite songs with my new best friends, we reach the front of the queue. We pick up our shiny silver tickets, marvelling that the system works and that the wait was so short. 'See you later!' says the deputy chief inspector of prisons, heading off into the rain.

I walk back via the beautiful Palais des Beaux-Arts, a stunning stone building with huge hoop-shaped windows overlooking a wide-open square. I stop by a bronze statue of a man on a horse, who turns out to be General Faidherbe, a nineteenth-century general who was born in Lille and became governor of Senegal, renaming the capital Dakar and subduing various Muslim attacks.

I wander about in the rain trying to find a shop selling Diet Coke (good for E's migraines) and end up buying one from a Subway fast-food shop for twice what you'd pay in a supermarket. Then I go back to La Maison Théodore, walking along Boulevard de la Liberté in the early evening drizzle and climbing the creaky stairs to our room.

E is better... much better (such is the miracle of Leonard Cohen). After swigging back the Diet Coke with another paracetamol, and a quick shower, she seems like a new person. We open a bottle of white wine we'd brought with us, and raise a toast to Lille and Cohen. And after a glass in our chic purple and red room, we retrace my steps from earlier and enter the cavernous industrial warehouse interior of Zenith Stadium. A good half of the audience seems to be British; concerts in Lille appear to be on the radar of British music lovers, and almost everyone is of a certain age – at least in their forties. I don't spot the deputy chief inspector of prisons or his 'high-class call girl' friend, and soon Cohen is before us. 'Thank you for your warm welcome: we'll give you everything we've got tonight,' he says simply, wearing his trademark fedora and black suit and launching into 'Dance Me To The End of Love'. I fetch a couple of plastic flutes of champagne and we listen to the sweet music swirling upwards through the darkened space. It's amazing to think that a seventy-six-year-old can perform with such intensity for three hours: but he does. We sip our champagnes and enjoy the show amid the Eurostar crowd. Before the Channel Tunnel opened in 1994, who would have imagined that hundreds of Brits would have visited a city in northern France to listen to a septuagenarian in a fedora sing about love and life? But we have – and it was superb.

In the morning, though, we have another mission: to visit the battlefields of World War One.

After several glasses of wine and champagne the night before, our 9 a.m. tour feels a little early. It's pouring down in Lille as we scamper through puddles and pass a strange man who decides to tell us that he doesn't like umbrellas: '*Je n'aime pas les parapluies.*' Each to their own, we're thinking, as we pass along empty pedestrianised streets and take in the wonderfully-named Mister City Bed Hotel, heading for the tourist office (and getting quite soaked, despite our *parapluie*). We eventually find the tourist office, and our small orange tour bus. We've made it just in time.

Moments later we're being driven through the wet streets of Lille in the direction of Fromelles, ten miles west of the city centre. We are about to learn all about the Battle of Fromelles, in which 1,547 British and 5,533 Australian soldiers were killed, wounded or taken prisoner on 19/20 July 1916 during a failed Allied action designed to gain an area of high ground known as 'Sugar Loaf' hill and act as a diversion for the Battle of the Somme, fifty miles to the south. A mass grave of soldiers was, remarkably, discovered on the edge of the village two years ago and a new cemetery has just opened, to which the tourist office arranges tours. The Australian losses were among the worst ever over a twenty-four-hour period, and there are several Australians on the bus with us making a pilgrimage.

On the way, we learn from Aurore, our twenty-something guide, that Lille was occupied by the Germans from 1914 to 1918, after a ten-day siege of the city. 'It was a terrible time for the occupants,' she says. 'There was deportation. The most beautiful women were sent to work in prostitution, while others were made to create weapons to attack the French. There was a 5 p.m. curfew and all the pigeons were killed as they could be used for sending messages. We have a pigeon monument in the city – it is unique in France.'

As she says this, the rain intensifies, pelting on the metal roof of the bus: it really is a dreadful downpour. 'During the Great War it was just the same: so much rain,' Aurore says. 'In this region it rains about 300 days a year. That's a lot of rain. Thanks to the good earth it's ideal conditions for fields growing cereals and vegetables. But the earth is muddy and heavy and sticky. Of course, that was such a terrible problem in the war. The water table is very close to the level of the earth.' This meant that trenches were often waterlogged or thick with mud, and also of course that soldiers suffered terribly from trench foot caused by wet socks and boots.

We drive through the village of Fournes-en-Weppe, which was almost totally destroyed during the Great War but was rebuilt afterwards. Just past Café de Sport and houses with window boxes full of geraniums, the bus slows down and Aurore points to a restored red-brick building, which we can just see through the steamy windows. 'That is number 966 – where Hitler lived during the war,' she says in hushed tones. 'He was a company runner: a messenger. He had a bicycle and daily he would cycle ten kilometres to deliver messages. A strange image of Hitler, don't you think?'

She waves for the driver to move on as villagers do not like tourist buses stopping. 'It is believed that during the war he had a love affair with a local lady. She later had a baby and everyone knew that it belonged to a German soldier. Nobody was sure if it was Hitler's but in the 1980s a British journalist took samples of DNA and found relatives and made a comparison. It was not Hitler's son.'

We keep going and arrive outside Fromelles (Pheasant Wood) Military Cemetery; the name comes from the site just over 100 m away in an area prone to flooding, where the bodies of 250 soldiers were discovered in 2008. There are symmetrical rows of headstones with flowers on a sloping lawn surrounded by a neat red-brick wall – created in the shape of the Cross of Sacrifice. And it is pouring down. From the shelter of the bus, Aurore explains that the mass grave was discovered after archaeologists puzzled over the fate of a group of soldiers.

'There were about a hundred and sixty who were unaccounted for,' she says. 'Of course one person could disappear in a shell blast. But a hundred and sixty? Where were they? In the end the archaeologists flew over the village in a little plane and noticed an area where the grass was a deeper green than elsewhere. That is often a sign of buried bodies and they were proved correct.'

The cemetery was built by the Commonwealth War Graves Commission and officially opened by the Prince of Wales a month or so before our visit; each of the bodies was reburied with full military honours. But before they were, something quite remarkable happened.

'The archaeologists took DNA samples from the bodies,' says Aurore – genetics again. 'By comparing DNA with those of relatives they have been able to positively identify ninety-six of the bodies so far.'

The result is that while many of the headstones are marked 'An Australian/British soldier of the Great War', others have the correct names of soldiers. Unlike so many World War One graveyards created soon after the conflict, the Fromelles cemetery has a personal feel.

The cemetery is both peaceful and chilling at the same time. E and I walk along the gravestones, taking in the names of those who died in the 'very badly constructed attack, remembered for its terrible violence', during which 'nothing was won and everything was lost' (Aurore's description). The ages of the soldiers on the stones, we see, range from nineteen to thirty-five. Neither of us has visited a Great War cemetery before.

'Isn't it sad?' E says quietly, speaking for us both, as we are joined by one of the Australians.

Kim is from Sydney but lives in Britain, working at a hotel in the New Forest. She too came over on Eurostar. 'My grandfather lost his eyes in the war,' she tells us as we huddle under our umbrellas. 'He was treated for three years for his injuries in the UK before being repatriated.'

Jim, also from Sydney, comes over and solemnly says: 'The French are doing a wonderful job here.'

He's talking about the memorials and we soon drive on to see several other sites, including a graveyard with a stupa devoted to Indian soldiers and another with Portuguese soldiers. The rain is relentless and looking out across muddy ploughed fields we get a strong sense of the sheer hopelessness of trench warfare; how futile it all must have felt.

By the Portuguese cemetery, we hear shots ringing out across the landscape. 'Probably after rabbits,' says Jim matter-of-factly, though it's almost disconcerting to listen to the echo of gunfire across fields so familiar with the sound of battle.

Then Aurore tells us a moving story. 'My great-grandfather was from the north of Portugal and he fought in the war,' she begins. 'While he was serving, he fell in love with a sixteen-year-old woman named Melanie. He didn't speak any French and she would come and visit him during the conflict. When the war ended, he refused to go home with the other troops. So he missed the boat and was considered a deserter; it was twenty-three years later before he was pardoned and allowed to re-enter Portugal without the risk of being jailed for desertion. He and Melanie married and had fourteen children, thirteen of whom are still alive.'

She pauses and looks across the graveyard. 'Now you can understand why I am so consumed with this – with this part of my history.'

It's an unforgettable half-day tour that puts a much broader perspective on the city than we'd have got just wandering about. Going down Rue Nationale towards the Grand Place, we now know that this was where German officers on leave went to requisitioned restaurants to unwind from the front line during the Great War. We know that the German HQ was in the Grand Place. We know that Allied prisoners were marched through the streets to boost German morale and depress locals. We know that a huge munitions explosion in January 1916 created a giant crater close to our B&B, destroying many houses and being heard as far away as Brussels.

We continue along wet cobblestones to the Grand Place, stopping for lunch at Café Paul, overlooking the columns and flamboyant stone figures carved into the façade of the city's opera house. There are tall buildings with decorative neoclassical designs all around the square and our cafe is at the foot of one of these. It's packed with people sheltering from the rain – we've definitely picked two of the city's 300 rainy days for this weekend break. We tuck into great flutes filled with *jambon* and *fromage* at a counter at the back. Café Paul, now an international chain, began in the small town of Croix just outside Lille in 1889, before moving to the city in the 1950s. It's still family owned and this seems to be the flagship shop.

'Delicious,' declares E, munching on her linseed flute in between sips of coffee, and then asking: 'So, where next?'

'Well, there's this new modern art museum,' I reply. The museum opened yesterday and has an incredibly long-winded name: LaM, Lille Metropole Musée d'Art Moderne, d'Art Contemporain et d'Art Brut. It's in the suburbs and is meant to be brilliant, if all the fanfare surrounding its opening is to be believed.

'How do you get there?' E asks.

'I'm not sure,' I reply. It seems quite a hike.

'Is there a bus, do you think? Or a taxi? A tram?' E suggests.

'Hmmm, I'm not sure,' I respond again, not knowing how long the journey will take.

This is how I end up handing over €30 to a grim-faced taxi driver (with no change) and then forking out an extra seven euros each to see LaM – which seems to be miles away from the centre of Lille. This had better be bloody good, I'm thinking as we enter after walking along a path in another monsoon-like downpour, my pockets considerably lighter.

The museum is in a series of low-level cube-like buildings. There are pink lights in the lobby and a lot of people wearing existential black. The Modern Art Lovers are in full luvvy mode as it's the first weekend, with lots of air kissing and exclamations and generally excited behaviour, amid the steam of folk drying out after the pelting rain. We enter a crowded room filled with the works of the Italian painter Amedeo Modigliani (1884–1920). Beautiful portraits of female nudes line the walls, with people in black peering closely at them. There are also female figures by André Derain (1880–1954) as well as a *Seated Nude Man* by Picasso (1881–1973). Everywhere we look there are nudes being scrutinised by Modern Art Lovers in black. Captions explain that certain works 'contribute to an expressive instability', while in others 'the light models the body, adding to its power and normality'.

'Really?' says E, reading this out.

The art is interesting even if the space is so crowded we can hardly see the pictures. We walk on through into another room full of giant multicoloured salt shakers.

'This is where it's starting to get very silly,' says E, as we pass a wall decorated with a map of France created out of pieces of teddy bears.

The room leads to a section on 'art brut'. I'd never known what this was before, but it turns out to be art created by people outside traditional art circles... people with no training who have nevertheless turned their hands to art. Some of the works are by inmates from mental asylums. Many are anonymous.

'If I'd created this junk, I'd leave it anonymous as well,' murmurs E, examining a portrait of a man with startlingly staring eyes.

'Hmmm... interesting,' she adds, taking in a black and white picture of a man in a garden surrounded by models of birds.

I don't think E is really taking to LaM.

We exit the museum through a maze of yellow and blue plastic cubes, and go to the cafe. There are more people in black here and E sits at a table while I queue for coffee. While she's there, I see her being confronted by a waiter with ginger hair. There seems to be a rather animated discussion – or is it a disagreement – taking place.

She comes over and says: 'Let's go.'

'Why?'

'That guy said I couldn't sit there as I didn't have a drink. He kept on saying: "Can you verify who you are?" And I kept saying that you were in the queue, and pointing over to you. But he refused to let us have a table. Honestly, this place is a complete joke.'

Yes, a completely bloody expensive one, I'm thinking. Outside, we wait in the rain and pick up a taxi that for some reason costs an eye-watering €40 to return to our B&B. I don't even want to think about how many euros LaM has set us back as I peel away the notes. Maybe we just went on the wrong day, maybe we should have worked out the public transport... maybe we were just in the wrong frame of mind to appreciate fully the splendours of 'art brut'.

But I don't think it was worth the best part of €100 (though at least we didn't have to pay for any coffees).

Our venture into the lovely world of LaM has also meant that we've missed out on the Palais des Beaux-Arts, home to masterpieces by the likes of Rubens, Constable and Turner, as it's too late in the afternoon and it's not open on Monday mornings. The gallery is considered one of the best in the whole of France. Instead we traipsed all the way out to LaM, and it cost an arm and a leg.

Well, you win some and you lose some, we're thinking as we relax back at the B&B for a while. I attempt to programme the television and fail at this task. Then we stroll along Rue de la Liberté and find ourselves turning into a side street and entering Tudor Inn Lille. This is a funky little bar with figures of panthers jutting out of the bar, rows of chandeliers hanging from low ceilings, and red-brick walls out of which a crazed face bulges outwards near our table. All the pink sofas are taken and we've found a spot near the bar.

Cool music plays as a cool waiter brings chilled glasses of Bourgogne Aligote; the wine we'd enjoyed so much back in Dijon.

'Absolutely delicious,' is E's verdict.

'When France goes wrong, there's always its wine,' I say.

'This is true,' says E.

'*Très vrai*,' I agree, waving to the waiter for one more.

We toast French *vin*. It's been a long day of sightseeing and it's good just to unwind and not think about tourist sights. The rain has finally stopped and it feels calm and quiet on a Sunday night. We have a couple of glasses and consider returning to the room and watching a bit of French TV.

'But it's still broken,' says E, quite accurately.

Instead, we go to a cinema around the corner and watch the film *Eat, Pray, Love* starring Julia Roberts. It's got French subtitles, and it's about finding yourself on your travels: and isn't that what going away is really all about? The film is also fun, if frankly way too long. Afterwards we stroll home through the empty streets of Sunday night Lille, feeling as though we've had a pretty full, but pretty different, day.

Breakfast at La Maison Théodore is served in the downstairs room with the weird wicker sculpture, and the spread on the kitchen table looks as though some kind of Lille festival day is about to begin. There are chocolate cakes, baskets full of baguettes and croissants, plates with neatly piled cheeses, jugs of fresh orange juice and milk, yoghurts, bowls of fruit, colourful jams lined neatly in pots. There's enough food for a dozen people, even though we are the only guests.

E's eyes widen at the sight of all the dishes. She's not hungry, and just fancies some fruit and a coffee. Chantal brings us lovely fresh pots of coffee. Then she says: 'Cake?' She pauses: 'I make zis cake myself.'

'*Ah, merci*,' I reply in my best French, as Chantal deftly places slabs of rich chocolate cake on both our plates and retreats to the kitchen. While she is there, E nonchalantly slides her slice onto my plate. I eat both (very good stuff) and Chantal returns.

She looks very pleased. 'Cheese?' she suggests. 'Zis cheese is zee hard cheese. Speciality of Lille.'

'*Ah, merci*,' I reply again, not sure what else to say: Chantal is so friendly it seems rude to say 'no'. She places slices of cheese on both of our plates and retreats once more to the kitchen, whereupon E, with a smile, swiftly transfers her cheese to my plate. I eat both portions of cheese before Chantal comes back.

The same routine is played out with chocolate croissants, ham of some sort, baguettes with 'zee traditional jam' and pieces of black chocolate; E is enjoying herself immensely and nodding appreciatively at every delicious offering.

'*Très bien*!' says Chantal, bringing another variety of cake. 'Zis is zee p-ee-can pie,' she comments, beaming. My eyes, and stomach, are more than beginning to bulge. E smuggles over her p-ee-can pie while Chantal is away.

'Don't want you to go hungry, love,' she says sweetly, watching me plough through both hefty slices of pie while grinning away and tucking a banana into her bag for later.

We say goodbye to Chantal, who has been a wonderful host, and wheel our bags across the city to the tourist office. I'm feeling a little bloated after the impromptu breakfast feast, but content, too. It's a bright-ish chilly day in Lille, no rain right now, though it does not seem too far away. We leave our bags behind the reception at the tourist office and catch a fifty-minute tour bus around the main sights. It's not something we'd planned to do, but the bus is there and about to go: why not?

'At least it'll be warm,' says E as we enter, handing over euros to a driver who had been in the middle of munching on a *croque-monsieur*.

It's more than that. We put on headphones and choose English as our language and are soon learning that the name Lille comes from the marshy land that the city was built on: Lille being a shortening of L'Isle (the island). We pass the closed Palais des Beaux-Arts and find out that it is the second biggest museum in France and that Rubens once came to the city. There is mention of the Dukes of Burgundy (but of course). We pass a fine statue of Louis Pasteur. We learn that the city has 220,000 inhabitants, although the metropolitan area covers a million people of whom 150,000 are students with many on courses covering 'engineering, journalism and business... it is a very young city'. We see the star-shaped walls of the Citadel, which dates from the seventeenth century and is still used by the military, though guided tours can be arranged in summer months. Then we pass, down narrow lanes, 'Le Why Not Restaurant' and a church where Charles de Gaulle was baptised. The leader of Free France during World War Two – who successfully fought to regain French colonies run by the pro-German Vichy regime, and famously called on the French to resist Hitler's occupation during a BBC radio interview in exile – was born in Lille in 1890. After the war he was made prime minister and later president of the country, when he granted independence to Algeria in 1962. He was a veteran of the Great War, fighting in many famous attacks in these parts including the Battle of Verdun, where he was captured after being wounded. He was injured several times during the Great War and his left hand was so damaged he had subsequently to wear his wedding ring on his right hand. He gained a reputation as an impassioned patriot during the struggle, five times valiantly attempting to escape when he was a prisoner of war.

His family house at 9 Rue Princesse is now a museum, we're told, though it's sadly closed today. According to the tour bus commentary, the museum tells the story of his remarkable life and contains a bullet-ridden Citroën in which a 1962 assassination attempt was made on de Gaulle in Paris by a far-right political group named the Organisation de l'Armée Secrète (OAS). This group opposed de Gaulle's liberal policy of independence for Algeria and their motto was: '*L'Algérie est française et le restera*' (Algeria is French and will remain so). This assassination attempt was recreated by the crime novelist Frederick Forsyth in his popular book *The Day of the Jackal*, published in 1971.

De Gaulle is considered by many to be the most important figure in post-war France – not a bad claim to fame for a wet industrial city just eighty minutes from north London that was also once home to the genius of Pasteur.

We continue onwards under a luminous grey sky, passing retro clothes shops, a downtrodden Romany woman in a yellow headscarf who is weeping silently near the grand nineteenth-century front of Gare de Lille Flandres (the domestic rail station), and the large concrete and glass shopping malls of Euralille.

This is a big development connected to Gare de Lille Europe (the international rail station), designed to capture business on the back of the trains from Britain and the extension of high-speed TGV services to Lille: a sign of how fast trains are quite literally beginning to change the face of European cities. There are big signs for global brands and a row of buses outside with '*Je roule au gaz naturel!*' written on their sides. It all looks very smart and futuristic, clearly designed to impress, with angular shaped annexes and shiny walls of glass, unlike any station we've seen yet – a brave new high-speed world that seems to be a foretaste of 186 mph travel elsewhere on the Continent.

E and I collect our bags and go to investigate Euralille at closer quarters. We enter the mall and walk past endless fashion shops and cafes. There are 'Wok & Sushi' and 'Tokyo' restaurants – Japanese food seems popular in Lille. There are DVD stores and posh toiletries shops. It's busy, even though it's midday on a Monday. We come to 'Brasserie Les Sports', where there's a table free. The cafe is decorated with old ice-hockey sticks, basketball nets, and pennants for American baseball teams: Cincinnati Reds, Baltimore Orioles and New York Yankees. We pay three euros for a Diet Coke and a Perrier, and settle down for a while – it's an hour before our train back.

'Drink up,' says E animatedly. Suddenly she seems eager to leave.

'What?' I ask.

'I've just spotted a Carrefour – look, over there,' she says, referring to a vast supermarket that's just round the corner. 'I just LOVE French supermarkets.'

And so we spend the last half hour of our trip before checking in doing exactly what just about every Lille weekend breaker does: stocking up on lovely French food. I pick up two bottles of Margaux red wine from the Bordeaux region (just €11 each).

'That would probably be £20 a go in Britain,' says E, dragging me away from the wines and heading for the refrigerated section.

'The French make the best yoghurts in the world,' she declares, selecting a sixteen-pack of Taillefine yoghurts. E has a thing about French yoghurts.

'Isn't that a bit big?' I ask dubiously, looking at the huge box.

'I think there's space in your backpack,' she replies casually, as we continue round the store collecting jams, olive oils, baguettes and more wine. By the time it's all packed and paid for, our bags (mine in particular) look ready to explode.

We join the crowds in the departure lounge, many of whom are carrying Carrefour plastic bags full of bottles. Booze cruises to Calais mean driving along the M20, waiting at the ferry terminal at Dover in long queues as enormous seagulls swoop above, squeezing into parking bays stinking of oil and diesel, waiting for ninety minutes in dreary surroundings as the ferry chugs across the Channel, disembarking and doing it all again on the way back. Yes, you can fit far more bottles in your car, but with a bit of planning (a decent-sized suitcase on wheels) and determination you could do pretty well on a weekend break to Lille. Slow booze cruise or fast booze train? I know which I prefer.

It's been an unusual weekend that's etched in both our memories. From a fantastic concert to moving battlefields, a quirky B&B and landlady, a crazy new art museum, famous old Frenchmen (Pasteur and de Gaulle), and just pottering about in a city that feels so easy to reach that it might be part of the UK. But it's not. It's in France. It's *French*. It's charming in a way that Leicester and Swindon, about the same journey times from London, will never and can never be.

Next stop on the fast trains is very different from the East Midlands and Wiltshire too. In a fortnight's time I'm about to visit a Grand Duchy in one of the smallest, least-visited and most mysterious spots in the whole of Europe.

CHAPTER FIVE

LUXEMBOURG CITY: 'LOST IN EUROLAND'

It's a mild Friday morning in early October. E and I are in Pret a Manger, our favourite St Pancras cafe, tucked away in a red booth at the back of the station, near a Boots, an M&S and the platforms for high-speed trains to parts of Kent.

These services began quite recently, piggybacking on the European fast tracks and shooting bleary-eyed commuters in a 140 mph streak across the Garden of England on Japanese-built trains. The introduction of the 'commuter bullets', slashing journeys from Ashford to London from 1 hr 23 min. to 37 min., was big news. The event was hailed by the then prime minister Gordon Brown as: 'A momentous day in the long and glorious history of British railways.' The trip from Dover to London had been cut from more than two hours to sixty-nine minutes. Many saw the trains as the start of a high-speed revolution within Britain. Lord Adonis, the then Transport Secretary, said: 'Journey times have shrunk dramatically, bringing regeneration and new opportunities for investment. This shows the potential of high-speed rail and we must now consider what it can do for the rest of the country.' Confident-sounding stuff: if Lord

Adonis is anything to go by, high-speed trains seem to be a fait accompli.

Maybe he's right, I'm thinking, in this corner of St Pancras that feels as though it's very much the future of British trains. Maybe we *will* all be jumping on 100 mph plus trains as a matter of course sometime soon. Perhaps trips between the likes of King's Cross and York, and Paddington and Bristol, will be cut to sixty-nine minutes too. Perhaps one day not so far away Edinburgh will only be a couple of hours away from where we're sitting right now. Maybe all of this is just inevitable, I'm thinking, no matter what the doubters and people whose homes will be affected by new tracks say.

'So what are you going to do in Luxembourg?' asks E, looking across the busy concourse. She can't make the trip as she has work to finish over the weekend.

I stop thinking about Japanese bullet trains speeding through the Cotswolds and answer a little vaguely that I'm going to see whatever comes my way, check out the sights. 'It'll probably be full of boring European Union officials and bankers,' I say, trying to play things down. Luxembourg City is home to the European Court of Auditors, the European Investment Bank, the European Court of Justice and the European Parliament's secretariat. It's also got 150 banks and is thought by many to be a tax haven. 'Not exactly the stuff of an exciting weekend break,' I say.

E regards me sceptically. 'So why are you going? I bet you're going to spend the whole time drinking wine and having fun,' E says.

She's got me here. Actually I am really looking forward to the trip, wondering what goes on in the tiny state that most people drive through almost without realising in twenty minutes on summer holidays.

I sip my coffee and assure her I would not dream of doing such terrible things – drinking wine and having fun.

She knows me too well. She eyes me closely. 'I bet you do: I bet you're going to have a great time.'

We sip our coffees. Commuters from Kent's bullet trains are queuing for drinks and the cafe is almost full, though many of the customers around us have bags and look as though they are about to head off to the Continent. Having been to this station so many times of late, we're getting used to the high-speed train buzz. St Pancras with its shiny upmarket shops and endless cafes may be unlike any other station in Britain, but it's beginning to feel normal to us now. Just as the station in Lille had an upbeat, futuristic atmosphere, so does William Henry Barlow's (much transformed) old shed.

E and I say goodbye amid the mini-forest of steel support pillars by the entrance to the departure gates. 'Text me: tell me what you're up to!' she says as we part. And I head into the departure lounge, take an escalator to the platform, and walk to carriage number 11, where I find myself at a table next to an elderly couple and their son. We're soon away and my neighbours, who are going to Lille, attempt to order drinks.

'I'd like a gin and tonic, please,' says the woman. We are in the Premium Leisure section, to which I've upgraded, not having told E.

'You must go to zee bar to buy that,' replies a snappy French steward in a charcoal-grey suit. He has a stand-offish manner and clearly doesn't want any messing about with G&Ts.

The woman settles for a mini bottle of wine, included in the Premier Leisure ticket price. Then she asks what food will be served. The expressionless steward points to a little menu on a piece of paper the size of a bookmark.

'Barbecued mushrooms and ham hock? Salami with black olives and Gouda cheese?' says the woman reading from the bookmark. 'Potato and salsify tortilla with smoked paprika?'

she continues. The menu appears to consist of tapas. 'Can't we just have a sandwich?'

'Hear, hear,' says her husband, sounding like a member of the House of Lords who's just woken up (and maybe he is).

The steward raises an eyebrow and says they can buy sandwiches from the buffet bar if they like. His look says: 'Zee British: phpffff!' Or something like that. He's not standing for any messing around. The woman and her husband settle for the tapas. And the husband promptly falls back asleep.

'What order does one eat this in?' asks the woman looking at the little plates, when the food eventually arrives. Her husband, awake again, and son shrug. She sips her wine. She looks at her glass, aghast. 'I'm hoping for something a little better this evening,' she comments. Nevertheless, she quickly polishes off the wine, and helps herself to her son's. 'It's only a skinny little thing,' she says, referring to the size of the bottle. Her son, who has a goatee and is in his forties, does not appear to mind in the slightest.

They discover I was in Lille a fortnight ago. I tell them about Fromelles and warn them about taxis to the modern art museum. 'What are you planning to do?' I ask.

'Eat and drink,' says the son, who is not a fellow of many words.

'We'll go to the main square and have a meal: enjoy the wine,' adds the woman.

The steward collects our trays. We move upwards out of the tunnel and speed across the familiar flat countryside. After a period of quiet, the woman's husband suddenly exclaims: 'Barbaric!'

We look at him. 'Absolutely barbaric!'

He's referring to *The Times* crossword, which he's been completing diligently. 'It's a barbaric system. I want to know who wrote the crossword. They used to tell you. They don't any more. Knowing who wrote it helps!'

He looks at his paper and continues: 'If we can't solve it, we don't speak to each other for the rest of the day.' He appears to be addressing me. 'It's not a joke, you know!'

We are pulling into Lille, and as they gather their bags, the man turns to me once again and says: 'Barbaric!' He shakes his paper and they depart.

The trip to Luxembourg is the longest one yet: 5 hrs 37 min., including a half hour wait at Brussels station for a connection. I left at 1 p.m. and will be arriving at 7.40 p.m. local time, one hour ahead. I settle into a double-decker train with lilac walls and grey seats, negotiate with a conductor who initially appears to want to throw me off as I don't show him the right ticket, and read *The Independent*. As we move past familiar graffiti on the edge of Brussels, I turn to a piece written by Simon Calder, the paper's senior travel editor. The headline is 'EUROSTAR UNVEILS NEW TRAIN TO REACH FURTHER INTO EUROPE... QUICKER.' The story explains that Eurostar has just ordered ten new trains from Siemens of Germany that will travel 20 kph faster than current trains, with a top speed of 199 mph. No date is given on the delivery of the trains, but the move would bring the journey time to Paris to just over two hours, down from 2 hrs 15 min., and open up the prospect of direct services to Amsterdam in under four hours and Geneva in five hours. Direct journeys to German cities, yet to be named, and French cities such as Bordeaux, Marseilles and Lyon are also being considered.

Our train moves out into ploughed countryside with wind farms on the horizon looking like a crop of space-age plants. I read on about the seemingly unstoppable spread of fast trains across Europe: getting that same sense of inevitability about high-speed railways I felt back at St Pancras. The German operator Deutsche Bahn is about to run test trains through the Channel Tunnel, with an eye to starting services to London from Cologne and Frankfurt. This depends on current regulations being relaxed to allow more companies to run cross-Channel trains. Apparently Italian rail firms have also expressed an interest. It does seem as though the Continent is about to open up completely to travel along the fast tracks.

But I can't help wondering if it will really make a difference. I'm not a fully signed up convert (yet, at least). Yes, new routes are beginning the whole time, but let's face it: 1) train tickets are usually, though not always, more expensive than flying on Ryanair or easyJet or even on 'traditional' services offered by British Airways and Air France, and 2) journeys can often take considerably longer. This trip cost more than £140 return, whereas a BA flight would have been £20 less. Flights from London to Luxembourg take 1 hr 20 min. – four hours quicker than by train if you don't include checking in early, transfers, and waiting at the baggage carousel. Put this together and it doesn't seem as though planes are on the way out at all, as articles like this one in *The Independent* might seem to suggest. They seem very much here to stay.

But then again: isn't that missing the point? Isn't the feeling on jumping on a train and heading for distant places what it's all about... and taking in what you can along the way? Isn't it the chance to see the Continent in a different, but still very fast, way? Isn't that what fast trains offer? Isn't that how they are changing things? It's the sensation, not just the statistics. It's all about the *experience*.

At least, that's the way I feel, as we pass between the apartment blocks and terraces of the city of Namur, which suffered heavy damage in both World War One and World War Two. It was on the front line during the Battle of the Ardennes in 1940 and the Battle of the Bulge in 1944. We plunge onwards into thick pine forests. A low yellow sun casts mottled beams between tall tree trunks, turning the landscape mellow orange as we move eastwards. At the small town of Marloie there are great stacks of logs shaped like Aztec temples waiting for freight trains. It's a beautiful ride, perhaps the prettiest yet. The sun drops quickly and it is dark as we reach Arlon, a town in Belgium close to the border with Luxembourg that is known for its Ferrero Rocher chocolate factory, and for having a mayor who was executed after collaborating with the Nazis during World War Two. We pause at Arlon. Then we move onwards, with mobile phones bleeping to announce our entry into Luxembourg. It is pitch-black as the train wheezes to a halt in the long train shed of Luxembourg City's station... bang on time.

It's a tiny, crowded station with piped music and a psychedelic, cartoon picture of a sun on the roof of the ticket hall. I stand by a sculpture of a fish and look at my map. Kids wearing hoodies are lurking in groups nearby, smoking cigarettes, swigging from cans of lager and generally acting furtively. I work out the way to the hotel and walk down a hill past bus stops, a McDonald's, a 'Snack Istanbul' restaurant, a beggar wrapped in a tatty blanket, and more teenagers with cans and smokes. Everything seems a bit rough around the edges. Luxembourg, with a population of about 500,000 and its strong banking reputation, is said to have the world's highest per capita GDP (about £43,700). But it doesn't seem so here. I keep on going down the hill, wondering if I've made a mistake visiting the city.

As I do, it all begins to change. The road leads to a bridge over a darkened gorge, with lights on spires and medieval walls on a bank on the far side. I cross the street to look out across the precipice. There are turrets, grand houses, churches and looming fortifications – which for many years gave the impenetrable city the nickname of the 'Gibraltar of the North'. There are sweeping bridges and a distant viaduct near a separate hill on which sits a cluster of neat skyscrapers, home to many of the European Union institutions. The city has a fairy-tale quality that immediately hits you. I'm not far from the station, just a three-minute stroll, and it's now almost eerily quiet: not a lager-drinking teenager in sight. I walk along a path overlooking the gorge and soon arrive at the hotel.

I'm staying at Sofitel Luxembourg Le Grand Ducal, a modern building overlooking the fortifications in the old town. Big Band music is playing in a minimalist lobby dotted with unusual pieces of modern art. A little multicoloured sculpture of a dog is inspecting a coffee table covered with a barcode-style design. There are pointillist paintings of looming figures. There are black and white leather daybeds. There are hoop-shaped chrome lamps. There are white candles flickering in tall silver candlesticks placed on the white marble floor. Looking around I realise that it's all very hip. I'd expected something corporate and bland, in keeping with Luxembourg City's boring-banker and Court of Auditor reputation. Instead, I've landed myself in some sort of stylish enclave, with blasé staff in charcoal outfits breezing about and jazz dancing lightly across the shiny surfaces.

A receptionist named Mario kindly presents me with a voucher for a free welcome drink at a top-floor cocktail bar. I take a lift in which the light shifts from red to pink to purple to blue. I walk down a hall decorated in lilac and pale pink polka dots. I enter a room with a purple chaise longue, a light shaped like a tall piece of seaside rock, and a shower in a glass box. The black and white carpet has a giddying pattern and there's a curved desk with finance magazines. It feels as though I've stepped into some kind of surreal dream.

I call E. 'It sounds very nice,' she says, referring to the hotel, with a slight undercurrent of: 'A bit too nice, why am I not there?'

I point out that she cóuld have come; that she could have brought her work with her as they've got Wi-Fi at the hotel. This is not perhaps the most helpful of comments.

There's silence at the end of the line. I describe the journey, the hoodies by the station and what I've seen of the pretty old town across the gorge.

'It sounds very nice,' she repeats, tight-lipped. Calling home is all very well, I'm realising, on a business trip. But if you're off on a fast-train weekend adventure with the sole aim of enjoying yourself while taking in an interesting new place (on your own), it's not the easiest of calls.

I don't mention the free cocktail voucher, and E tells me about her work. She's been commissioned to write an article for a national newspaper for the first time, after recently leaving a job connected to education. 'It's impossible!' she declares. She's having a hard time with it. 'They want 1,200 words. How can I say it in 1,200 words! I feel like I'm summing everything up. It takes all the colour out of it!'

I sympathise, make a few probably hopeless suggestions – and we say goodnight.

'No gallivanting!' she says, somehow managing to sense that I might be about to go out.

'Oh no, of course not,' I reply.

Then I go to the cocktail lounge. This is called Coco Mango and it's on the eighth floor. It's even more hip than the rest of the hotel. As I exit the lift, I turn left and almost bump into a DJ who has stepped aside from his turntables and is in the process of a peculiar solo dance. Music with a congo beat thuds across a long, busy room with scoop-shaped 1970s retro seats. There are pink neon strips of light along the floor and a bar covered in more polka dots. The DJ skips from one foot to another looking like a heron in the midst of some sort of mating ritual. I sit at a bar stool not far from a row of smokers, with a view through windows of the gleaming towers of EU offices and international banks, and take a look at the cocktail list, which offers drinks with names like Dirty Sanchez and Un Bango. Not sure which to order, I ask for a gin and tonic. A barman with a purple tie says: '*S'il vous plait, monsieur.*'

He rattles off something quickly in French. '*Je ne comprend pas*,' I reply.

'Which type of gin, sir?' he asks, deadpan.

There are three types. I go for Bombay Sapphire and he pours a vast measure in a glass with ice, places a bottle of tonic by its side and slides across little bowls filled with olives and pieces of cheddar.

I drink my G&T while reading Graham Greene's *The Ministry of Fear* – which E had slipped into my bag while I'd been buying coffees at St Pancras – and overhearing a conversation between a group of three British bankers wearing off-duty shirts and chinos. 'It took ages for us to win that product,' says one.

'Oh yeah, Dave was very disappointed,' says another.

'Oh yeah. Yeah, right, yeah I agree with you. I agree. He was right to be disappointed,' says another.

'He's a very smart guy,' says the third.

They drink their wine and light cigarettes. The room is already enveloped in a hazy fug. So this is how the people who shift Europe's mysterious tax-free millions take it easy on a Friday night.

Then one of them talks about a train trip to Brussels the previous weekend. 'It was a last-minute thing,' he says, drawing on his cigarette. 'We left at 8.30 p.m. and arrived late. We drank half a bottle of vodka along the way and went to three hotels and couldn't find a room. We were half-cut with nowhere to stay, but we got somewhere eventually. Then we hit the town.'

'Sounds like a laugh,' says one of the chino wearers.

'Oh yeah,' he replies. High-speed trains, it seems, have got Euro-bankers zooming about the Continent for impromptu binge nights out. With this story they stub out their fags and amble over to a minimalist restaurant in a far corner.

I turn to *The Ministry of Fear*. It's a gripping tale about a main character, Rowe, who becomes inadvertently mixed up with an underground group of Nazi sympathisers in London who are attempting to send secrets to Hitler during the war. On one level it's a comedy – Rowe's troubles begin in amusing circumstances when he wins a guess-the-weight cake at a local fair run by the undercover group – but on another it's about the pointlessness of war and of intervention in people's lives. 'One can't love humanity. One can only love people,' says Rowe early on, reacting against the idea that those who organise society necessarily know better than the people they are organising. I read on, finish my G&T and order another (why not, I'm on holiday), as Rowe continues: 'Knowledge was a great thing – not abstract knowledge in which Dr Forester [one of the Nazi sympathisers] had been so rich, the theories which lead one enticingly on with their appearance of nobility, of transcendent virtue, but detailed, passionate, trivial human knowledge.'

It's a thought-provoking book. And as my new drink arrives, I look through the tall windows towards the offices of one of the biggest governmental institutions in the world, responsible for rules in twenty-seven countries, feeling as though I'm reading this in the right place. After all, wasn't the EU partly the result of the desire to bring harmony in Europe after one (very evil) theory of organising society that led to World War Two? And isn't it now, in turn, responsible for organising our lives again? I gaze out towards the tower blocks, wondering which ones are home to the politicians who make rules on 'bendy bananas'.

I consider another G&T as I re-read the sentence about 'detailed, passionate, trivial human knowledge'. In a funny way, along with the straightforward experience of catching the fast trains across Europe, it feels as though that is what I'm searching for on these trips: slices of life at the end of the tracks, detailed, passionate, trivial or whatever comes my way.

And with these Bombay Sapphire thoughts (OK, I admit it, I stayed for another, the view was just too good) I return to my mad polka dot room in the heart of Euro-banker land. I've got a busy day ahead.

It starts early, on a bright clear morning with just a hint of mist in the gorge in front of the old town. Luxembourg looks beautiful in the golden light, even more like a fairy-tale city than it did last night. Terraces of terracotta, ruby and pale-yellow houses run in line above the cliff-like fortifications, partially covered in great vines. Trees in the valley below are displaying their full autumnal splendour: warm browns, soft yellows, hints of red, touches of silver. Turrets and spires stand out against a royal blue sky. The EU tower blocks are gleaming. A few folk are walking dogs, some taking steep paths into the valley, where I can see a small calm river. It is wonderfully quiet.

Taking all of this in, I'm approached by a man holding a brochure. He has a goatee beard, a blue overcoat and must be in his mid sixties. His name is Steve Lyons, and he's a retired broker from Britain. Without E around to check out the sights with me,

I've decided to book a city guide for the morning. He is, I soon discover, a fount of all knowledge regarding Luxembourg City.

We head down one of the tracks into the valley, towards the old houses by the river in an area known as Grund. As we do, I ask Steve why so few people are about.

'Commuters, that's why,' he replies, treading carefully to avoid damp leaves on the cobbled path. 'There are 150,000 people who commute into work here each week. The main reason is that it's a very expensive place to live. The permanent population is just 85,000.'

This means that the city is almost dead at the weekends, which either makes it a very dull or a very relaxing place to visit... which I guess I'm about to find out. 'There were a lot of people at the hotel bar last night,' I say.

'Oh yes, Luxembourg is in the top ten for alcohol consumption in the world,' Steve responds. He's a great one for figures and statistics. 'Our excise duty is very low, so it's a very good place for booze.'

'It is also in the top ten for suicides per capita in the world. There are often obits that say that someone "died suddenly",' Steve continues, almost cheerfully. He really is not your average guide. 'Yes, this may be one of the wealthiest countries in the world. But money isn't everything.' He pauses for a moment and adds matter-of-factly: 'Unfortunately.'

Statistics are soon flying about as we stroll beneath weeping willows along the River Alzette in the Grund valley. 'The last population count was 502,000 for the whole country,' Steve says. 'Of this, forty-four per cent are foreigners, with the largest group being Portuguese, about 80,000. They came during the Salazar regime [the authoritarian right-wing government of António de Oliveira Salazar ran Portugal from 1932 to 1968] and they came looking for work. They did the jobs the people of

Luxembourg did not want to do.' As if to prove their presence, we pass a cafe with a red and green Portuguese flag hanging above the entrance.

He tells me that there are about 5,000 Britons living in Luxembourg, and that he came to work here in 1974, meeting his wife and settling down. Then we cross a charming bridge and skirt past Scott's Pub, where a sign is advertising a gig by a band called the MEPs. I ask Steve about the local food. 'Luxembourg cuisine is heavily based on pork,' he replies. 'Sliced collar of ham served hot with broad beans in a sauce and boiled potatoes. Sauerkraut with pig's trotters: that kind of thing,' he says, making me think of how E, a vegetarian, would really have enjoyed it here.

We ascend a path on the other side of the river, after walking along a narrow snaking road with little houses. This leads upwards past neat rows of vineyards on shelves of land sheltered beneath great stone city walls dating from medieval times. Above us are the blackened cave-like holes of ancient casements, from which tunnels weave through this corner of the old town.

These tunnels have a story to tell (one that helps explain the unusual history of this peculiar little European state). In the tenth century, I learn from Steve, the strategically important hills and territory around the city were taken over by an influential dignitary. Count Siegfried I acquired the land through a deal struck with monks in the nearby German city of Trier; in one fell swoop creating Luxembourg as it more or less remains today. Local legend goes that Melusina, his wife, made a request when they were married: she was to have one day and night each month when she would be left totally alone. Siegfried granted this and for many years Melusina would retire into her chambers deep in the tunnels of the city, until one day Siegfried was so curious that he peeked in to take a look. He saw her in a bath with a fishtail in place of her legs. She sensed his presence and leapt out of one of the casements into the River Alzette below, and swam away never to be seen again.

So the story goes, but more importantly Siegfried's legacy remained. An independent tradition was begun and Luxembourg maintained its autonomy for 400 years during the Holy Roman Empire, until Holy Roman Emperor Charles IV turned the land into a duchy and made himself the duke. Over the years the fortifications that we are walking up to were fought over and eventually taken in turn by the Spanish, the Austrians and the French. It was a French politician who, after a seven-month siege, during one of the many skirmishes, declared the city to be 'the best [fortress] in the world, except Gibraltar'.

After the fall of Napoleon and the Treaty of Vienna in 1815, Steve continues, the territory was made a Grand Duchy and given as a personal possession to William I, King of the Netherlands and the Prince of Orange-Nassau. When Napoleon III attempted to buy the land from the third grand duke in 1866, Otto von Bismarck, the Prussian chancellor, stepped in and opposed the sale, saying that Luxembourg was too strategically important to be ruled by the French. The result was the 'Luxembourg Crisis' and the Treaty of London in 1867 that led to many of the tunnels and fortifications being destroyed. The small territory was too much of a stronghold and it was decided that neither the Germans nor the French should ever be in control of the position.

The result? The state, about the size of Derbyshire, was declared neutral and to be forever ruled by the House of Nassau (although the Germans, of course, invaded during both world wars). It is still run by the House of Nassau today, under a democratic system of constitutional monarchy, with Grand Duke Henri in charge.

We make our way up the cobbled steps to the old town. The sun is shining and my head is spinning. Steve really does seem to know everything you need to know about Luxembourg. We stand on a bridge overlooking the tunnel openings, and he begins to tell me about banking.

'We're a tax haven,' he says matter-of-factly. 'There are strict bank secrecy laws. Yes, there is a small "holding tax" of about 15 per cent on interest. Luxembourg keeps a quarter of that and the rest goes to the country of domicile.'

These taxes were introduced relatively recently, after the 1970s and 1980s when 'it was pretty possible not to pay any tax at all'.

'But if you have to pay some tax now then surely it's not a tax haven,' I say, as we cross the bridge to look at the EU tower blocks.

Steve pauses. 'People pay taxes... in theory at least,' he says, striding on without further comment.

Down below us is a viaduct built by the British in the 1860s for the first railway. Not so far from this, Steve points out the birthplace of Robert Schuman, one of the early campaigners for European integration, whose enthusiasm led to the formation of the European Coal and Steel Community in 1952, a forerunner of the EU, which in turn now employs 14,000 Eurocrats in Luxembourg. 'We always call them employees, not workers,' Steve says conspiratorially, implying that they don't actually work all that much.

'They get very good salaries and tax benefits,' he continues, warming to his theme. 'Every three years they get to buy a tax-free car. They have to keep it a couple of years, before they can sell it on. There are terrific clubs and fitness centres up there as well.'

When he says 'up there' he points to the buildings on the opposite hill.

We walk into a square where there's a flea market selling all sorts of antiques including delicate pieces of locally made Villeroy & Boch porcelain, old lamps and wooden furniture. The square is surrounded by plane trees and cafes. 'It's a bit of a tourist trap,' says Steve.

We take in the imposing sixteenth-century grand ducal palace, which was a Nazi headquarters during the war and left in such a state that Grand Duchess Charlotte chose to move to a palace outside the city in Colmar-Berg when she returned after the conflict. And then we pass the prime minister's office. 'The current PM likes to come out and talk to tourists,' my very knowledgeable guide tells me. 'One time I was here for ten minutes with him and a group of Japanese tourists. Oh, he's a great man.'

We say goodbye. What a tour: I get the sneaking impression that Steve could have talked about Luxembourg until a whole new chapter of its history began to unravel, requiring yet more explanation. He's been great, but I'm shattered. I'm also hungry. On a high street, near a shop in which you can pick up free posters displaying portraits of the bigwigs in the European Commission – what a terrific Christmas present that would be – I slump into a small restaurant named Maison des Brasseurs.

I find myself sitting at a walnut-effect table in a narrow, gloomy room next to a row of elderly women looking outwards while eating steaming pots of mussels. A waitress in a red and white dress comes over and I point to a dish on the menu, which appears to be written in Luxembourgish. This is the local language, although people also speak French and German. The woman nods as though this is an excellent choice and departs.

I peruse a 'Welcome to the European Parliament' booklet I picked up after popping into the EU shop round the corner. If

I was beginning to feel sleepy when I came in, this publication is in danger of pushing me into dreamland. More than half a billion people live in the EU, I read, and 'all of us, whatever our situation, young or not so young, students, workers or pensioners, and certainly as consumers, are affected by European laws, sometimes without realising it'. These laws protect human rights and democracy, allow freedom of movement and provide 'healthier food on our plates'. As I read this, contemplating the rather sinister phrase 'sometimes without realising it' and thinking back to Graham Greene's *The Ministry of Fear* in a state of semi-slumber, my food arrives.

This makes me wake up pretty sharpish. I've ordered *judd mat gaardebounen*, a dish consisting of neck of smoked pork, runner beans and potatoes. There are three enormous slabs of pork resting on a pile of runner beans on a plate next to a metal bowl of boiled potatoes that seem to have been mixed with little pieces of pork scratchings. Each piece of pork would reasonably be considered a 'large portion' in just about every other country I've ever visited.

I eat one of the slabs of pork, with the row of women watching; maybe I'm being paranoid, but it definitely feels as though they are regarding me as some kind of spectacle. I dig into the foothills of the runner-bean mountain and have a go at the potatoes covered in pork scratchings. Lovely. But I already feel full. And there is *a lot* of food left: masses of it. The women regard me, chattering among themselves and seemingly enjoying watching 'the tourist who ordered the huge dish for three people and now can't eat it all'. It must be for more than one person, I'm thinking, as I embark on the neck of smoked pork number two. It's slow going. But I get through my pork and beans and potatoes and pork scratchings in the dimly lit wood-panelled room. There isn't another tourist in the restaurant, as far as I can see. The women on the long bench smile and appear to be genuinely surprised I polished off the whole lot (perhaps they were taking bets).

Afterwards, feeling as though I could live for a few days on the food I've just eaten, I take a look in the tunnels. They cost a couple of euros to enter and are... tunnels. I don't know what more to say, other than they have great views where they open onto the cliff face, though you get the same views from above. I walk along the fortifications in the sunshine enjoying the autumnal colours across the valley back towards my hotel. It's quite spectacularly beautiful, especially walking across the arched bridge that is Pont Adolphe. The Bank Museum on the other side is closed, and I can't pretend that this leaves me heartbroken. I go back to the hotel, take a rest, and venture back out in the early evening to visit Casino Luxembourg. This is not an actual casino: it's a modern art complex with exhibitions displaying neon lights and odd sculptures shaped like tortured human faces. The neon lights are shaped into sentences in English: 'LOSING FOCUS', says one, while another reads: 'THERE'S NO PLEASURE IN HAVING NOTHING TO DO, THE FUN IS IN HAVING LOTS TO DO AND NOT DOING IT.' Pondering these words of wisdom, I stop off at the Cathédrale de Notre Dame, where I hand over a euro to a fellow with scraggly hair and sorrowful eyes who is begging outside (a down-on-his-luck banker perhaps) and take a look at the Madonna by the altar, amid high columns and a smell of incense. I stop off at Scott's Pub after taking a public lift down to the valley, where I listen to a couple of songs including 'Sympathy for the Devil' by the MEPs while having a pint of lager. Then I return to my hotel where there's a private party on the eighth floor and music is booming throughout the building. I read more of *The Ministry of Fear*, enjoying the sense of menace that Greene builds up as

Rowe haplessly finds himself drawn into the strange world of the Nazi sympathisers, and finally fall asleep to the upstairs sound of bankers and Eurocrats at play.

In the morning I 'follow the Chinese'. This had been Steve's advice: 'Just follow the Chinese.' He was talking about the Chinese tourists who visit the Trier, about twenty-five miles north-east of Luxembourg City, just across the Moselle River and the border into Germany. I do as he says, boarding an eight-euro-return train, where I find oriental faces that I take to be Chinese in my carriage. We cross the old British viaduct, passing the sun-splashed cliffs of the old town and travel through deep forest, before opening into sloping fields full of piebald cows and yellowing vineyards. We cross the olive expanse of the Moselle and pull up in Trier, the oldest city in Germany.

The Chinese and I disembark, and walk along a wide boulevard into the centre, heading for the birthplace of Karl Marx. Until fairly recently Museum Karl-Marx-Haus would attract the odd tourist visiting the spot in the charming city where Marx was born in 1818. But since the Chinese began travelling on holiday, there has been a steady flow of visitors in search of the origins of the man who penned *The Communist Manifesto*. I am among them as we make our way to a superb Roman gate named Porta Nigra, a UNESCO World Heritage Site. This 1,800-year-old structure has four storeys and you can, for three euros, climb to the top. I do so, skirting a group being led by a man dressed as a Roman soldier, and enjoying the views across the rooftops towards the glistening sweep of the Moselle. It's amazing to think that the gateway has remained intact so long. It's also a place that can't help but give pause for thought about the sheer scope of Roman endeavour. While most of Europe was scratching an existence from the land, Hadrian, Caesar and their likes were constructing vast gateways and walls that would last forever.

Down below, I walk onwards to a square in which locals are drinking hot wine at a circular bar near a brass band playing jolly German songs. Everyone's having a grand old time on Sunday morning in the middle of Trier. I pass a McDonald's and a fashion shop called 'More and More', of which Marx might have approved: after all, his theory on the collapse of capitalism was based on greed bringing its downfall. And then, beyond a Chinese restaurant, I come to his old home, a baroque house on an undistinguished side street. Before I go in, I take a picture of the front, just as a homeless man with a long grey beard passes, pulling an old cooler bucket on a trolley with his worldly possessions piled on top. I hadn't seen him before I held up the camera and he swiftly walks on round a corner, looking a little like the old German philosopher himself.

Inside there are Chinese, everywhere. In the queue for tickets I get talking to Nick 'Happy' Young, aged twenty-seven from Dalian in north-east China's Liaoning Province. 'We are on business trip in Wittlich,' he says, referring to a nearby town. 'We work for Dunlop tyres. One month I am here. I'm an engineer.'

Is he visiting the museum because he admires Marx? Is he a hero?

'Actually, he's famous, but he is not a hero,' he responds, quietly. 'I don't think his theory is helpful to China.'

Next to him is Lan Jiang, aged thirty, a translator on Happy's business trip. 'I also think he is not a hero,' she says. 'I don't know why. Maybe this is the view of the young, not the old. I think that maybe for young women in China, fashion is more important than politics. We have come because we are... a little curious.'

Capitalism seems to be going strong in the gift shop of Marx's birthplace: Marx's father was a lawyer and Marx, the third of nine children, spent his childhood and youth in the city. T-shirts bearing his famous visage are on sale for €20; special leather-bound editions of *Das Kapital* are available for €155; there are miniature Marx busts for €25. I scoot around, learning that the Nazis stormed the building in 1933 and claimed to have 'liberated' a 'house of damnation'. A section is devoted to Marx's rowdy days as a student in the city, when he is known to have been incarcerated for drunken behaviour and the possession of 'illegal weapons'. It's also interesting to find out that Marx used stories gathered locally about the plight of the Moselle vine-growing peasantry in his early journalism about the conditions of the poor.

Downstairs I find Happy signing the visitors' book. He points to his entry and invites me to read it. 'Freedom, the human rights and equality are not the basic things of communism,' says his entry, 'They are the basic things of the whole world.'

I follow the Chinese back up to Trier station, where I call E and tell her about the art gallery last night.

'Oh God,' she says. 'I know those places... full of weird plastic stuff.'

'Exactly,' I say.

I tell her about Karl Marx and the Chinese. 'How bizarre,' she says, not sounding as though she's missing the origins of *The Communist Manifesto* too much – it's a freak heatwave in London and she's sunbathing on her balcony.

She quizzes me on how many beers I had at Scott's Pub last night. Then she asks: 'Would people really want to go to Luxembourg?'

My answer comes straight out: 'Yes, it's very nice. Quite stunning really.' I've enjoyed the visit; there is something about the city that's extremely laid back and relaxed. It's *not* quiet in a dull way.

But before I go I have one more mission. Back in Luxembourg City, I walk into the old town where I stop at a sign on the side of an old building that says: '*Mir woelle bleiwe wat mir sin.*' On my tour yesterday Steve had told me that this comes from a local song called 'The Fire Wagon', written to celebrate the coming of railways in 1859, just a few years before the Grand Duchy was declared 'neutral' after the Luxembourg Crisis. The saying means: 'We want to remain as we are.'

In many ways, though, I don't think they have stuck to it. I walk on to Kirchberg, the hill where all the EU institutions are built. I climb the steep incline, stop at MUDAM, another wacky modern art museum with a commanding view back across the city, and then wander along virtually empty streets, taking in the golden mirrored-glass front of the European Court of Justice and the glistening plate glass of the European Parliament's secretariat. The only people about are a few teenagers skateboarding along the edges of stone walkways and benches. Apart from their occasional scrape and clatter, there is almost total silence.

I cross John F. Kennedy Avenue, a big dual carriageway without a car in view in either direction. Big buildings loom all about. There are empty construction sites where more governmental buildings are due to rise. And it's clear that while the 'We want to remain as we are' slogan remains true of the status of the Grand Duchy – Luxembourg has, after all, not been incorporated into any of its neighbours – there clearly has been huge change over recent years.

It's all quite *1984* and it also reminds me again of *The Ministry of Fear*, written six years before George Orwell's dystopia. Amid all the looming structures and the deserted walkways, the anonymity and sheer scale of the institutions bear down on you. For five minutes I don't see another soul. Greene's story about *people* mattering – rather than big ideas and theories – seems somehow to resonate here.

With these thoughts, I walk back to the hotel and to the station. I've enjoyed Luxembourg. It's an intriguing, rather curious place (well worth a weekend). In a fortnight I'll be heading back in this direction, passing even further still on a fast train… to a city deep in Marx's homeland.

CHAPTER SIX

FRANKFURT: 'BANKERS, JUNKIES AND VANISHING CABARET ACTS'

There's a buzz of mobile phones as we enter Germany, and a nasal voice clicks on the speaker system. 'Vee are very sorry,' says a guard. 'Zis train is running seven minutes late. Zere was a problem with zee high-speed line in zee run-up to Liège.'

Our journey so far has gone like clockwork. We've shared the journey to Brussels with a carriage full of cheerful Geordies drinking Kronenberg and discussing football ('they were 300-1, it were champion when that came in for me, absolutely champion,' a fellow was boasting in the seat in front). We've waited twenty minutes in a pleasant lime-green cafe in the bowels of Brussels station before catching our connecting ICE train to Frankfurt. And we're on schedule to arrive – more or less on time, just under six hours from St Pancras – in Germany's banking capital at 7 p.m. on this chilly Friday evening in late October.

'Imagine that back in Britain,' says E. 'So polite: apologising in advance about a tiny delay to a three and a half hour journey.'

We've just passed through a city called Aachen, known for being the site of the palace chapel of Charlemagne, the powerful Holy Roman Emperor, and for its thermal baths (the hottest north of the Alps). Now we're speeding out of Cologne station, with the huge cathedral looming up, and crossing a bridge flanked by statues of proud figures on horses across the wide expanse of the River Rhine. It's a busy carriage with comfortable red seats, and I'm reading guidebooks that say that Frankfurt is the wealthiest German city in terms of per capita income and that it really ought to have been made capital of West Germany after World War Two. But it wasn't, I'm informed, because Chancellor Adenauer, who made the decision, came from a town near Bonn. Like Luxembourg, it's a place of both high finance and European regulations, home to the country's main stock exchange and the European Central Bank; some nickname the city 'Bankfurt'. One in every ninety-nine people is also said to be a lawyer, which seems like rather a lot for a population of 660,000. The city is home to 'trance music' and drug pushers, junkies and prostitutes are a big problem around the station. 'You will see junkies self-medicating,' warns the Lonely Planet. 'Men should expect a few shouts from the street prostitutes.'

I read this out to E.

'Great,' she says. 'I look forward to the reception party.'

As if to prepare us for the worst, we are soon moving past rundown allotments, grim apartment blocks, a beast of a power station billowing steam across the Main River, derelict warehouses plastered with graffiti, and empty yards covered in weeds in the run-up to the city: Frankfurt does not exactly sell itself to you on the approach by train. 'It isn't the most beautiful place, is it?' I comment.

'You're right, it's really ugly,' says E, who has flown to visit her banker brother here in the past. 'This bit at least is ugly,' E adds. 'Other parts are OK.'

With these less than brilliant first impressions, we pull into Frankfurt Hauptbahnhof, precisely seven minutes late. We do not see any self-medicating junkies and I am not bellowed at by prostitutes. Instead, we catch a taxi for a short drive across the river to our hotel.

We're staying at Villa Kennedy, set back from a main street named Kennedyallee in a quiet neighbourhood. We pull up outside a Gothic stone entrance of an old residential house and enter a stylish lobby with purple flowers in vases, staff in charcoal-coloured suits, marble counters, and provocative modern art depicting a woman wearing a bikini-thong with her back turned to the painting. 'Very classy,' says E as we make our way to the lifts, passing a central courtyard and a snazzy bar.

But our room is indeed classy – with daybed-style sofas, tasteful modern art and a courtyard view. There is also a 'Pillow Menu'. This is a new one to us. E picks up the menu and inspects the offerings. There are 'soft grain' pillows, 'cherry stone' pillows (literally consisting of cherry stones), 'flat horsehair pillows' and 'exclusive neck-supporting pillows'.

'Let's order new pillows, what the hell!' says E, amused by the concept. 'Let's call them and say: "The current pillows are not to my liking: bring me new pillows!"'

'We could perhaps do that,' I say.

'Yes, we shall. But we shall do it at our leisure,' says E, in her best lady-of-the-manor voice.

She puts the pillow menu to one side and enters the bathroom. It's full of shiny marble and has a big bathtub. Gentle classical music emanates from hidden speakers. 'Wow,' says E. 'Let's just hang out in the bathroom for a while. Do we really need to see this sodding city? I just want to see this hotel.'

We decide to save Frankfurt investigations (proper) for tomorrow. Instead, we take a walk round the block, which consists of a series of vast Gothic houses, and nip into an On the Run garage to pick up water and a decent bottle of wine – no point in breaking the bank with hotel prices.

A nice theory, but on the way we stop for a drink in the Villa Kennedy bar. With its red velvet armchairs bathed in soft lemon-coloured light emanating from thistle-shaped chandeliers, it looks too good to resist. I tuck the clinking On the Run bag under a chair. There is a 'Favour your Flavour' cocktail promotion in which you can choose fruit juices to go with your drink, and a menu on the table shows a very fruity cocktail. 'Does that picture bewitch your senses?' a caption asks.

A waiter arrives, his eyes appearing immediately to lock on the glaring red petrol station bag, though he says nothing about it. We order two glasses of house white, ignoring the promotion, and take in the surroundings.

There are two other drinkers in the bar: a woman who has clearly had plastic surgery and is pecking at a mobile phone, and a businessman sitting in a far corner. The barman arrives with the wine. 'Enjoy!' he says. And then a tall woman with long straight blonde hair, high heels and a black miniskirt materialises. She walks to the bar and asks the barman a question. He indicates the direction of the man in the corner. The woman smiles and saunters over to him, whereupon they are soon in intimate conversation.

'What do you make of that?' I ask E.

'What do *you* make of it?' she replies, raising an eyebrow.

We order another glass of wine, totally ruining our On the Run plans to keep costs down. E asks for glasses of tap water as well, and we are given a bottle of mineral water, which is opened and poured before we realise what's going on. We discuss our

Frankfurt plans and mark a few sights on a tourist map. Then I sign a bill for €44 (so much for economising), and we head back. Our luxurious, pillow-menu abode awaits.

Saturday morning is crisp and sunny and we're driving in a car full of kids' toys through the south of Frankfurt. We are with E's sister-in-law, Kat, who has kindly picked us up and is cheerfully giving us an insider's view of the city.

'Frankfurt in general is affluent,' she says, beaming a big smile. 'And this area, Sachsenhausen, is one of the nicest areas.' Our hotel is on the edge of Sachsenhausen, and Kat, who works in banking and is originally from Bonn, tells us that Goldman Sachs held their Christmas party at the hotel restaurant last year. The huge investments bank, which had just made news in the UK with average annual salary and bonus packages of £269,000, has one of its headquarters in the city.

Kat is full of enthusiasm for Frankfurt. 'Yes, this is a good area: for young bankers and their families,' she says, as we pass along cobbled streets with yellow and turquoise trams occasionally sliding by. 'Here in Sachsenhausen it is also a traditional place for going out. Drinking *ebbelwoi* [an alcoholic apple cider] is very big here. It's really strong: knocks your socks off!'

We drive along the river for a short stretch and soon turn on to a road into Oberrad, where Kat and Phil, E's brother, live with their two young boys. The suburban neighbourhood has a laid-back, sleepy feel. We pass the small Al Capone Pizzeria and a courtyard where a man 'has thousands of apples and he crushes them and sells apple juice – it's really healthy'. We suddenly feel as though we're a long away from the skyscrapers we'd seen a few minutes earlier on the north side of the river, and coming here is a reminder that as 'inner city' as things may be around the railway station, Frankfurt is in reality a relatively small place; about a fifth of the size of London when you take in the full metropolitan area.

'It's like a little village where we live,' says Kat. 'We have farmers as neighbours. Everything is quite rural, but I can cycle in half an hour to my work in the city in the morning.'

We enter a door to a pale pink building and we're soon meeting Phil and the boys in their spacious but modest flat. Phil is an extremely chilled out guy, whose calm eye served him well at the major bank he recently left to take some time out of the rat race. He and the boys are playing a game of 'house poker' with cards and casino-style chips on the circular red carpet of their living room, which is lined with packed bookshelves and has a computer whirring away in a corner. 'They've just lost their pocket money,' says Phil, chuckling as he goes to the kitchen to fetch fresh coffee.

As Kat and E chat and the boys begin an impromptu violin concert amid all the casino chips, Phil is soon telling me that he fancied a break from banking and that he's been taking part in poker tournaments over the past few months. He's been creating a stir. 'I played at a couple of live events,' he says casually. 'It was quite unusual. The other players were degenerates, terrible people most of them. All of them smoked – it was constant – and their cards were unbelievably loose.'

'How did you do, did you win anything?'

'Oh yeah, I won,' he says, smiling from under his grey baseball cap. 'It's the intellectual challenge I enjoy. The intellectual challenge of chess... but you're making money as well.' He has rows of well-thumbed poker books by his computer and an unflappability that seems made for the game.

'I feel quite sorry for your opponents,' I say, wondering if they stand much of a chance.

He chuckles again and goes to make more coffee, joined by E. The two of them are as thick as thieves: you only have to look at them to realise they're brother and sister.

Kat tells me about the differences between her hometown Bonn and Frankfurt. 'Bonn has Beethoven, Frankfurt has Goethe,' she says, gazing through her half-rimmed specs. 'Bonn is more snobbish than Frankfurt. But Frankfurt has the literary establishment, the annual book fair and many people working in publishing. It also has a bit of an older population: people living in the villages like this one, people who don't go out so much.'

She discusses Berlin: 'It's more for poor, hippy people.'

Then she talks about cities in Germany as a whole, giving me an insight into the country that I hadn't had before. 'Germany does not have a major city as such,' she says. 'It's because the country only came together at the end of the nineteenth century.' For this reason, she explains, each city has its own flavour and pride of place, without a sense that it lives in the shadow of a capital city in the way other places in Britain may feel about London. Regarding Frankfurt, Kat adds: 'Historically it's very interesting. But you've got to dig deep.' She pauses and beams another big smile. 'It's really not a place that is so,' she pauses again, seeming to be searching for the right word, 'so *lovely*... you have to dig deep in Frankfurt.'

We spend the morning chatting away. Phil tells me all about his efforts to set up a cricket league (much to the surprise of the locals) and how his team, the Corinthians, recently lost the Frankfurt 'Ashes' against a team of 'broken down pub hacks' who had sneakily recruited Indian bankers to gain an advantage. Then E and I say goodbye to him and the boys and return with Kat to the city centre. On the way, though, we stop at their family allotment. It is huge with cherry and plum trees, rows of vegetables (runner beans, sweetcorn, butternut squash), a barbecue, garden furniture, and a big shed. The plot of land is about 30 metres wide and 40 metres long, in a secluded area surrounded by trees and other allotments. 'Almost everyone has one, it costs just four hundred euros a year to rent from the council,' says Kat, as though having such a large area of what is effectively countryside to themselves is a matter of course.

'I love it here,' says E.

'We love it too,' replies Kat.

Kat drops us at Römerberg, the old cobbled central square on the north side of the river, not far from the skyscrapers – just a fifteen-minute drive away. This is home to the rose-stoned town hall where she and Phil were married. It's an eye-catching building with step-shaped gables, carved figures of saints, and large European Union and German flags flying outside. There is a smell of fresh bread coming from somewhere... and a waft of hot dogs, too.

We are, after all, in Frankfurt – so I go and buy an 'original Frankfurter *würstchen*', while E tucks into a cheese sandwich from a Starbucks round the corner: the city's hot-dog kiosks are not the best for vegetarian offerings. We sit on the steps of the town hall and eat our lunches. My *würstchen* is made of pork, though I could have opted for an identical-looking *rindswurst* made of beef. It cost €2.80 and comes on a paper plate with a large dollop of mustard and a napkin.

'Good lord,' says E, smiling, her eyes bulging in vegetarian alarm as I tuck into the *würstchen*, with mustard and *würstchen* juices going everywhere.

It is quite simply delicious. Silence descends as E eats her sandwich and I munch through my hot dog in the spiritual home of hot dogs. People pass by munching hot dogs of their own, while others are intently doing the same sitting at picnic tables and standing by upturned barrels near the stall. Some of the groups are also drinking beer and laughter rises from their direction, echoing across the cobbles. Around us tall, distinguished buildings with pink and black exteriors with decorative wooden criss-cross shapes wobble upwards. They look ancient, yet most of the structures round here were reconstructed after World War Two, when Allied raids in March 1944 destroyed about 80 per cent of the city centre. We take in the pretty square. Jolly chatter echoes across the cobbles. The sun is out and all is well among the hot dog eaters of Frankfurt.

I fetch another, a *rindswurst*. 'It's good to test out the different types,' I explain to E.

'Good lord,' she replies, smiling again, her eyes widening.

'They're a bargain: only two euros eighty,' I say evangelically. It's easy to become evangelical about the hot dogs of Frankfurt.

'Have you got enough mustard?' E asks, with what I take to be a slightly sarcastic tone: I have a huge amount of mustard.

'I'm quite fine,' I reply.

'Because I could get you some more,' she says, laughing now and looking at the small sea of mustard on my plate. 'Just ask if you want more mustard,' she adds, enjoying her 'mustard joke'.

'Thanks,' I mumble in between a bite of *rindswurst*, which I think I prefer to *würstchen* as it's a bit richer and less watery.

I finish my second hot dog, feeling quite full. And we walk round the corner to the pink-stone St Paul's Church, where the country's first parliament met in 1848–49 in one of the early attempts to create a constitution for a unified Germany. This project ended when Prussian troops stormed the building to protect the interests of the Prussian monarch, who did not want to lose his grip on power. It was here that John F. Kennedy once spoke of the city as the 'cradle of German democracy' and outside there is a plaque with a bust of the youthful president commemorating the speech on 24 June 1963, two days before his more famous 'Ich bin ein Berliner' address in front of the town hall in Berlin and almost exactly five months before his death. We look inside the tall, domed structure with its whitewashed walls and rows of flags representing the states of the German federation. There is something moving about imagining JFK's words floating upwards through the wide open hall of the church, which was rebuilt after the war. We pick up a copy of his speech and flick through the short document.

Aside from President Obama perhaps, I can't think of anyone in politics today who matches the strength, clarity and vision of JFK's power of communication. During his brief talk on a visit to Germany to bolster international togetherness, which attracted politicians from across the country and acted as a forerunner to the rally of more than 120,000 people in Berlin, Kennedy cleverly drew on the words of Johann Wolfgang von Goethe, the genius of German literature who was born in the city and lived a few hundred yards away in the late eighteenth and early nineteenth centuries.

'Goethe tells us in his greatest poem that Faust lost the liberty of his soul when he said to the passing moment: "Stay, thou art so fair",' JFK intoned, standing not far from where we read this. 'And our liberty, too, is endangered if we pause for the passing moment, if we rest on our achievements, if we resist the pace of progress. For time and the world do not stand still. Change is the law of life. And those who look to the past and present are certain to miss the future.'

He goes on to call for 'the reunion of Europe… bringing a permanent end to the civil wars that have repeatedly wracked the world' – reminding me of the European Union buildings in Luxembourg. He stresses the importance of economic cooperation and growth: 'As they say on my own Cape Cod: "A rising tide lifts all boats"' – reminding me of recent global financial woes and the concerted response to banking crises. The speech ends by calling once again to protect liberty – 'highest wisdom, the best that mankind ever knew'.

It's moving stuff. When we leave St Paul's, which has become a symbolic centre of European peace over the years partly because of JFK's speech, we have an entirely new perspective on the city. Haunting music played by buskers with violins and cellos floats across the cobbles as we continue onwards a short distance to the looming tower of the Frankfurter Dom. Frankfurt is a city in which you keep feeling the impulse to go upwards – there are all sorts of skyscrapers with observation decks and restaurants and bars on top floors. But this is the city's original scraper, started in the fifteenth century and completed in the 1860s. It is one of the few structures to have survived the war and we are soon climbing its corkscrew staircase to the 95-metre summit; perhaps not the best plan of action when you've just polished off a double portion of local sausages.

The climb is worth the effort, if only to see the fabulous Gothic gargoyles at close quarters. As we near the top we look out of a portal and see marvellously grotesque faces grimacing outwards as though warding off evil spirits (and Allied bombs). Delicate turrets that seem too thin to have survived the test of time, let alone raids during the war, rise from below. On the circular viewing platform, the walls are covered with graffiti, some dating from 1963, when Kennedy must surely have come up here to see the view.

It has changed beyond recognition since then. Over a simple metal rail we take in a skyline of office block towers that strikingly reminds me of the downtown of an American city. Squint your eyes and you could easily imagine yourself in St

Louis or Dallas, the city of Kennedy's assassination. It's almost uncanny. I haven't visited anywhere in Europe that looks quite so American.

E and I gaze along the sweep of the tree-lined River Main, with its pretty metal-hoop bridges. We can see the green of the suburbs, with all the allotments. We can see the neighbourhood of Gothic buildings near our hotel.

'It's wonderful up here,' says E, looking out towards the skyscrapers. We take pictures amid the gargoyles and anti-pigeon spikes, with an icy wind blasting across us.

A gust catches E's dress and she offers some impromptu advice: 'Do not go up the Dom wearing a shirt-dress... unless you want to show the entire city of Frankfurt your knickers!'

And with that we descend the Frankfurter Dom.

Back on terra firma, we walk along the Zeil, a rather bland, pedestrianised shopping street that's full of international brands of the Footlocker and H&M variety. There are beggars on almost every corner, noticeably more than in any other city we've visited so far. Back in Luxembourg I can only remember the fellow I took to be a down-on-his-luck banker by the cathedral. But there are homeless everywhere here, wrapped in blankets and huddled on pieces of cardboard. Some have missing limbs. Some look shifty and pale, as though they might be in need of a fix. All seem lost – and cold.

There are also lots of shiny shopping malls; Frankfurt is a place of extremes, and the wealthy in Germany's richest city need somewhere to spend their cash. We enter a mall that's bizarrely full of wooden sculptures of Buddhas. We walk around the fashion and jewellery shops followed by the gaze of dozens of enlightened eyes. Then we amble back in the direction of the hotel, stopping at a succession of mini-supermarkets and corner shops where we try without luck to find Sprite Zero, E's favourite soft drink.

'I can categorically report that they do not do Sprite Zeros in Frankfurt!' E declares, seeming to have taken it upon herself today to issue random travellers' tips.

'Do you have any further pronouncements?' I ask.

'Yes,' E replies. 'It is time to go back to the hotel!'

I agree. It is very cold. It's also getting late in the afternoon. So we catch a taxi across the river to Villa Kennedy, where we retreat to the pool in the basement. Gentle jazz plays as we splash about in the water and leap into the hot tub and then make our way to the steam room. It's busy in the pool area, and in true German style we claim our sunloungers with our towels as soon as they are free, drawing approving looks from fellow guests nearby, who appear to be German. After all the sightseeing it's a great place to relax and while away an hour or so.

We think about going out in the evening. We think about it, but don't. What's the point of wearing ourselves out? It's too nice in the hotel anyway. We have another drink at the bar – shunning the €620 bottles of Dom Pérignon, and watching the peculiar goings on of tall blonde women in high heels. We order room service – the JFK burgers for me (no hot dogs on the menu) and a salad for E. And in the morning we set off early on perhaps the most unusual tour of our lives.

It starts at the tourist office at the centre of the busy concourse at the Hauptbahnhof. Railways began in Germany in the 1830s, and just as in Belgium they were considered a way of bringing political unity to its many states. With such an enormous area of land to join together, figures such as Goethe were well aware of the power of trains to connect the country. When it was realised that building lines would also be profitable and help speed up industrialisation, more tracks were laid. By the time of Otto von Bismarck's rise to power and his 1870 war with France, which lead to the annexation of Alsace-Lorraine, the states felt closer together than ever. On 18 January 1871, Germany was unified under Bismarck, nicknamed the 'Iron Chancellor' for his tough negotiating style. The importance of railways was not lost on him, and the country soon had more miles of track than anywhere in Europe, overtaking Great Britain. Put simply, were it not for railways, Germany might not have become Germany as we know it today.

We learn all of this standing outside the curving stone façade of the Hauptbahnhof, where we have been met by Elizabeth Lucke, a guide from the tourist office wearing a leather jacket and Art Deco-style glasses. We are about to embark on an 'On the Streets' tour designed to take in 'the poor Frankfurt: drugs, prostitution and homelessness'.

'Are you sure we want to do this?' whispers E.

'Well, it is different,' I whisper back.

'We're on a weekend break and we're going to see druggies and hookers?' she asks as Elizabeth walks a few steps ahead.

'It would appear so,' I reply, ignoring the fact that I booked it for the very reason that it sounded so offbeat.

E makes a muffled comment that I can't quite catch in the wind.

Soon Elizabeth is turning to face the station from across the street next to a building where Oskar Schindler lived in a small apartment after the war. During his time in the city during the 1960s he failed to make a cement factory business work and he was eventually reduced to living on a small pension; the man credited with saving the lives of almost 1,200 Jews during the war died penniless in 1974. There is a small plaque on the apartment block.

But Elizabeth brings our attention to the train shed. 'It was built at the end of the nineteenth century,' she says. 'And the houses around here once made up an elegant residential neighbourhood for around 11,000 people. When the station was first made it looked really spectacular and people said: "It's far too big." But they were wrong and in the 1920s the station was extended. Now there are 1,700 trains a day.'

We walk along narrow streets, passing 'Dr Müller's Erotik Shop' and a run of seedy fast-food joints, where the tour proper begins. 'We have a big drugs problem. About 70 per cent of Germany's drugs are imported through the airport,' she says matter-of-factly. 'In the 1980s Frankfurt was considered the crack capital of Germany. But since then we have adopted a system of offering clean syringes in clean facilities. It has taken a lot of the drugs off the street.'

Since 2002, we learn, laws have also been introduced to legalise prostitution, giving women the right to sue men who do not pay and also providing health insurance and a pension fund. The area we are walking through now is known both as the 'Red Light District' and also, officially, as a 'Tolerance Area'. The vast majority of the prostitutes are from Eastern Europe, only 3 per cent are German, and they work in buildings with set standards of hygiene for which they pay landlords a set rent per day. We pass one of these, named Crazy Sexy, with mannequins of scantily-clad women draped over the balconies of its many floors. Streetwalking is not officially allowed. The turnover from prostitution in Germany is, according to Elizabeth, €14.5 billion annually with 1.2 million men asking for the services of prostitutes each day.

'They are not forced to do so,' says Elizabeth, who is middle-aged and might pass for a librarian. She's referring to the prostitutes, not their customers. 'It's their thing. It's OK. That's my personal view. It's the oldest profession in the world. At noon you see bankers coming over every day at lunch. Prices start at around twenty-five to thirty euros.'

We continue, taking in the garish red and yellow façade of Showcentre: Sexyland and a Blue Movie Kino Centre. We're told that there are male prostitutes working on the streets near the station. 'Many are from Romania and they are not homosexual – they come to work here but can't find jobs, so they work on the streets and send money home telling their families they work in construction,' Elizabeth says. 'Most have drug habits. When they get older, in their thirties, they get into sadomasochistic techniques. They do it for the money. They are desperate.'

We continue past *kebap* shops as we are told that there are 1,700 homeless people in the city, including many illegal immigrants and mentally ill, and that buses drive round the city centre at night distributing sleeping bags and hot drinks. A short walk along, we enter a park with pleasant benches and landscaped gardens. At the far side in front of a row of skyscrapers there's a blue sculpture in the form of the euro's currency symbol. Beyond this, on the other side of the park, is the Euro Tower, headquarters of the European Central Bank, founded in 1998 in readiness for the introduction of the new currency across much of Europe on 1 January 1999. At the base of this, we find a shop selling commemorative coins and old German mark notes. After what we have seen a couple of hundred yards away, it's almost hard to come to terms with the stark contrast: bankers on one side of the park, bedlam on the other.

As we walk back towards the Red Light District, Elizabeth tells us about the fateful night of 22 March 1944: 'There was a moon and no clouds and the Royal Air Force carpet-bombed the city. Fewer than 2,000 people died, people hid in basements and in tunnels.'

E comments: 'We are so sorry about that.'

To which Elizabeth immediately and firmly responds: 'But we started it.'

We come to a shuttered venue called Cabaret Pik Dame, where we stop and are told that this is one of the more respectable places to see a cabaret act: 'Even women can go in there and watch: no problem. It was founded in 1963.'

As she says this, a woman who does not look as though she spends her spare cash on attending cabarets scurries by, as though agitated. She has a pinched, pallid face and might be eighteen or could be fifty. She's wearing a puffa jacket and calling excitedly to a friend down the street. 'They're as high as kites,' says E. She's right. We watch the waif-like figures disappear in a hurry round a corner, looking like lost souls.

And then we come across a spectacle we have never seen before and hope never to again. We are on a narrow side street where there is a complex with a 'consumption room' with clean needles for heroin addicts. But the users we see have not bothered to go inside. Instead, we watch four men with jerky puppet-like motions come to a halt at a windowsill outside the building. They hurriedly retrieve objects from pockets and, totally disregarding everyone and everything around them (including two tourists with a guide across the street watching them) begin to prepare their drugs for shooting up. They fix their heads downwards, intently involved in the task at hand, their bodies twitching. The four are in a row, but each is so absorbed that he pays no attention whatsoever to the others: none. They remind me of chickens poking at grain left on a barn floor. Nothing else matters. Then one turns outwards and strips off his hooded jacket. His eyes are the colour of ash and he has deep lines in his young face. He pulls a tourniquet round the top of his arm and injects his concoction. The others do not even glance in his direction as he does so. Then, one by one, they do the same. The group becomes animated in a way that seems totally alien to their former states of existence. They appear jovial and relieved: they have got where they want to be. Nothing now matters, in a different way. And even though they have clearly 'arrived', they still seem as though they are living in entirely separate spheres. They may be wired in to what they were seeking. They may be brothers in needle-pricked arms. But they are as alone now as they were when they were twitching at the windowsill.

They still don't notice us. Why would they? We are irrelevant.

On the wall of a derelict building next to the drug clinic there are bright posters advertising music concerts. It seems a very odd place to have pasted them. The twitching junkies are standing a few yards from a poster advertising a Katherine Jenkins show. There's a picture of the smiling blonde singer from Wales, known as the 'voice of an angel', looking very angelic indeed in this depressing street. The whole scene feels sordid, sad, desperate and wrong.

We walk back in silence to our starting point at the station, turning past the entrance to Oskar Schindler's old flat. As we near the entrance, Elizabeth simply says: 'You can never have a society without drugs.'

Maybe not. But after what we've seen of the streets around the Hauptbahnhof, you can certainly hope for one.

We thank her for her tour, and then E and I head for a coffee at a cafe in the station. E collects her bag where we'd left it at the tourist office. She is catching the train back in an hour so she can get to work on Monday, while I'm staying on for another night. We eat sandwiches and drink espressos at a cafe in a food hall, where a persistent beggar with a twitch that we now recognise as being the sign of only one thing asks table after table for spare change.

E disappears on a grey and red, bullet-shaped ICE train and I return to the city centre passing the World of Sex and shops with window displays featuring items boasting of 'cordless technology' and 'high performance lithium batteries'. Shortly afterwards, I'm in the Euro-banker zone with its upmarket wine bars and skyscrapers; it's such a peculiar city and again I'm reminded of inner-city USA. Not only does Frankfurt look American, it also feels as though it belongs on the other side of the Atlantic. The extremes of wealth and poverty, combined with the businesslike local acceptance that this is just the way it is, are so like what I've seen in New York or Philadelphia. I pay five euros to go to the top of Main Tower, clearing security and rising 200 metres in a 20 kph lift playing German pop music to a circular platform on the roof that I share with a couple of other tourists. Down in the station, the trains look like toothpicks. Beyond the offices of DZ Bank, AG and Commerzbank, I can see the traditional buildings of Römerberg beyond St Paul's Church. In the distance there are green rolling hills.

I go back down and walk a short distance to the city's opera house. It's covered in scaffolding and the Finnish Philharmonic Orchestra is playing tonight. But I've got something other than Finnish classical music in mind for the evening. I walk to the sandstone classical columns of the Börse, Germany's main stock exchange. Outside there is a sculpture of a bull and a bear that I recognise from news reports.

Not far away I stop at the Goethe-Haus and adjoining Goethe-Museum. This was where the author was born in 1749. The distinguished pale-yellow building with a gable on the top floor, in which Goethe had his study in later years, is on a tiny lane just south of all the shops on the Zeil. I go through rooms full of antiques and smelling of polish, listening to an audio guide outlining the story of Faust and the young scholar's deal with the devil to enjoy earthly pleasures (including a pretty woman he has his eye on) in return for serving the devil in hell. The house is decorated as it would have been in Goethe's time and as I walk into an 'oriental room' with crimson silk fabric it is interesting to learn that the writer was not in favour of a unified Germany. He was conservative by nature and preferred the idea of German states run by powerful individuals with people's interests at heart. He was himself in politics and I hear the tale of his involvement in a controversial case in which a mother who had killed her baby is sentenced to death. Goethe is said to have been part of the panel that agreed to her death penalty – which for me casts a whole new light on the writer.

On the top floor, there is an olive-green room with a bureau by a window. 'This is Goethe's realm,' says the audio, explaining that he wrote a version of *Faust* here and *The Sorrows of Young Werther*, about a young man who becomes obsessed with a woman, finds his love unrequited and commits suicide. A cheery tale; I read a line from the work, published in 1774: 'Alas! The void the fearful void, which I feel in my bosom! Sometimes I think, if I could only once but once, press her to my heart, this dreadful void would be filled.'

I'm feeling a void of my own – a void involving German beer. To remedy this situation, I walk across a green metal pedestrian bridge to Sachsenhausen. Tug boats slide along the mercury surface of the river as the afternoon light fades. I negotiate cyclists and joggers and walk along a street that for some reason has a promising beer-hall feel to it. This proves to be a good hunch, and after passing a few trendy sushi restaurants and fashion shops that almost have me turning back, I come across the Adolf Wagner Apple Wine Tavern. It looks old and no nonsense, with long wood tables and staff in black waistcoats and white shirts wielding trays laden with glasses and heaps of steaming food.

I am directed by a waiter who says 'We do not have a table for one, but you can have one place at a table' to a spot near the back where my neighbours are a jolly middle-aged man with a moustache and a cackling blonde woman. Behind me is a group of Japanese businesspeople. They are already three sheets to the wind, and have been ordering the most expensive bottles of red wine and champagne on the menu. There is laughter and ribaldry aplenty. I ask for a glass of *ebbelwoi*, the apple wine. I'd forgotten that was the local tipple; beer can wait. Then I order *Handkäse mit Musik,* cheese with oil vinegar, chopped onions, bread and butter, followed by *Frankfurter Grüne Sosse,* green sauce with brisket of beef and home-fried potatoes – as these are said to be the local specialities. There are also liver dumplings with 'bacongravy' and sauerkraut, as well as 'meat filled cabbage rolls', also served with the intriguing 'bacongravy', though I am not sure I'll have room for these as well. The 'vegetarian' main courses, as far as I can tell, consist of two salads, one of which is made up of 'fried feta cheese with olives, pepperoni, onions and bread' (a rather strange interpretation of 'vegetarian'). My drink and the dishes come with remarkable speed, and I'm soon tackling another superb Continental pile-up of meat and potatoes. The *Handkäse mit Musik* is delicious, even though its name is a little off-putting: the *musik* is referring to the dish's tendency to give you wind. I drink my apple wine and order another. The blonde woman cackles. The Japanese shriek with laughter. The waiters in black waistcoats scoot about and, as I'm leaving, I notice on a picture board by the kitchen that this place must be famous: Chancellor Kohl, Nicholas Cage and Lionel Richie are all photographed enjoying the local fare.

Outside, I wander back in the direction of the river, and find myself crossing over and entering the quieter streets of the skyscraper zone. At a building near the Main Tower, I go up a lift to Bar 22, on the 22nd floor. It's a small place with black leather armchairs, subdued lighting and a pianist with a goatee playing bluesy numbers. Through the thick glass windows and past another office block a yellow moon is so clear in the sky you can almost make out the craters. I order a house special cocktail and am delivered a bright blue drink that makes we wish I hadn't. It tastes almost healthy. I listen to the blues music for a while, catch the lift down and walk towards the hotel. On the way, I pass the 'tourist friendly' Pik Dame cabaret club. I stop outside. There's a greasy-faced bouncer with a black jacket. He addresses me, appearing to ask if I want to go in.

'OK,' I say.

He blocks my way. 'Ticket! Entry five euros,' he says.

I hesitate. 'Five euros!' he says.

I only have a fifty-euro note. He seizes this and disappears inside, indicating that I follow him. We enter a darkened room with black walls. There is no music. There is no cabaret act. There is nobody else at all. It's just me and the bouncer, who has lit up a cigarette and is holding my fifty-euro note in his other hand.

I ask for my money back. 'There's nothing here,' I say.

'Two minutes!' he replies, as though all will be well in two minutes.

'Give me my money,' I reply.

He holds the note away from me. I lean forward and take it. He looks most annoyed. And I leave. So much for seeing a cabaret act in Frankfurt.

Before catching my train back the next morning, I return to the Börse (stock exchange). I'd reserved a place for a free visit yesterday; you must book a day in advance. And so I spend my last hour in the city watching traders with expensive watches in front of digital displays flashing up numbers of stock prices. They look decidedly bored amid their swivel chairs and computers, and it feels a little like a human zoo. Apparently 3,000 people are employed by the exchange, though there are just a dozen down in this 'enclosure'. There's a display about 'diversified risk, fixed investment income, bonds are debt instruments...' but it loses me. Near the exit though, there are some literary quotes about money. 'Money may well make you a worse person, but a lack of money certainly won't make you a better one,' says John Steinbeck, while Mark Twain's contribution is: 'October: this is one of the most dangerous months to speculate in stocks. The others are July, January, September, April, November, May, March, June, December, August and February.' Which sounds about right these days. And with these words from two Americans, I depart from this American-feeling city. Next stop, another country, another fortnight away.

CHAPTER SEVEN

LAUSANNE: 'BEAUTIFUL LAKE... BEAUTIFUL PEOPLE'

The man leaving the metro as we board stands out – quite literally. He's about seven feet tall and looks as though he must be a professional basketball player. He ducks out of the carriage. But as he does so, we realise something. He's wearing roller skates. We also notice something else: he's pulling a pram. We board the metro and watch as the giant fellow, made even taller by his skates, casually scoots along the platform pushing his baby. It's an arresting sight – even more so, when we see him somehow managing to roller-skate *up a steep street* outside the station, as though this is the most normal thing in the world.

E and I regard the man skating upwards with his pram, hardly believing our eyes, and we find a place to stand with our bags. The doors close behind us to the sound of waves crashing on a beach. Each station in the metro has its own sound: be it birdsong or rattling pebbles. Then we head down a slope... quickly.

It's a far cry from the Tube. The train plunges away, stopping every few hundred yards at tiny stations, before dropping altitude rapidly again. We're at the top of the carriage, so high up that we can't see through the front window of the short train.

'This is cool, love,' says E clutching one of the rails – which you have to or else risk flying downwards.

We are in Lausanne, a hillside city on the edge of Lake Geneva, in the south-west of Switzerland about fifty miles north of Geneva. We've spent the best part of the day, six and a half hours, travelling from St Pancras through to Paris, where we caught a train from Gare du Nord to Gare de Lyon (avoiding pushy commuters the best we could), and on to this city that both of us knew virtually nothing about before coming. The journey has been one of the most picturesque yet. We've passed through Dijon, where we saw familiar steeples and the beach by Lake Kir where we had a swim not so long ago. We've seen wide landscapes full of vineyards. We've moved into the foothills of the Alps, with snow-capped peaks all around and long green prairies full of fat black cows. And we've entered Switzerland with a bright yellow sun shining across pretty villages of A-shaped wooden houses.

Now we're on the last leg of the trip – not feeling at all tired from the travel, which has been relaxed and enjoyable (pushy Parisians aside).

'It is cool,' I say to E, referring to Lausanne and our whole experience so far.

'I *really* like it here,' says E, gushing a bit as we angle past smart apartment blocks and bijoux parks with flowerbeds and benches.

'Look, we're almost here,' she adds. By 'here' she is referring to Ouchy, the final stop on the metro, down by the lake. It had looked like a long journey on the map. But it's not. The metro takes a matter of minutes and runs like clockwork – as you'd expect in Switzerland, of course.

E continues to rave about Lausanne. 'The youths are dressed well,' she says; the teenagers are not as scruffy as the ones back home. 'The down-and-outs look pretty good as well,' she continues; we'd seen a couple of unexpectedly dapper beggars at the main station; one had been wearing a tie. I can't remember E taking to a place quite so quickly.

The carriage draws to a halt, and a handful of us disembark.

'Switzerland is good,' E suddenly announces, as though this is spoken from the bottom of her heart. 'I know some people think it's a bit sterile, but I like it here,' she says. And on that positive note we exit Ouchy station to what sounds like cows mooing over the metro's speaker system.

It's the most beautiful arrival so far. It's 5.30 p.m. on a Friday evening in early November. But the weather's mild and people are roller-skating and skateboarding on paths in a neat park. The sun is a blazing ball of orange that's about to drop behind a ridge of mountains on the other side of Lake Geneva. Streaks of golden light shimmer across the magnesium surface of the still lake. Seagulls swoop above a giant chessboard, at which elderly fellows are intently focused on a game. A player makes a move and voices rise in heated discussion. They're drinking from blue beer cans and having a grand old time. Nearby, children are playing on a carousel and climbing frames with slides. A woman who must be in her eighties jogs by. Rollerbladers skate past, pirouetting and wheeling backwards. Kids on push-along scooters zip along the promenade by the water's edge. Cyclists whizz by. A chap in a reclining bike that looks like some kind of converted armchair pedals along, appearing extremely content.

'What do you call those things?' E asks.

'I'm not sure,' I reply. 'Lying-down bikes?'

'Hmm,' she says, sounding unconvinced that I've got the terminology right.

E and I stand by the water watching the sporty people of Lausanne, as the sun dips beneath the mountains, casting pink light across a delicate blue sky. The timing is perfect; as though the sunset has been waiting for us. Then we stroll onwards past elderly couples taking evening perambulations, more kids on scooters and an octogenarian man energetically rollerblading towards Ouchy station (nobody bats an eyelid). On first impressions Lausanne feels like some kind of perfect society, with people of all ages happily and healthily going about their business. We ascend a path where we come across two teenagers on unicycles. So we can pass on the narrow pavement, they somehow slow down, which seems impossible on the steep slope, and start *hopping on the spot* next to a parked car. Unbelievable. We say *merci* as this is the French-speaking part of Switzerland and they politely say *pas de problème* – such good manners in Lausanne – and we stroll on to our hotel, just round the corner.

The Beau-Rivage Palace is a grand affair in a tall chateau-like building by the lake. The entrance is guarded by marble hounds and the reception is palatial indeed, with crystal chandeliers, tall white flowers and Corinthian columns leading to a high ceiling. We walk along a corridor with glass displays revealing Rolex and Cartier watches and stop by a sumptuous ballroom in which a champagne reception has begun. A sign on a board says '*SOS Enfants: Association Humanitaire*'. People in suits and flowing dresses mingle with African dignitaries in traditional costumes. We skulk onwards in trainers and jeans to a lift next to a sweeping staircase. But we're not the only ones wearing trainers. As we wait for the lift, an elderly oriental man, about 5 ft tall, walks past flanked by two young women in gold miniskirts. They teeter along in high heels towering above him, while he shuffles by in a black suit with a grey polo neck. A pair of elaborate silver Nike trainers completes his look, along with a broad cat-that-got-the-cream smile. They glance at us waiting for the lift and proceed to climb the stairs, seeming reluctant to share the journey up. We watch the trio disappear: they make quite a sight.

'He looked like a happy fellow,' comments E, arching an eyebrow.

'Very happy indeed,' I reply.

There's no sign of them on our floor as we make our way down a long corridor; it's a monster of a building. At the end we enter an elegant room with antiques, plush carpets and old oil paintings. There's a large bed, a writer's desk and a spotless marble bathroom. I open the doors to a balcony revealing the last of the lovely pink sunset – and a quite extraordinary sight.

Above a churchyard by the lake, hundreds upon hundreds of starlings are swooping in a mesmerising swirl of flickering black. The birds are silhouetted perfectly against the dimming light, dancing across the sky, forming giant question marks in one moment, long snake-like tubes in another, erratically-shaped stars and almost perfect circles. It's breathtaking. We stand absolutely still as though moving might distract them. The birds continue their mind-boggling show, occasionally breaking apart and then rejoining above the steeple of the church. For a few seconds they swoop in our direction coming so close we can hear the patter of a thousand wings. It's as though they've come to say hello. Then they angle away, mysteriously landing on a tall fir tree in the grounds of the hotel. The tree is turned completely black. Then they're off again, flipping back across the lake in another wild burst of energy, looking as though they're having the time of their lives.

What a performance.

We get changed and go for a drink in a downstairs bar, near the humanitarian party. There are mirrors everywhere and smart, healthy-looking Swiss people of all ages relaxing on Friday night. 'Maybe there are so many mirrors because the Swiss are so beautiful,' comments E. Everything seems to sparkle. A waiter in a suit with a Chairman Mao collar brings us glasses of wine, olives and cashew nuts. We sit back in brown velvet chairs, taking in the refined atmosphere. Of all the fast-train destinations we've visited, this is the classiest and the most romantic by a long shot.

In the morning we head for one of the reasons the city, with its population of just 122,000, is so outdoorsy and sporty. Lausanne is the headquarters of the International Olympic Committee and it is home to a huge museum celebrating the history of the Olympic Games and containing artefacts from some of the greatest moments in sport. The museum is up the hill just round the corner from our hotel, and as if to prove the general all-round fitness levels of the local community, two more octogenarian women jog past as we turn into the entrance. It's another bright, sunny day by Lake Geneva, also known locally by its French name of Lac Léman. France is on the other side of the lake, about a half hour's boat ride away; you can catch a ferry from near the museum to Évian-les-Bains, the source of Evian mineral water, beyond which lie the distant peaks of Mont Blanc.

Outside the museum are sculptures of athletes in a landscaped park. And soon we're entering a large white building with a dizzying array of medals, flags from Games past, swimming caps, running shoes, bobsleighs and Olympic torches – each with a story to tell. The IOC settled in Lausanne after Pierre de Coubertin, a Parisian aristocrat who founded the modern Olympic movement in 1894, chose the city as his home. Coubertin was a believer in 'fortifying character' and developing 'the muscular moral of man'. He believed that the success of the British Empire at the time resulted from the playing of competitive sports at public schools; in his twenties he visited

Rugby School to get first-hand experience of what British children were being taught. Having seen France defeated in the Franco-Prussian war when he was growing up (during the rise of Bismarck), he wanted to encourage 'the recovery of the nation through the practice of sport'.

But his passion for sport took him further than that and the result of his enthusiasm was the first modern Olympics in Athens in 1896. At this Games 241 athletes from fourteen countries took part with swimming events held in the Mediterranean Sea close to the port of Piraeus and athletics in the ancient marble Panathinaiko Stadium. There are old black and white pictures from those Games, including an intriguing shot of the line-up for the 100 m final, when only one of the competitors began with his hands placed on the track before him. This American, Thomas Burke, won gold and had invented the modern starting posture of the sprinter.

Nuggets like this abound. We're both sports fans, and enjoy taking in stickers advocating the boycott of the 1980 Olympics in Moscow, and basketballs from the 1992 Barcelona Games signed by the 'dream team' consisting of Magic Johnson, Michael Jordan and Larry Bird. Beyond this, there's a tennis costume belonging to Swiss hero Roger Federer, the running shoes worn by the 100 m gold medallist Carl Lewis at the 1984 Olympics in Los Angeles, and a swimming cap donned by Mark Spitz when he picked up seven gold medals at the 1972 Games in Munich. We stop to take a look at a skating costume that was worn by Katerina Witt of East Germany, and the two-man bob used by Trinidad & Tobago's unexpected Winter Olympics team in 1994. There's also a (very small) section devoted to doping scandals and tests on athletes to weed out cheats. 'NON AU DOPAGE!' says a headline next to empty sample bottles.

It's an intriguing place to spend an hour, but it's still sunny outside and we want to enjoy the scenery and the weather. We're also on a mission. There's a train that travels along the edge of Lake Geneva, passing through vineyards and mountains before stopping at the town of Vevey, where silent film star Charlie Chaplin spent his later years, moving to Switzerland to escape McCarthyism in the 1950s, and where Graham Greene died in 1991 (he's buried in a tiny local cemetery). After this, the train continues to Montreux, where the famous jazz festival is held each July. Then it rolls on to Château de Chillon, the 'most visited historical monument in Switzerland', just over half an hour away from Lausanne. This chateau, which we'd never heard of before, is built on an oval island a stone's throw from the shore and is known for having attracted artists and writers over the years including Lord Byron, Jean-Jacques Rousseau, Victor Hugo, Delacroix and Courbet. When I asked a Swiss friend back in London what she likes most about Lausanne, her answer was immediate: 'It's simple.' She had paused as though withholding a secret. 'The best thing is the lake – the beautiful lake.' She'd paused once more, as though deep in thought. 'And you must go to Château de Chillon – the beautiful chateau!'

But before heading to the beautiful chateau, we go to the main station in the centre of town, travelling up on the funny metro and disembarking at Place de la Riponne. We find ourselves in a fine old square with a busy market in full flow. We walk along bright stalls selling quinces, cabbages, carrots, spring onions, squashes, cauliflowers, mushrooms and onions.

'Everything's a bit messed up,' says E.

'What do you mean? You don't like the look of it?'

'No, it means it's all probably very good. Organic, not mass produced,' she answers. 'It's not often you see vegetables looking so perfectly roughed up.'

Even the things that don't look perfect are perfect in Lausanne.

And then we walk one to one of the neatest, almost ridiculously tidy flea markets we've ever seen – the cliché about Swiss orderliness definitely seems to hold true in this very orderly city. Oriental rugs are spread out for sale on the stone central courtyard, making the whole square look like someone's very large living room. The sun beats down on this sedate scene. We take in eclectic stalls selling old gendarme hats, Buddha sculptures, tea sets, African masks, fur coats, old watches and jewellery. Everything is lined up carefully, no higgledy-piggledy mess that you'd get in a market like this or a car boot sale back home.

E likes the look of a purple-stone ring, tries it on and asks about its price.

'That ring?' says the stallholder in perfect English. 'That one's fifteen euros.'

We look at it and then walk away, undecided, towards a stall selling great lumps of cheese and packets of Gruyère mixes used for fondues. 'Hold on a second. Wait here,' I say to E, and go back to the stall, out of view round a corner.

While €15 seems like a pretty damn good deal, I try to negotiate a price with the stallholder. '*Dix euros?*' I ask nonchalantly in French, hoping to knock him down five euros.

'That one is still fifteen euros,' he replies in perfect English, with a deadpan gaze.

'*Douze euros?*' I ask tentatively.

'It is fifteen,' he replies without hesitation.

'OK, here you go,' I say in English, handing over €15.

'*Merci, mon ami,*' he says, smiling and tucking the notes into a pocket as I do the same with the ring.

No wonder the Swiss are so damn wealthy.

E and I walk along steep, spotlessly clean, cobbled streets lined with florists and smart cafes, no multinational chains in sight. A man is selling a beer called Docteur Gab's at a stall on the way to the station and I'm tempted to pick up a six-pack of *bière blonde double malt combine force de caractère et amertume subtile*, though E points out that this would probably not be the best thing to carry about during the rest of the day's sightseeing. She does have a point.

And then we catch the train to Château de Chillon. This must be one of the most charming rail journeys in the world, especially in the autumn. Within minutes we are moving through a spectacular landscape of golden vineyards on slopes on either side of the track. The vines spread as though stretching forever, shades of gold and yellow mixing with the speckled shadows of the leaves, creating a blaze of warmth running upwards to the crisp blue sky. It's a spectacular setting. The yellowing vines are staggered on shelves of land positioned between grey-stone walls, as well-constructed as some kind of ancient temple. It's no wonder that UNESCO has nominated the vineyards of the village of Lavaux, which stretch for 30 km between Lausanne and Château de Chillon, a World Heritage Site. There's evidence that vines have grown here since Roman times, although most date from Benedictine and Cistercian monasteries from the eleventh century. Were it not a UNESCO registered site, also protected by local planning orders, this land would undoubtedly fall prey to property developers.

Looking across the lake, we can see the jagged, snow-capped peaks of the Alps. The water is placid and pastel blue, an empty expanse without a boat in view. Misty clouds hang over the mountains on the far side. It is indeed a very beautiful lake and as we move through even steeper ridges of golden vines it's hard to know which view to enjoy. Stunning vineyards on one side or mystical lake on the other... take your pick.

On the edge of Vevey, there are expensive-looking modern apartments with ceiling-to-floor windows. 'What an amazing place to live,' says E. We can see into sitting rooms that belong in the pages of *Wallpaper** magazine: blond wood dining tables surrounded by retro orange dining chairs – anglepoise lamps and pieces of abstract art everywhere. Everything seems so perfectly arranged, so *exactly right*. They look like show apartments waiting for estate agents to take round potential buyers for the first time.

'The views must be stunning,' says E, who seems to be about to start her very own Swiss Appreciation Society. 'They sure know how to live round here.' Greene chose a wonderful place to spend his final years; and we wish we had time to search for his grave, which is apparently marked simply: 'Graham Greene 1904–1991'.

We roll into the station, where there's a sign for a railway museum that's only open from May to October. '*Yes!*' cheers E, afraid that I might have dragged her round it otherwise (which indeed I might).

This is a slow train, but a steady one. We leave Vevey with its adverts for a lottery: 'PROCHAIN ARRÊT MILLIONAIRE!' says a sign on the platform. The next stop is another small town called Villeneuve. This is the one for the chateau. We disembark, walk past a little stone church and a *charcuterie*, pick up a late baguette lunch from a supermarket, and read the temperature on a digital display in the town centre. It's 21°C – extraordinary for November. We catch a bus along the waterfront and arrive at Château de Chillon.

It is indeed a very beautiful chateau, with cone-shaped turrets and tall cream-stone walls with thin window-slits. The fairy-tale castle looms out of the still water with a red national flag above the entrance. There are almost no other tourists and the attendant on the ticket gate waves us through as apparently it's a 'free day' to visit. Inside, we walk across a courtyard to a dark passage leading to a vaulted chamber. This room, we soon learn, has a story to tell... a tragic, captivating tale.

In the sixteenth century, a monk named François Bonivard was imprisoned here for six years. His father had been burnt at the stake for his religious beliefs and he was the sole survivor of six brothers, each of whom perished in terrible ways at the hands of their enemies. Two died before his very eyes in this room while chained to columns we see before us. Against all the odds, however, Bonivard somehow held on and survived. And many years later his story captivated two tourists from the very early days of Swiss tourism who arrived at the chateau on a sailing trip across the lake.

These adventurous travellers were Lord Byron and Percy Bysshe Shelley, who visited in June 1816. They adored the chateau and were taken by Bonivard's plight; Byron being particularly moved. They sailed back across the lake in the direction of Geneva, but bad weather drew in. So they stopped very close to our hotel, where they stayed in lodgings and had some time on their hands while they waited for the storm to pass. The result is a poem entitled *The Prisoner of Chillon*.

We pick up a copy at the chateau. It's a gripping read:

'There are seven pillars of gothic mould,
In Chillon's dungeons deep and old.
There are seven columns, massy and grey,
Dim with a dull imprison'd ray,
A sunbeam which hath lost its way,
And through the crevice and the cleft,
Of the thick wall is fallen and left...'

Thus begins the 392-line poem, which vividly describes Chillon, with its 'snow-white battlements' above while Bonivard perishes in a 'living grave' below. In this 'dark vault' he listens to the water 'ripple night and day' while witnessing his brothers die one by one, leaving only 'the accursed breath of dungeon-dew' in the chamber. He continues on in 'stagnant idleness' for 'months, or years, or days, I kept no count', making friends with spiders and mice, and sinking so low that 'fetter'd or fetterless to be, I learn'd to love despair'. When he is eventually freed, not understanding why, he leaves the chamber, which has become his home and steps out into the world. 'I regain'd my freedom with a sigh,' the verse ends.

Bonivard went on to live another thirty-four years. On one of the thick dungeon walls there is a simple plaque that says: 'BYRON, JUIN 1816, IN MEMORIAM 1788–1824', right next to the 'fifth pillar' where Bonivard was held. We walk back through the story-filled chamber, take a look at the battlements and peer through the slit-windows to the lake, before eating a late lunch at a wooden jetty in the sun outside the entrance to the castle. The surface is almost eerily still, reflecting the cliff-topped mountains above Villeneuve: such a picturesque setting.

'I love the fact that there are no tourists around,' says E, collecting evidence for her Swiss Appreciation Society, which I'm thinking of joining too. We've had this 'most visited historical monument in Switzerland' more or less to ourselves. The tiny jetty with its view across to the Alps, where the ski season is soon to get underway, is completely empty. Who cares if it's November? Maybe we've just been lucky, but it feels as though any time of year is a good time to visit these parts.

We catch a bus to Montreux, then wait in the station at the Paradise Café. Just about everyone we've come across has been polite and charming so far; even the tough-dealing stallholder had been full of smiles (once he'd got his €15, admittedly). But at the Paradise Café, we have a different sort of welcome. A sour-faced woman looks at us as though she would prefer us to leave her in peace, even though we're her only customers.

'*Deux cafés noirs, s'il vous plait*,' I ask, E sniggering a bit at my accent.

'Yes?' the woman replies snappily. 'What do you want?'

I repeat my order in French.

She says nothing and turns away from us. We sit on blue plastic chairs in the orange glow of the lighting in Paradise Café. A sign on a board says that credit cards are not accepted. Tinny pop music plays and there's a stale smell of cigarette smoke. After a long wait, the woman places the coffee on the counter.

'*C'est combien?*' I ask.

She snaps the price in English. I hand over a ten-euro note. She turns away and leaves me standing at the counter, while she wipes a surface, seeming to have forgotten my existence. I go back to the seat. We've finished our very average coffees and need to catch our train.

I ask for our change. 'OK, OK, I will get this for you,' she replies, and swiftly hands over a few coins. The drinks were not cheap.

And so we leave 'paradise', wondering what we've done to offend its keeper.

It's almost a relief to find that everything is not always so perfect in these parts. Anyway, a bit of brusqueness never did anyone any harm.

Back in Lausanne, E and I pick up a bottle of local Valais wine from a Co-Op supermarket near the hotel – and I carry the bright orange plastic bag past the marble hounds and the smart staff back to our room. It's the late afternoon and while E has a bath and a rest, I go back to the lobby, where I have an appointment.

My Swiss friend back in London has arranged a meeting through a local contact with a Lausanne man who is as close as the city has to a living legend. His name is Renato Hausler and he is the 'nightwatchman'. Lausanne is the last place on the Continent to continue the ancient tradition of calling out the hour in the night; a practice that goes back to medieval times when fires were common, sweeping rapidly through wooden dwellings unless they were spotted quickly. Renato's job is to cry out on the hour from 10 p.m. to 2 a.m.: '*C'est le guet; il a sonné l'heure*' from the tower of the pretty cathedral near the market square. This translates as: 'This is the nightwatch; the hour has struck.'

He is a short, stocky man in a blue ski jacket, which he does not take off. He's sitting by a pile of 'Luxury' magazines, one with the headline 'EVEN THE WEALTHY DREAM', beneath the crystal chandelier. Not far away the Rolex displays glisten and there's a Sotheby's board advertising six-bedroom villas with pools for rent for £11,000 a month. It is a very fancy hotel, by far the fanciest E and I have stayed at so far (a treat as it was E's birthday a week ago).

'I have not been in this place before,' he says, looking around the sparkling lobby. I order coffees as Renato explains how he became a nightwatchman.

'I was twenty-nine and I had no family and no fixed job. I was asked if I would like to help. So I said "yes",' he says. 'It was not such a heavy demand to be there up in the cathedral each night.

155

Actually, it was quite amazing being all alone in such a very old building.'

That was back in 1987 and for twenty-four years now Renato has been the principal watchman, covering the watch for five nights a week, while a deputy is responsible for the other two nights. This practice dates back to 4 November 1405, and every single night since then the hours have been called. 'It is a tradition that is part of our history,' he says proudly, adding that he carries a lantern and wears an old farmer's hat when he is on duty.

Renato tells me quite a lot – really quite a lot – about the provenance of the old church bells of Lausanne, losing me a bit. 'Is the nightwatchman tradition anything to do with the Swiss love of watches and timeliness?' I ask, trying to get him to shift tack. 'Why is it that Swiss people are so obsessed with watches and clocks?'

There's a pause as Renato considers this. 'I don't know why exactly,' he responds, sounding a little as though this matter is an itch he would like to scratch, if only he could reach the scratch. 'Perhaps it is because of the Huguenots who came here escaping persecution in France in the seventeenth and eighteenth centuries: they had great expertise and knowledge of watches.' Many Huguenots fled to non-Catholic Switzerland to avoid the wrath of King Louis XIV, who regarded the minority as a threat to his authority. 'But it is more than that.'

His voice trails off, and then Lausanne's nightwatchman becomes quite existential. 'Time doesn't exist, you know,' he says. 'The present is soon the past, but we attach a lot of importance to "time". I was three minutes late arriving here, as I did not know the time. Yet if we are catching a train or a bus, we need to be on time. If time exists,' he pauses once again, scratches his chin, and picks up his train of thought. 'If time exists... it exists as a very special notion.' He falls silent and appears pensive. 'I think about this a lot.'

We shake hands, and I head back to the room. I'd promised E that I wouldn't be longer than an hour (the very special notion of time playing, it's very special part for me). We open the Co-Op wine. The starlings of Lake Geneva are not dancing in the twilight tonight as E and I enjoy glasses of the fruity and strong local plonk on our balcony.

'Different,' says E. 'But I like it. It's got more to it than Chardonnay.'

'It's hitting the spot very nicely,' I reply, glad of wine of any description after our full day of sightseeing. And for eight euros a bottle I'm not complaining. Eight euros wouldn't have got us a glass of the stuff we had last night down in the bar.

'We've earned it,' says E.

'Yes, we have,' I reply, topping up our glasses.

'It's very good research,' says E.

'Never a truer word spoken,' I reply.

It's mild, quiet and still in Ouchy. There is something about the lake, with the mountains looming beyond and its gentle swelling surface, that feels incredibly tranquil. It's definitely the calmest fast-train stop-off yet.

In a good frame of mind, we stroll down the short hill from the hotel, not sure where we're heading. We haven't booked a table at a restaurant; maybe we'll stumble upon a great little fondue joint. But we don't. We're tired and we're two glasses of Valais to the good. We find ourselves entering the first bar we see, the White Horse. This is to all intents and purposes a *very British pub*. We walk across a tartan carpet and find a place at the bar near a Wurlitzer jukebox as a song with a refrain that sounds like 'bad to di bone' plays and a TV in a corner shows South Africa against Ireland in a rugby match. There's a 'Big Buck Hunter' pinball machine with a picture of a stag and lights flashing energetically. In an alcove with wood panels, apparently designed to look like those in an English country house, there are several pictures of Louis Armstrong. A Swiss man sitting a couple of stools away is drinking Guinness from a pint mug, seeming doleful. It may be a British-style pub, but we are the only apparent Brits.

'What a ropey old joint,' is E's verdict. 'But I like it.'

I like it, too. We order glasses of white wine from a barmaid who doesn't say anything (a 'right little so and so,' says E, amused by her surliness). We stick two-euro coins in the Wurlitzer and play old Beatles and Rolling Stones songs. We drink our wines, listening to the occasional cheer from the far corner, where the rugby is being watched by three chaps who don't appear to be either Irish or South African. We order more glasses from the right little so and so (who's actually very nice this time). We generally make plans about the future – buying a house together (but where?), travelling across America next year (but how can we get time off?) – and set the world to rights on a few key points, feeling totally anonymous and tucked away from things in the tartan depths of the White Horse pub. More wine flows. 'Excellent local stuff,' is E's verdict by this stage. Then we return to the hotel, where we polish off the Valais and I order a room service hamburger that arrives with side chips in an unusual crumpled-ceramic McDonald's-style 'chip bag'… totally blowing any earlier efforts to economise.

One of our many and varied plans at the bar of the White Horse included 'going to France'. After a quick breakfast with a very large, and very necessary, pot of coffee, we do just this in the morning, walking the short distance to a small quay with a ferry and buying tickets for a crossing to Évian-les-Bains.

This is how we find ourselves on rolling pencil-grey water under a milky white sky. The weather has changed and the lake is choppy. It begins to rain. We can just make out the peaks of mountains in the distance. It's nice feeling that we're out in the middle of this strange inland sea, heading into the unknown.

It's not so nice, however, feeling the bumpy water after polishing off quite so much 'research wine' last night.

'Is there anything worth seeing in Évian-les-Bains?' I ask E. She's not sure, she replies tetchily. We haven't got a French guidebook with us.

'I mean, do you think Évian is such a good idea?' I continue, a little loudly perhaps. 'Will there really be anything worth doing?'

'Stop shouting out "is there anything worth doing in Évian?"' whispers E, who I sense would prefer it if I just kept quiet for a while. 'There are probably loads of locals who speak English here.'

Silence descends. I pick up a tourist pamphlet about Lausanne near an automatic coffee machine. The brochure mentions a Musée de la Main (Museum of the Hand), which we hadn't come across yesterday. It was founded, I read, by a local professor involved in reconstructive hand surgery.

'Did you know there's a Museum of the Hand founded by a local professor involved in reconstructive hand surgery named Claude Verdan, who died in 2006?' I ask E.

She casts me a slightly disbelieving look.

'How about we go to the Museum of the Hand when we get back?'

E looks at me. And silence descends once more.

Then she pipes up. 'Talk to the hand!' she pronounces, as though fending off a paparazzi photographer, before adding:

'Talk to the wrist, coz the hand is pissed… that's what they say in America.'

She has a chuckle about this. I take it she does not want to go to Lausanne's Museum of the Hand. I keep quiet for a while.

After half an hour or so, we arrive in Évian-les-Bains and disembark. It is raining. It is also chilly. Everything looks closed, as you might expect it to on a Sunday morning. There's a row of cafes with lights out and a boarded up *tabac* across the street. We take one wet look at Évian-les-Bains. Then we walk back to the ferry, which is returning to Lausanne in a moment or two. The ferry staff appears amused, though not surprised. We're sure the hometown of Evian mineral water is a very charming place… when you haven't been hitting the Valais the night before.

Anyway, being out on the lake was fun in its own way and on our return we stroll past the hotel to a museum that has nothing to do with hands. It's called the Musée de l'Elysée and it's devoted to photography. We're feeling a bit better now. And we're soon walking around an unusual old building filled with brilliant pictures taken by the American photographer Irving Penn (1917–2009), who worked for many years for *Vogue* magazine.

The walls are plastered with black and white portraits of characters from different walks of life. There are mailmen, knife sharpeners, beer barrel boys, newspaper salesmen, scrubber women, lorry loaders and window cleaners, mainly from the 1950s. It's as though another world has come to life. The ghostly, expressive faces of chimney sweeps, fishmongers, contortionists and cucumber salesmen peer out as though from behind the grave. Each is captured against a plain background with the accompaniments of their trade. The newspaper salesman clutches a bundle of papers and a notice announcing: 'FOOTBALL RESULTS: EVENING NEWS'. He's wearing a mad scarf, has a cabbage-shaped face and looks manic and slightly crazed. 'That's you, that is,' says E, chuckling to herself once more.

It's a lovely museum, with plain white walls below and an unusual attic gallery with exposed beams and a smell of wood above. The perfect size: not too big or small – just right for whiling away an hour on a damp, possibly hungover Sunday morning by the shores of Lake Geneva.

We return to the hotel and wheel our bags past all the octogenarian joggers and teenage unicyclists to the metro. A sloping carriage takes us once again to the main train station, where we sit in the Euro Café with a quiz show on TV fizzing in a corner. Nearby, teenagers are horsing about and eating hot dogs. A man who might be a down-on-his-luck artist is drinking a beer by the bar.

It's not the most glamorous setting. Frankly, it's pretty damn unglamorous. As we sip coffees though, the setting makes me think of the early days of rail travel in Switzerland, when things were a whole lot more glitzy.

Before coming to Lausanne, I'd picked up a book entitled *Blood, Iron and Gold: How the Railways Transformed the World*, written by Christian Wolmar, perhaps Britain's leading 'train expert' and the former transport correspondent of *The Independent*. While the title may sound slightly trainspotter-ish – and Wolmar admits to having been one until the age of fourteen when he 'became interested in girls' – it tells the fascinating story of the early days of railways, with an illuminating section on Switzerland.

In the 1870s, when rail travel was taking off under Bismarck in Germany, there were few trains in its less industrially developed and much hillier neighbour. Bismarck, as E and I learnt back in Frankfurt, was desperate to build a strong, united Germany to create cohesion among its states and fend off potential attacks from France and Russia. When he looked at Switzerland, he saw an enormous potential for a rail line through the mountains to export coal and other goods to Italy, where there were vast profits to be made.

But what about the Alps? And what about the expense of building a track through them? The result was an agreement in 1871 to create a nine-mile tunnel through the St Gotthard pass, financed by the three countries, with Switzerland and Germany paying for just a quarter of the costs each, and Italy for half. The idea worked and in 1882 the longest tunnel in the world opened, setting off a German export boom to Italy, where there was a desperate need for coal.

And in the process of all of this, Switzerland ceased to be a country that shut down during its bitter, snow-covered winters. Rail travel had arrived, changing the landscape forever.

Train mania soon took off, as it had just about everywhere else in Europe. By the turn of the twentieth century, lots of mountain short cuts had been created including the Simplon Tunnel, which opened in 1906 allowing glamorous new Orient-Express trains – the brainchild of a Belgian named George Nagelmackers – to pass through Lausanne to Venice, Zagreb, Belgrade and Istanbul. Luxurious mahogany-panelled couchettes, restaurant cars serving seven-course dinners, and waiters dressed in blue silk became the way of things for the well-to-do. Back in those days, train travel felt *exciting* for everyone, especially for the affluent on Nagelmacker's dazzling trains, which began to attract all sorts of wild gossip. Stories of high-class prostitutes, high jinks, spies and even murders (thanks to Agatha Christie) abounded.

It's nice to think of those days gone by as our SNCF train pulls in, bang on time, if not full of mahogany cabins, aristocrats or waiters dressed in silk. We board. And soon we're away through the mountains, speeding through tunnels that have completely transformed Switzerland over the past hundred years or so.

Watching the rocky landscape pass by, I wonder whether *that's* why the trains are so punctual in Switzerland: because they mean so much to the country's past. Perhaps *that's* why the Swiss love their watches so much: they want to be on time for the 8.52 to Bern or Geneva or Zurich. It's all about the trains.

We enter a gorge with a waterfall. I go to the buffet car and buy a little bottle of red wine.

'I'm trying to evoke the spirit of the Orient-Express,' I say to E.

She gives me a look.

'It's hair of the dog,' I say, trying another tack.

'It's called falling off the wagon,' E replies, sticking to a Diet Coke.

There's an announcement as we plunge into a tunnel. 'Ladies and gentlemen, as we have just crossed the border, may we take the opportunity to welcome you to France,' says a polite woman over a speaker.

And we rocket through the mountains at a rate at which our ancestors could only have dreamed. It's been an almost perfect weekend in an almost perfect place. My next stop in Fast Train Europe is a little rougher round the edges – without a snow-capped peak in sight.

CHAPTER EIGHT

ROTTERDAM: 'OH, WHAT A ROTTA'

It's late November at the Eurostar office in St Pancras. My ticket to Rotterdam won't print out of the self-service machine. I'm sitting on a star-shaped leather sofa by a sign that says: 'CONNECT SEAMLESSLY TO 100s OF CONTINENTAL DESTINATIONS. WAKE UP TO A BREAKFAST OF HOMEMADE JAMS AND PASTRIES SERVED IN THE MIDDLE OF A BIRD SANCTUARY. LES ORANGERIES, POITIERS: 4H 45M.' Minutes tick by as my mind wanders and I ponder what it's like to open your eyes in the morning to find birds fluttering about your breakfast pastries (perhaps it's a little too early to be thinking straight). I'm beginning to worry about making the train as it's getting close to the thirty-minute check-in time. What is it about Eurostar ticket machines? Already on these trips, they've been a source of many unprintable mutterings: sometimes simply out of order, other times seizing up – though I've kept quiet about them up till now as they haven't been that bad really, and anyway, I've been looking forward to the trips too much to complain.

But this is a first total failure. I turn to look at the counter, where a man who asked me to wait is punching details into a computer. Near him, another sign says: 'FEEDBACK FOR THOUGHT. TEXT US TO TELL US HOW WE'RE DOING.' Has anyone, I wonder, ever seen this and bothered to take out their mobile and tap in: 'Well done Eurostar, super service today', or 'These delays are a disgrace.' Is a Eurostar employee sitting next to a company mobile somewhere near here ready to spring into action at the sound of a text pinging through? Looking at the row of slightly shivering staff at the counters, it seems fairly unlikely.

The tickets arrive with an apology from an assistant, just in time, and I make the thirty-minute check-in. In the departure lounge it's a madhouse on this Saturday morning. I'm in need of a coffee before the off, so I queue at the Caffè Nero. The line of people runs into the concourse and it's hard to believe that there is only this one cafe when you get through security, expected to serve so many passengers in the lounge. The only other 'refreshment' option is a pub, where I see middle-aged couples, the men drinking pints of lager and the women with wines. It is 8.45 a.m. They sit there wordlessly and quite contentedly. Meanwhile, we shuffle forwards with our bags, past a row of feeble sandwiches and bottles of Coke that seem to be twice the price they are in supermarkets. It's a good ten-minute wait.

'Black Americano please,' I ask, when I finally reach a counter packed with overpriced slabs of flapjack.

'Would you like milk with that?' asks an attendant, keenly pressing buttons on the till.

'No. Black, please.'

'Without milk?'

'Yes,' I reply.

The attendant shoots me a look that seems to say 'we've got a difficult one here'. I hand over the best part of £2 and take my coffee straight to the train.

We're soon pulling away under a dirty grey sky past familiar warehouses and graffiti that says 'TOXIC CUT'. It is a grim winter's morning. I hunker down, sitting next to a man intently playing Sudoku, and look at my *Rough Guide to The Netherlands*.

Rotterdam, four hours and nine minutes away via Brussels, seems to be an unusual choice for a weekend break. I read about the devastating damage suffered during a Nazi attack on 14 May 1940, when the centre was almost totally flattened. I discover that the city has an 'earthy character... its tough grittiness is part of its appeal'. I learn that it boasts Europe's first pedestrianised shopping precinct (though this is described as 'tired and sad'), as well as many 'boisterous bars and clubs'. I gather that the city has the highest population density in Europe and has the largest port in the world, though the one in Shanghai may just be about to take over this title. Rotterdam is slightly smaller than Amsterdam with a population of 600,000 compared to 740,000 – while the entire country consists of 16.5 million, which seems quite a lot for such a small geographical space. It is known for its modern architecture and contains a series of houses shaped like giant sugar cubes. Aside from this, the place was a 'turbo charged hotbed of hippy action' in the 1960s and the Pilgrim Fathers set sail for America from Rotterdam in 1620 'changing to the more reliable *Mayflower* in Plymouth'.

What am I about to let myself in for, I'm thinking to myself. No wonder E ducked out of this one, vaguely citing an 'unmissable' family birthday.

The journey goes smoothly and at Brussels, there's a pleasingly quick connection for the onwards train. It wouldn't have mattered if I'd missed it, though I'd have had to wait another hour. We're soon passing through wispy woodland, apartment blocks and power stations billowing steam. I buy a 'bacon oeufs' sandwich and a bottle of water from a woman pushing a trolley. A grey-haired ticket inspector who looks a little like Seamus Heaney appears.

'Amsterdam?' he asks.

'No, Rotterdam,' I reply, wondering if the ticket is wrong.

'Oh, whatever,' he says casually, and moves along the carriage.

There's soft winter sunlight across the flat, open landscape. Ploughed fields with symmetrical lines disappear into the horizon. Solitary red-brick barns look as though they belong on the American prairies. I sit back, reading *St Pancras Station* by the architectural historian Simon Bradley. It explains how the station was built in 1867–77 by the Midland Railway Company – I'd picked it up at Foyles on an impulse earlier. Maybe I'm turning into some sort of trainspotter or train obsessive (E has suggested as much) or maybe not, but either way I'm suddenly engrossed in the history of St Pancras railway station.

I already knew about the train shed built by William Henry Barlow, the Victorian engineer whose marvellous roof above the terminal inspired lines of poetry and the campaign to save the station in the 1960s by John Betjeman. But now I find out about George Gilbert Scott, the Victorian architect who created the vast red-brick building at the front of the station. This building, with its columns and turrets and grand V-shaped windows has always seemed a mystery to me; standing proudly by the Euston Road and looking as though it houses a major museum of some sort. For some time when I was younger I thought it must be something to do with the next door British Library. It has long been closed to the public, and during these weekends away it's been fenced off with builders at work.

In the space of a few pages, as we zoom through the Low Countries under an ice-blue sky, I learn that the early Christian Saint Pancras may never have existed, and that many graves from an old church bearing the saint's name had to be excavated to make way for the tracks (with Thomas Hardy, before he turned to full-time writing, overseeing the excavations during an apprenticeship with a company building the station). George Gilbert Scott, the enormously prolific Victorian architect responsible for more than 800 churches, many workhouses and the Albert Memorial (for which he was knighted), won a competition to design a hotel at the front of Barlow's train shed. It was a pivotal moment in his career. Just before embarking on St Pancras, Scott had suffered a very public snub by the prime minister Lord Palmerston over his plans to build a neo-Gothic version of the Foreign Office in Whitehall. Instead, much against his instincts, he was instructed to finish the Foreign Office in a 'safer' Italian Renaissance design.

He was annoyed. And the result was that he threw all his gusto and greatest Gothic ambitions into St Pancras. Stones were brought down by train from the Midlands, sculptors carved images of railwaymen into halls with enormously high ceilings, great staircases went up, towers with clock-faces arose, turrets and columns shot up just about everywhere, as did vaulted ceilings, iron balustrades, oriel windows and gables. To hell with Lord Palmerston! The Midland Railway Company had wanted 'the grandest hotel in the realm' and in sheer outlandishness they got it. Scott, who through his relentless work ever since starting in the business at the age of fourteen seemed to represent the archetypal self-made Victorian, had left his (very large) mark on London. St Pancras was a 'child of the Gothic Revival at its creative zenith', says Bradley. Like the prime minister, not everyone enjoyed this revival, which deliberately harked back to aspects of medieval Britain at a time when the country was conquering the world. But at St Pancras they got one of its best examples ever created.

I put down the book. Maybe E is right, I suddenly realise, after being totally immersed in the world of George Gilbert Scott while speeding northwards towards Rotterdam – maybe I am transforming into some kind of 'train nut'. Maybe I should hold back. Perhaps there *is* an unhealthy level of train and station knowledge, and perhaps I'm heading towards it? But I don't care. At least I haven't started marking down the types of engines and locomotive names... yet.

A text buzzes to say 'Welcome to the Netherlands'. I look up, realising that we went through Antwerp some time back and are now crossing a large river lit up by a low yellow sun. Beyond, strips of water in the ploughed fields look like long thin mirrors reflecting the sky. There's a cube-shaped office block. We pass two brown ponies munching grass by a canal and a couple of teenagers standing beneath a willow tree sharing what might be grass of a different type (this is, after all, Holland). We enter Dordrecht, the fourth biggest Dutch town, apparently almost completely untouched by bombs during the war, as Allied attention was focused on its larger northerly neighbour – my destination. Then we come to a beautiful iron cage bridge over another river, snake past a mosque with twin minarets and domes, and duck into a tunnel.

And so we arrive in Rotterdam. This station is not neo-Gothic. It doesn't seem to be neo anything, or have any architectural style at all. It's a mess, under renovation of some kind, with a board near the platform describing grand plans. It begins

'The best impression is the first impression...' In this instance, that impression is of overcrowding, the sound of drills and a sense of something approaching mayhem. Realising this is being perhaps a touch unfair if the place is about to have some sort of elaborate makeover, I follow confusing signs to a tourist office that appears to be attached to a restaurant named 'Engels'.

I enter a reception with purple sofas, opposite a room full of people eating late lunch. This seems to be the tourist office as there are brochures and a counter at the far end, behind which a woman sits with her eyes fixed to a computer screen.

I go over and show the woman my hotel's name. She presents me with a map.

'Take tram number 20,' she says, straight away. 'Or else it is a forty-minute walk.'

What about a taxi, how much would that be? 'Twenty euros,' she replies. She's not big on chit-chat, though she's polite and friendly.

I ask which way it is to the trams. 'Right... I mean left,' she says, waving an arm in the direction of the restaurant.

I take the map and am about to walk away.

'One euro,' she says, her eyes falling on the map.

I pass over a euro.

The tram arrives promptly and soon passes from the madness of the station to a calm canal lined with tall, burgundy-coloured houses with A-shaped roofs. There are Chinese and Surinamese restaurants on corners and modern sculptures in a strip of park along the canal. It looks quaint and old here, lots of narrow buildings with typical Dutch gables and high windows. But then we turn off the canal, and the devastating effects of World War Two are soon clear to see.

Anything 'old' seems to have vanished. Contemporary buildings shoot up with angular designs and abstract shapes –

from the top of one tall structure a long rectangular section hangs outwards, looking a little like a hammerhead shark. Gleaming new skyscrapers intermingle with low-level blocks clearly built in the mid twentieth century. One of these houses the office of a tour operator specialising in trips to the Caribbean island of Curacao, a former Dutch dependency just off the coast of Venezuela; the pictures of white sand beaches and palm trees look a little incongruous in 'gritty, earthy' Rotterdam. But it's not gritty in a depressing way. Actually, the city is having a very different effect. This is nothing like Britain's war-flattened Coventry, with its dull buildings, noisy roads and the heart-dropping sense of life having moved on elsewhere. Far from it: the first impression, after the crazy station, is of a place that is growing and modern and full of life.

This sense of vitality hits you quickly. And it seems at its strongest as the tram crosses Erasmus Bridge – named after the Renaissance humanist who was born in the city.

It's a beauty. We move with electric quiet up a gentle incline towards the centre of the delicate, harp-like suspension bridge, which dates from 1996 and connects the north and south parts of the city. I'm staying in the south (which frankly I hadn't quite realised when booking my hotel), though most of the city centre is in the north. The local nickname for the bridge is 'The Swan', because of the elegant white curve of the white pylon on the south side that supports the many cables that hold up the structure.

Looking back across the wide expanse of the River New Meuse I take in the towers lining the river in the north. There's the hammerhead shark. There's a row of neat buildings that look like executive apartment blocks, with ski jump roofs and unusual red cage-like exteriors. The river is wide and grey, the bridge is 800 metres across, with an island below with residential housing and more offices. In the distance I can see metal-framed bridges, with one in the shape of giant goalposts, which looks as though it was built to lift cargo. In the distance in the opposite direction – to the west – there are a thousand cranes in the Europort area, built after World War Two as a much bigger replacement to the battered central docks. Across the river to the south there are a couple of shiny skyscrapers that seem very new with 'Deloitte' and 'AKD' written on them, as well as a strange lime-green building with a giant digital display on its façade. What a view and what a city: I've been here less than an hour and already I can tell that Rotterdam seems to be going places. It's big and it's bold... and I like it.

After a struggle with the map and a walk along an enormous empty dock lined with well-to-do apartments, an unexpectedly rundown building that looks as though it's full of squatters and a diner called 'Manhattan: You Still Got To Eat', I find Hotel Pincoffs, where I enter an old red-brick building with a modern whitewashed lobby.

Here I meet Wouter, a young receptionist in a grey V-neck jumper – who likes to talk (quite a lot). 'Welcome to Rotterdam,' he says. 'We are a small hotel with seventeen rooms. I am a trainee manager here. This used to be the immigration office. We are a 100 per cent green hotel. We used old doors to create this shelf,' as he says this he points to a shelf on which a row of DVDs sits. 'Yes, old doors. We are the only hotel in Rotterdam with a "Green Key" award,' as he points to a certificate.

Then he walks me into an adjoining room with leather armchairs bathed in lemon-yellow light. He draws my attention to a giant safe in a corner. 'See, we did not throw this away. We are green.'

'What do you use it for now?'

'We keep the whisky and the brandy there,' he replies 'We also have a fridge inside, for cold beers.' He pauses for a split second, and switches to discussing the hotel food. 'Biological produce from biological farms. We are Michelin-recommended 'green'. See these key chains,' he indicates towards a cabinet near the lift, where we've walked round to now. 'Old bike tyres,' he says. 'That's what they're made of. These purses: old bike tyres too.'

He shows me the breakfast room. This is, naturally, a green zone as well. 'Old doors,' he announces once again. 'The breakfast counter is made of old doors. And see that old piano?' I do see an old piano sitting in a corner. 'It didn't work. So we converted it,' he opens the piano cover. 'See: cutlery and tea and coffee things.'

Several clocks above the piano are stuck at 1.50, though it's later than that now. 'This is a happy time,' Wouter explains, when I ask. 'It's always a smiley face when the hands are at that time.'

Sensing that Wouter might be a fount of all local knowledge, I inquire about the rundown building, which we can see through the window, with the gleaming Deloitte skyscraper just beyond. 'Old hippies,' he replies casually. 'They call themselves a living community. They're in a kind of dispute: the city of Rotterdam and them. The city wants them to go, but they don't want to. This whole neighbourhood used to be bad. Lower-class society used to live here, mostly industrial dockers. It was dangerous. Tough. But it has really been developed in the past thirty years. The Deloitte building went up last year. Really it is all changing.'

We catch the lift up to my room as I learn about the name of the hotel. I'm feeling a bit travel weary, but Wouter is full of beans. 'It was a very big scandal,' he says, referring to a man named Louis Pincoffs, a nineteenth-century businessman who was responsible for the development of much of the city docks.

'A very powerful businessman, but he committed fraud. It was some kind of pyramid scheme... like Bernie Madoff. When people began to find out he fled to New York City and started a cigar shop. It bellied up and he died quite a poor man.'

All of the rooms, I learn, are named after friends or enemies of Pincoffs. Mine is called Prins Hendrik, who Wouter says was a friend until he discovered he had lost money. The room is literally green, with olive walls decorated with a long chain of white flowers. These flowers lead to a strange doorway opening on to a narrow private staircase to the floor below. 'This was Pincoffs' bedroom and this staircase led to his office,' he says. 'He liked to be able to move about without people knowing: legend has it. This is just one of the hotel's funny little stories.'

He pauses, drawing a breath, and looking thoughtful for a moment. 'Old doors!' he says pointing to a side table with a coffee-maker. And with that Wouter departs – leaving me alone in the greenest hotel in Rotterdam.

It's 4 p.m., too late to go to any 'attractions', too early to go out for the evening. So I do what comes naturally after a bus, a Tube journey, two international trains, a tram, a dockside walk and an impromptu history of the old hippies, tyre products and doors of my hotel – I fall asleep. I don't see why not. I've got no appointments this weekend. There is nothing I am urgently required to do. It's a Saturday afternoon in a European city that very few people consider visiting. There's no hurry to see anything. Why not take it easy?

I doze off and wake an hour or so later to the sound of seagulls – wondering where on earth I am. I stare at the chain of flowers on the olive-green walls of my room, and I remember. I consider what to do: I could easily just stay here, order room service and take it easy. It's dark out on the river. There's a big unfamiliar city out there.

I call E and explain I'm in an eco-hotel next to a hippy commune on the wrong side of the river.

She seems pleased about this. 'Really,' she says, with an undertone of 'there but for the grace of God go I'. I hear her chuckling. 'You say that most of it was flattened in the war,' she continues.

'Yes,' I reply. 'It was.' I pause and, realising this does not exactly sound enticing, add: 'But there are a lot of nice modern buildings.'

'Really?' she replies, enjoying this and chuckling a bit more, before slyly declaring: 'I guess there's a reason why it's called *Rotterdam*.'

I ignore this. And then E, who's clearly on perky form, adds: 'You may have pulled the wool over my eyes about Antwerp, but you were never going to get me to go to Rotterdam! Weekend break! More like make or break!'

E is already at her family party and seems to be enjoying taking the Mickey: imagining me lost in a cold industrial city in a north-west corner of Europe. She doesn't really mean it (and it sounds as though she may have been at the family sherry). Anyway, E seemed to like Antwerp.

I get back to the city at hand. 'Actually, it's very upbeat,' I say. 'Very modern... futuristic.'

'So it's got skyscrapers,' E replies, cutting me short, and giggling a bit.

'Yes, lots of them,' I say, suddenly feeling defensive about Rotterdam. 'And they're very modern ones.'

'Right,' she replies. More chuckles.

'Right,' I reply.

'I hope you're having a good time,' E says, sounding as though she definitely is.

'I am,' I respond, trying to come across as blasé about Rotterdam. 'Very much so.'

We say goodnight warmly, with the sound of laughter in the background at her family get-together.

And then I do what I suppose a lot of Hollanders do at this time of evening on a Saturday night. I jump on a tram and head for a 'coffee shop' – determined now to 'have a good time' in the biggest port in Europe.

This course of action sees me crossing Erasmus Bridge and ending up by Witte de Withstraat, next to the canal. As I enter the street two female police officers are walking in the opposite direction on the other side of the road. They are both six feet tall with long blonde hair tied in ponytails that poke from under baseball caps. To say that they would stick out back in the UK is an understatement – they might even induce a mini crime-wave. Here, no one bats an eyelid. I stroll on along the street finding cool jazz bars filled with middle-aged folk dressed in black. There's a stylish Indian restaurant called Bollywood Lounge (filled with television screens showing Bollywood films) and a funny little place called the Spooky Café, where chicken nuggets and kebabs are on offer and there are pictures of ghosts drawn all over the walls. Beyond, an artist in a bohemian gallery is putting the final touches to a work that consists of sculptures of eagles mixed with lit candles and a sign saying 'DISINTEGRATION'. Further on, I find the very bizarre Hotel Bazar, with an elaborately gilded lobby filled with Middle Eastern ornaments.

In short, it's eclectic, eye-catching and plain strange. I'd never have guessed the street would hold so many surprises: the buildings had looked nondescript and dull when I'd first turned in. 'I'm having a good time in Rotterdam, very much so,' I say to myself as a kind of mantra. But I still can't find Witte de With, one of the city's 'more amenable cannabis coffee shops', according to the *Rough Guide*.

Finally, I do. I'd walked straight past it earlier. It's against the law for coffee shops to advertise their wares explicitly from the outside, though this one – I now notice – has large paintings of cannabis leaves on the front. Neon blue lettering says: COFFEE SHOP OPEN'. I'm not entirely sure how I hadn't spotted the place.

Two guys are hanging about outside – appropriately wearing puffa jackets – as I enter. They grin inanely at me, looking happily dishevelled. I descend a couple of steps and find myself in a tiny, dark chamber with a kiosk on one side. A youngish man, also wearing a puffa jacket, with 'Stone Island' written on the back, is in the middle of a complicated purchase. This gives me time to assess my surroundings and work out what to do. I'd imagined I'd be able to sit down somewhere and order a lime-juice or something and soak up the atmosphere while watching the cannabis smokers of Rotterdam at play. But here there only appears to be the kiosk, a CCTV camera, and a scuffed door into a backroom. I check the handle: it's locked.

Behind the kiosk there's a long list of the (many) different types of cannabis on offer. Some of the names hint at the effects: Napalm, Amnesia, Haze. Others identify the supposed country of origin: Colombia and Jamaica. Next to each of the types are little bags containing green leaves and brown seeds. Scribbled prices show that a gram costs from seven to twelve euros. Pipes in Rastafarian colours are for sale and a sweet smell emanates from under the locked door.

I consider my options as puffa jacket completes his purchase. He shuffles to the back door and is, apparently, buzzed in.

So that's how it works. I catch a glimpse of the hazy inner sanctum; a kind of holy of the holies for the smokies. It looks pretty grim and the clientele are not quite the beat-poet types I'd expected. The guy behind the kiosk turns his attention to me, as I'm now the only customer in the antechamber.

Here are my thoughts at this moment: 1) I gave up smoking eight years ago: do I want to risk triggering off the evil weed addiction again? No, I definitely don't. Giving up was a nightmare; 2) But why not get in the spirit and just give it a go? Don't be so lame. You only live once. Anyway, you're meant to be having a good time; 3) On the last occasion I tried this stuff, many moons ago on a stag do in Amsterdam, I was struck with such intense paranoia that I truly felt, to paraphrase my all-time favourite tennis player John McEnroe, that I'd entered 'the pits of the earth'; 4) This was perhaps because I didn't know how to smoke it properly; 5) On the basis of all this, what am I doing coming here in the first place?

So concludes my foray into the subterranean drug culture of Rotterdam.

Anyway, I fancied a drink in the first place. I stroll back towards the canal and find myself passing Zaras and River Islands on a dull shopping precinct, before entering a cool-looking hideaway on a side street. Soul music is playing in the Rotown bar, and I sit at a table on a scuffed wood floor near the window and order a glass of Sauvignon Blanc from a polite waitress.

'Large, sir?' she asks.

'Yes, please,' I reply.

'With you shortly, sir.'

Everyone seems to speak excellent English round here – well, excellent enough to arrange a decent glass of cool white wine, which is excellent enough for me.

This is more like it. A board advertises live music and a band has just entered, heaping guitar cases by the bar. Like so many other Rotterdammers, they're an ultra stylish lot. Their dressed-down, almost down-at-heel look at first seems to be 'charity shop hip' – as though their clothes were picked up in second-hand shops for next to nothing – except then I realise that actually all their stuff seems brand new and probably very expensive. The guys wear large boots with jeans tucked haphazardly inside, while the women are in dungarees or ultra-miniskirts. There are designer glasses and angular haircuts aplenty. I sit at my table glancing through *Rotterdam in Your Pocket,* a mini guide I picked up from a shelf by the bar. It's a useful little booklet, with each area of the city mapped out, and with things to see in each area. An advert for high-speed Thalys trains catches my eye. 'GOOD NEWS: 20 MINUTES FASTER FROM ROTTERDAM TO AMSTERDAM,' it says, stressing that this is the quickest way to get to Amsterdam: now just forty minutes. Another advert showing a railway track leading to the Eiffel Tower – which appears to be bathed in heavenly light – gives the latest time to Paris as 2 hrs 30 min. This is thirty-nine minutes less than before.

I continue to read up on high-speed train times amid the various hipster band members. This is not, I reflect, a high moment of my 'cool'. One should not, possibly, be reading about high-speed trains on one's own on Saturday nights in cool Rotterdam bars. 'So what,' I say to myself. 'I'm enjoying myself.' And I am. I order another glass and listen to the soul music, before catching the tram back, for a final sharpener in the hotel – no sign of 'Old Doors' Wouter – and hit the sack.

One of the best ways to see the city is by bike, or so it says in *Rotterdam in Your Pocket.* So on Sunday morning I do just that. I catch yet another tram to the main station, where I get off outside the office of Rotterdam ArchiGuides. Here I join a group of tourists on a two-hour cycle round the sights, learning about the local architectural highlights.

It is a bright, but extremely chilly, morning in the south-west of the Netherlands as we pedal towards our first stop at Schouwburgplein. By the time we arrive, my hands are frozen as we look out across a square covered in a metallic raised platform, which shines in the morning light (squint your eyes and it looks a little like an ice rink). There are half a dozen of us on the tour and we stop and shiver as a cheery woman named Eeva tells us about this creation, which is surrounded by lamps shaped like harbour-side cranes. 'It is meant to look like a dock,' she informs us. 'But there have been problems. In fact for the average citizen, there have been very many problems with this square.'

She pauses as she looks across the glistening metal, as I have a surreal moment: am I really about to find out about the technical drawbacks of a public square while sitting on an odd green bike in the middle of an industrial city on a frozen Sunday morning in the middle of winter?

The answer is: yes, I am.

'Drainage,' says Eeva. 'At first it wasn't draining. That meant it was smelly. That was fixed in 1996.' This was six years after the completion of the square. 'It is also very slippery. People started slipping over, especially when it was icy or when it snowed. This is very dangerous. This also is being fixed.'

She urges us to push our bikes across the square rather than risk slipping – and points out that the little holes in the metal surface have also caused 'problems with the high heels'. We obediently follow on foot; glancing at one another with looks that appear to suggest: 'It is very cold. Why didn't we go to the art gallery?'

On one corner of the square there's a strange shoebox-like building containing a cinema. 'It looks dirty,' one of our group pipes up.

She's right, it does look pretty filthy.

'They tried to clean it but used the wrong product,' replies Eeva, sounding a little let down by the enquiry. 'That was another problem.' She pauses, and ruefully adds, 'people are always complaining about modern architects. Unfortunately...' she tails off for a moment as though trying to find the right words '...many times they are right.'

We take a look at a theatre with odd twisting metal objects rotating on the outside and pedal on along excellent cycle lanes to a place called Lijnbaan, one of the dull shopping precincts I'd had the dubious pleasure to walk through yesterday. But this is not just any dull shopping precinct, we soon discover, it is the *world's first* dull shopping precinct. 'It opened in 1952,' says Eeva, 'the first car-free shopping street in the world. Japanese and American architects came here to see it. It was quite radical. There was a big master plan: a vision of a modern city. The idea was to have shops here, with housing in separate towers.'

These towers loom on each side of the shops. They look at first glance like archetypal council blocks, though on closer inspection I can see they're very well-kept versions of archetypal council blocks, with plants on balconies and smart Rotterdammers on bikes with groceries in baskets cycling up to the entrances. It's very quiet round here, but although we are in a big city centre, it does feel as though there's a life in the neighbourhood, even on a cold Sunday morning. 'Rotterdam may not be as beautiful as Amsterdam,' says Eeva, who's wearing a beret and a black coat. She's in her mid twenties and has, we soon realise, a charming honesty. It's as though we are being taken round by a local with a bit of time to spare, not a robotic guide with information to deliver at certain points. 'But once you know the city, it really gets to you. Artists think it has a better atmosphere than Amsterdam. I lived in Amsterdam for a year and a half. But the city doesn't get *personal*. Everyone likes to go there, but it is not *personal*.'

We cycle onwards past the City Hall and an ornate post office; two of the only buildings to have survived the horrendous 14 May 1940 bombardment by the Nazis. This attack was almost called off at the last minute as negotiations for the surrender of the city had been frantically agreed, but this message had not reached the Luftwaffe as they were out of radio contact. The result was the wiping out of the centre of one of Netherlands' oldest and finest cities (first dating from around 900).

Pondering this, we arrive at a tourist office overlooked by a semicircular office block with blue-tinged mirror windows. Eeva locks up our bikes. 'Every Dutchman has three bikes stolen in his lifetime,' she informs us, as a way of explaining her caution as we enter.

It's a fairly typical tourist office with windmill-shaped pens, porcelain clogs, tulip bulbs and 'I LOVE ROTTA' T-shirts – the original name of 'Rotterdam' comes from *rot* (muddy) and *a* (water). I can tell some of the group, a mixture of Canadians and Americans, are thinking: 'Why have we come here?' And I'm wondering that a bit, too.

But our question is soon answered when we come to four large black and white aerial pictures of the city. The first is taken in 1932. It shows a city cluttered with old terraced houses. The next is taken in 1946. Save for the Town Hall, the post office and a church, there is virtually nothing. The rubble has been cleared away leaving dark patches where neighbourhoods used to be and thin strips of whiter land where the roads once were. The land is so empty it almost feels as though the few remaining old buildings were superimposed.

'The bombardment only lasted ten minutes,' says Eeva. 'But that day the wind changed direction and the fires really picked up: 260 hectares was destroyed. More than 800 people died and about 25,000 houses were ruined. Many of the canals were filled in with the rubble. People from Rotterdam are obsessed by the "pre-war". It is still a big trauma for the elderly people living here.'

The next picture shows 1967. Modern buildings have sprouted up, including the apartments near Lijnbaan. There are still many empty lots of land. The final photograph shows the city in 2008, with all the skyscrapers and Erasmus Bridge linking to the south side of the river. 'What happened is that the modernists won over the traditionalists,' Eeva explains. 'So Rotterdam was modelled on an American city. They thought we'd all go and live in the suburbs and commute. For that reason only 10,000 of the 25,000 homes were rebuilt in the centre. A grid pattern was created for the roads and we became the most American city in Holland.'

She continues her history of Rotterdam, which I can tell the Americans are particularly enjoying. But Eeva changes tack. 'Now the opposite is the case,' she says. The Americans – who had been basking in glory for a minute or two, and acting all 'Stars and Stripes' – look a little put-out. 'We want people to live in the city centre. In the 1980s the city felt dead at night and on Sundays. No one was there. Now we have many more apartments in the centre. Foreigners understand that this is a cool way of doing things: that this is a cool city. But Dutch people like canals. And we don't have many. The average Dutchman says: "This does not look like a Dutch city to me."'

Our bikes have not been stolen, and we cycle on, seeing example after example of modern building; Rotterdam is an architect's dream. We learn that the city hall is soon to be transformed with some kind of amazing glass roof by the local star architect Rem Koolhaas – 'one of the three biggest architects in the world'. We discover that Katendrecht, an area on a peninsula in the south of the city near my hotel, was once 'full of opium dens and sailors after hookers, it was really rough'. The reason why there is such a large Chinese community in the city – something I'd noticed when walking past Chinese restaurants near the bar last night – is that 'cheap Chinese workers were brought in to break a dockers' strike in 1910... afterwards they stayed and now we've got the biggest Chinese community in Europe'. Katendrecht still has social problems and for a while 'if there was any trouble the police just closed off the peninsula'. We stop by a statue of Erasmus, who was born in the city in 1469 and lived here for four years. You might have thought the city would make more of being the home of 'the first Dutch cosmopolitan', as Eeva describes him. 'He went to Paris and to England to tutor the kings' kids – he was a reformist and his books were printed all over Europe, an inspiration for Martin Luther.'

'Gee, is this it?' says one of the Americans, looking at the statue, which shows Erasmus wearing a floppy hat and with his head buried in a book. He seems surprised, as I am, that there is so little by way of commemoration.

'Yes it is,' says Eeva.

And with that we cycle on, leaving one of Europe's greatest ever thinkers on his own next to a nondescript apartment block.

We pedal and pedal and see a rare old building dating from 1898 that once claimed to be the highest office tower in Europe (45 metres high), as well as a stylish new Red Apple tower block, which is covered in bright red cladding and, Eeva says, has 'some great penthouse suites, I've been in them'. And then we lock up our bikes again at the 'cube buildings'.

It is difficult to be a tourist in Rotterdam without seeing the 'cube buildings'.

These odd houses seem to be mentioned in just about every tourist guide to the city. There are thirty-eight of them and they are coloured yellow and grey. They are indeed shaped like giant sugar cubes and they look like giddying places in which to live. They were completed in 1984 as part of the drive to get more people to live in the city centre, but they were not a great success with residents, who found them, as you might expect, quite odd. Plans to build more were cancelled, but the ones that remained became somehow iconic and symbolic, in a positive way, of Rotterdam's efforts at post-war rebuilding. We walk up to one that has been opened to members of the public by an enterprising local guy.

'When he realised his house could work for him,' says Eeva, 'He gave up work.'

The interior is extremely peculiar: cramped and awkward. Where you might usually expect floors, there are sloping walls. We spend the whole time ducking and moving into squashed corners to let other tourists past. A steep staircase runs narrowly upwards. Wooden Buddhas are dotted here and there, amid the occasional African mask. There's also a fine set of metal figures depicting witches and wizards.

Rotterdam's Cube House is a very peculiar place indeed.

But in two hours we've seen vast swathes of the city. It's been a superb way to get a sense of how Rotterdam has changed, and is still changing. And it's the cycling that's done it. We've seen a hell of a lot of 'Rotta'. We may have only stopped here and there, but it feels as though the city has somehow sunk in.

I catch a tram south – skirting Schouwburgplein with all its intriguing technical design faults. On the old canal, I get off and pass the coffee shop on Witte de Withstraat, looking for a place to eat. I end up having a late lunch, a very good baguette served by the cheerful bald owner of Spooky Café – good service, cheap prices, clean tables, nice ghost pictures. And then I walk to Boijmans Van Beuningen art museum.

Rotterdam may not be blessed with too many historical sights; a void that seems to have been filled by its passion for modern architecture. But the city has a fine collection of art. I spend a happy hour or so examining Dürers, Rembrandts, Picassos and Monets. In the Flemish and Netherlandish section, there are four fabulously memorable pictures by Hieronymus Bosch (1450–1516), including one entitled *The Peddler*, which shows the Prodigal Son sloping away from a brothel in tattered trousers, while holding a crooked stick and looking gaunt. In the same room there is the marvellously enigmatic *Tower of Babel* by Pieter Bruegel the Elder (1525–1569), with the gargantuan half-built tower enveloped in cloud, tiny figures scampering at the base and the whole world seeming as though it's gone quite mad. For some reason, perhaps because Rotterdam seems to be in the midst of so much construction, this painting almost feels as though it serves as some kind of local warning: go so far… but don't go crazy.

After an afternoon nap back at Rotterdam's greenest hotel, I get a final and very different perspective on the city by taking a water taxi from outside the hotel to Euromast. This is a 185-metre observation tower in the west of the city in the direction of the docks. A little yellow-and-black boat arrives, looking a bit like a bumblebee, and the taxi driver asks in Dutch where I want to go.

'Euromast,' I say, keeping things simple.

'The big tower?' he answers in faltering English.

'Ja,' I reply, in a flourish of Dutch.

And off the bumblebee buzzes across the choppy grey water in the early evening gloom. The neon lights of the city's skyscrapers are all around as we zip under Erasmus Bridge and stop at a quay next to a ship shaped like a pagoda housing the 'Ocean Paradise' Chinese restaurant. I walk over to the tower, which opened in 1960 and was extended a decade later. The lift flies up towards the 'crow's nest' observation deck, and soon I'm looking out across the sodium lights and haze of Rotterdam. Yuppie apartment blocks are all around this part of the city. The river looks coal black heading for the North Sea. Prompted to enter by an attendant, I step into a room with 'Euroscoop' written on the door. I expect that this will include some sort of information panels. Instead, I'm projected on a twisting, corkscrew ride to the tower's peak. Having had no idea this was going to happen (and being a vertigo sufferer), this is not an experience I'm going to forget in a hurry. Facts and figures come over a commentary, while I listen in a haze. The ride twists up seemingly forever, and then down seemingly forever, too – the modern architecture of Rotterdam looking very small below.

I get out and head for the lift. I take the lift down. And I catch a water taxi back across the river to the New York Hotel, not far from where I'm staying, having perhaps cracked the Euroscoop to New York Hotel speed record. This is how I find myself in the former headquarters of the Holland-America Line, completed in 1919. Inside, it's buzzing even though it's a Sunday night. There's a cavernous open-plan restaurant with exposed brick walls, chandeliers and a pleasingly rough and ready atmosphere. Many hundreds of thousands of immigrants left for the New World after passing through this hall, I learn from a bar menu 'history', the final ship departing in 1971. It was from just across the water here that the Pilgrim Fathers sailed, via Plymouth, to America.

I sit by the bar drinking a beer, pleased to be on terra firma with a cool Dutch lager. In this happy state, I am approached. A woman in a yellow dress comes up, smiles and says something in Dutch as though she knows me.

'Excuse me,' I reply, wondering who she is. She really does appear to think I'm an old friend or something. 'Can I help you? I don't speak Dutch.'

'Oh, sorry!' she says, and goes down the bar to someone else – the man she was supposed to meet.

I drink my beer and realise I *have* had a good time in Rotterdam. It's full of surprises, vibrant, modern, 'green' (with all its bikes and recycled doors) and generally feels as though it's going places. There's not the sense of 'what if things had been different' that I've felt in Coventry – that other war-wrecked city back home. There's more a feeling of 'whatever next'? The Nazi bombs are not forgotten, but it's the future that's on people's minds.

CHAPTER NINE

MARSEILLES: 'ON THE SNOW TRAIN TO THE MED'

Forget erratic ticket machines and queues at Caffè Nero. There's snow on the high-speed lines, and there is nothing short of mayhem at St Pancras.

Amid Christmas trees shaped out of bottles of champagne and promotions advertising shopping discounts, groups of travellers are gathering near the security gates, looking like crowds denied entry to a football stadium. A member of staff informs us that it's 'first come, first served' on journeys today due to cancellations caused by freezing weather; weather forecasters in the papers this morning say we are embarking on the coldest winter since 1927.

We're about to find out whether it's a very good or a very mad time to be going on a weekend break to the French Riviera.

With yellow stickers on our tickets reallocating our seats, we enter the departure lounge to find our fellow high-speed passengers draped over seats and chairs and bags, and whatever is to hand. A board says that our train to Paris will leave an hour and a half late. We find a corner. I fetch coffees. Time moves slowly. E mutters: 'What's the big deal? It's snowed. Snow happens in the winter.' We board our train. We roll slowly past warehouses covered in icicles into a white-out landscape. An announcement says: 'Because of snow speed restrictions, expect delays of up to ninety minutes.' That will make us three hours late in total. We're going to miss our connection to Marseilles, but assume – rightly or wrongly – that we'll be OK to travel on from Gare de Lyon.

We'll just have to jump that hurdle when we get to it. On the plus side, we soon realise, this is a spectacular ride. A bright sun looms above; a great white orb glowing through the snow clouds. Kent is frozen, turned into a fairy-tale landscape with even the electricity pylons looking picturesque. There are occasional flurries as we look out of our packed carriage, listening to a group of Americans seated in front.

'We don't have high-speed trains back home,' says one, talking to a British neighbour. He's wearing polished cowboy boots with a suit, and has a deep Texan drawl. 'I live in Dallas and it would be amazin' to have 'em there, man: go by train to San Antonio, truly amazin'. New York to Chicago, man, we could do with that, too. Man, I spend so much goddamn time at goddamn airports.'

'Why aren't there any high-speed trains?' asks the Brit.

'The car lobby,' he replies. 'In the 1950s and the 1960s, it was them that blocked it. The railroads never recovered, man. The infrastructure is there: it was just those damn lobbyists from those goddamn car companies.'

He returns to checking share prices on his laptop. We go through the tunnel and come out in an even whiter landscape; in places we can't even see across the tracks through a thick soupy mist. Through the gap in the seat, E looks with fascination at the jewellery belonging to the American's wife. 'She's dripping with diamonds,' she whispers. 'They're huge: I mean huge. Proper jewellery. Look at the bling!'

I regard the bling; it's impressive bling.

'They've got to be oil magnates,' E decides. 'Loaded, absolutely loaded.'

We fall into silence, with the carriage inside almost glowing white. It feels as though we're taking some kind of train through the clouds. Even though we're running late and going slow, there's something deeply soothing about the journey.

We hear the Brit ask the Texans where they are staying in Paris. 'The Ritz,' the wife replies nonchalantly, raising a hand full of rocks and gesticulating vaguely in the direction of the French capital.

'But of course,' chuckles the Brit.

'Well, it was either The Ritz or the other one... The George V,' says the wife.

We reach Paris at 3 p.m. Our original train was due to leave at 8.55 a.m., and even though the journey's been relaxing it feels as though we've been on-the-go quite a while now. We make it across the French capital and stand by a screen in the bowels of Gare de Lyon waiting for the next train to Marseilles. There is one, but it's delayed and the departure time keeps shifting backwards. We stare upwards at the monitor like goldfish waiting to be fed. We've got no choice.

It's crowded and cold. We're near a restaurant named 'Bonne Journée', which doesn't feel quite right to describe ours so far. A bit further along though, there's another place called 'Croq Voyage'.

'Crock indeed,' says E, acidly.

Our platform number eventually flicks up: we virtually sprint to the train and, even so, are lucky to find seats on the upper deck. It's now 5 p.m. and we learn this journey is going to be delayed even further due to the snowy conditions. Instead of the quickest time of three hours for this route, it will be five hours instead. As if to rub this in, there's an announcement that the buffet is closed.

'I can understand "no sandwiches", but just to say "we've closed the buffet", *that* doesn't make sense,' murmurs E, who has been murmuring various other pronouncements on the state of European fast-train travel. 'High speed, eh?' she says glancing at her watch, and then looking at me. 'I only wish it was high speed.' She's only putting on an act... we're both enjoying this (slightly crazy) adventure.

We move through the quiet darkness of snow-covered France. As we do so, E falls into a deep sleep and I think back to the beginnings of fast trains... There may be no sandwiches or even a buffet on this TGV, but there's more than enough time for reflection on the way to Marseilles.

To start from the very beginning, the whole point of trains has always been that they're quick. Even when the world's first proper line opened, the Liverpool and Manchester Railway on 15 September 1830, the top speed was a pretty damn fast 35 mph; much speedier than galloping horses (around 25 mph at full pelt) and obviously capable of sustaining this rate over a much longer distance. Though 35 mph may seem piddling to us now, back then this was frightening stuff. Doctors were consulted in advance of the official opening to ensure that eyes would not be damaged taking in scenery as carriages whizzed by and that there would be no problems with breathing at such heady speeds. Huge crowds used to stagecoaches lined the tracks waiting in awe of what lay in store.

It turned out to be both a momentous and a tragic day. With the brilliant engineer George Stephenson at the helm of the *Arrow* and the Duke of Wellington on board (the hero of Waterloo was by then prime minister), the Victorians were wowed as the locomotives set off from Manchester to Liverpool and moved across the landscape as though by magic along the thirty-one-mile route. It must have been a triumphant sight, with steam and smoke billowing across the landscape and a sense that this was a world first, connecting two of the proud pioneering cities of industrialisation. All was going swimmingly, that is until the *Arrow* stopped to take on water, when various dignitaries disembarked, some of them venturing on to the track, despite many warnings. This was when tragedy struck. Before disbelieving eyes, a former cabinet minister strayed in front of *The Rocket*, Stephenson's original groundbreaking locomotive and was knocked over and crushed, the sound of crunching bones horrifying onlookers. He died in agonising circumstances a few hours later in hospital.

But this inauspicious accident did not dampen enthusiasm for trains. Far from it: the day marked the start of 'railway mania'. Almost immediately, across the world there was great excitement at the potential offered by this fast new form of travel. Everyone's eyes were on what was happening in Britain, where success seemed to be leading to success, bringing advances in many walks of life. Even though there were many doubters, including some who were worried that cows near lines would be too frightened to produce milk and that sheep might be blackened by smoke, within ten years there was a train network up and down the length of England.

People ditched slow, bumpy old stagecoaches, bringing an end to tiresomely lengthy journeys via coaching inns. Fish 'n' chips became popular thanks to fresh catches brought in daily from the coast. Express dairy milk came in on trains from the country, meaning filthy city-centre cows could be removed. Industrialisation boomed on the back of the cheaper movement of coal and goods, canal owners becoming terribly upset at lost business. The country felt more robust, vibrant and stronger as a direct result. Prosperity and standards of living for all grew. The first train holidays began, organised by one Thomas Cook, a twenty-three-year-old cabinetmaker and former Baptist preacher. On 5 July 1841, he took a group of 500 teetotallers on a twelve-mile trip from Leicester to Loughborough to attend a temperance meeting. The cost? Just a shilling (a little more expensive than this fare down to Marseilles, which was £119 return).

Other countries, including France with its vast interior we're zooming through now, were soon following suit. Belgium was one of the first, as E and I discovered a few weeks back in Antwerp. It took Belgium just six years after the Liverpool and Manchester Railway's triumph to build a line from Brussels to Antwerp, George Stephenson himself helping with the engineering. France, Germany, Italy and others were next, with Bismarck's enthusiasm proving so important to Germany's swift advances in the 1870s. The Orient-Express was soon up and running, offering exotic journeys via Switzerland's Lausanne to Venice and Istanbul.

Further afield, in the United States, the 'Golden Spike' was hammered into place at Promontory Point just north of Great Salt Lake in Utah on 10 May 1869, thus connecting America 'from sea to shining sea', both an incredibly symbolic and a strategically crucial moment in the United States of America. In India, meanwhile, British influence meant railways had been established across the huge colony in the 1850s.

All these advantages came from *quicker* travel, which in a few short years was transforming the world in all sorts of ways... but what about *real speed*? When did trains really start to go fast? This 'slow' train from Paris to Marseilles – still moving quietly through the darkness – in fact has a pretty decent average of 97 mph along its 487-mile route; admittedly a long way below the usual 160 mph plus, but still not bad. In the 1930s, this journey we're on now would have taken ten hours at something like 48 mph – which might just have prompted a few wry comments from E along the way.

Apart from a surprisingly speedy train created in 1939 during the rule of Benito Mussolini in Italy, averaging 102 mph on the 200-mile journey from Florence to Milan (going some way to establishing the dictator's reputation for 'trains running on time'), and 75 mph services between Hamburg and Berlin promoted by Hitler, both of which ceased after the war, there were no recognised high-speed routes as we know them for many years. But then came the Japanese bullet train, or *Shinkansen*.

This changed everything. Built between Tokyo and Osaka in time for the 1964 Olympics, the *Shinkansen* achieved an average speed of 125 mph and cut the journey time between the two cities from 6 hrs 40 min. to 3 hrs 10 min. This was so fast that carriages had to be pressurised to prevent pain in ears and toilet bowls spurting water when trains zipped through tunnels (which can't have been too pleasant during tests). The idea was to go in straight lines to prevent slow sections or deviations caused by curves. It proved a huge success in the crowded country, and showed the world what was possible with fast trains.

The *Shinkansen* were not, however, immediately followed in Europe, where best average speeds had stuck for many years at around 70 mph on old tracks, many of which had not changed much since the days of Stephenson. This was partly because of the boom in car travel on motorways and partly due to cheap flights; investment in faster lines was seen as unnecessary as there was simply not enough demand for rail. It looked for a while as though trains, in Europe at least, were yesterday's way of getting about.

But then in 1983, on the very route we're travelling along now, Europe got its first fully-fledged high-speed railway, capable of top speeds of 186 mph. Just as the Tokyo-Osaka line had worked wonders in Japan, so did the *Ligne à Grande Vitesse Paris–Sud-Est* in France, making travel by train the preferred choice for many between Paris and Lyon, as well as opening up the Mediterranean to the French capital. France began to consider additional routes. Neighbouring countries watched on with interest. And so began the era of the fast trains on the Continent, eventually leading to other nations linking up with the growing French network. The opening of the Channel Tunnel in 1994 seemed a symbolic moment for the spread of the high-speed train bug, though it took Britain more than a dozen years to complete its first sixty-seven-mile track from the coast to St Pancras – meaning that trains had, embarrassingly, to slow down on arrival in the UK.

The shape of travel in Europe had started to look different.

All of which is a little ironic as we trudge onwards towards Marseilles on an iconic line, going quickly enough for drinks to slide on tables on bends, but not exactly burning across Europe. E wakes up after Avignon, where half the passengers disembark. She's sleepy after the early start, and had a hectic, late-night rush to meet a deadline for another newspaper article yesterday: her first a few weeks back went down well. We watch an episode of *Downton Abbey* on my laptop to pass the final hour (a gay butler propositions a Turkish lord, who later collapses of a heart attack after a midnight fling with a lady of the house). 'Very amusing shenanigans; I enjoyed that,' says E, cheering up. And as we finally come to Marseilles we make sure we're by the front carriage so we can zip to the taxi rank.

It's 10 p.m. as we arrive. We are among the first few people at the rank and catch a cab with a man who will in our minds always take the title of The Worst Cab Driver in France. And that really is saying something. Sure, we've had some awful ones in Paris, Lille and Dijon, but this guy is something else. For a start he's dressed in a white tracksuit and looking as though he wants to join a break-dancing crew – even though he's in his fifties and not exactly sprightly. He drives sedately out of the station and turns a corner. And just as we're admiring a pretty church, he puts his foot down. We go down hills at a terrifying speed, we see the Mediterranean flash by our windows, we dive into tunnels, we dive out of tunnels, and we zoom up ramps feeling the car tilting with all the weight seemingly on two wheels. I ask him to slow down. He pays no attention whatsoever. We arrive at our hotel, the Sofitel Vieux Port, very quickly indeed. After a day of go-slow, we've had five mad minutes of go-very-fast. The fifty-something break-dancing lunatic snatches €14, does not smile and accelerates away.

Welcome to Marseilles. 'What was all that about?' I ask E.

'I don't know. He was totally insane,' she replies, as we watch the black Mercedes tear down the hotel drive.

'You have to laugh,' I say.

'Now we're in one piece, we do,' says E, raising an eyebrow.

And then we collapse in a room with a view of the cream stone buildings and old fortifications of the harbour below. We're shattered and just about capable of ordering room service (we're starving from the buffet-less train). We eat and go to bed.

So much for the high-speed rail experience when snow hits the tracks.

We wake to the sound of the mistral fizzing against our window, seagulls and thousands of pings coming from the rigging of yachts in the harbour. It's a crisp, sunny day. Police boats are churning through the water below. Across the way, to the south, we can see the remains of the old fort of St Jean and the stripy stone towers and domes of Cathédrale de la Nouvelle Major. Streets of tightly packed houses and apartments with terracotta roofs run down towards a ferry quay at the centre of the *vieux port*. The sea is an undulating metallic blue. Of all the places we've visited, this feels the most exotic and far away (which of course it is). Marseilles, France's second biggest city, with a population of about three million when you take in its sprawling suburbs, almost seems as though it doesn't belong in the country. There's something about the domes on the cathedral and the tight, winding streets leading up the hill from the harbour opposite that just doesn't look French.

Adding to the general sense of otherworldliness after our journey south through blizzards into a sunny Mediterranean port, we soon find that the hotel reception is filled with rows of white flashing plastic Christmas trees and slightly psychedelic-looking reindeer. A receptionist named Djanita gives us a city map and promptly tells us: 'Sarkozy and Carla Bruni stayed here before he was elected. We've had Gérard Depardieu, Jay-Z, Beyoncé, Tom Cruise. It makes us very proud.' She points out the way to the cathedral of Notre-Dame de la Garde, the best place to get a view of the city: 'It is a taxi or a long walk up the hill. There are a lot of hills in Marseilles.' I ask about her name: 'It is Algerian. Oh, my family came here to France a long time ago.' Many people moved to Marseilles from Algeria, just across the Mediterranean, when the former colony was granted independence by de Gaulle in 1962.

We wait for a taxi next to a row of palm trees and are soon travelling up a steep hill with long streets and then narrower and narrower lanes. The driver is quite sane, which makes a nice change. We soon reach the cathedral, dating from the nineteenth century with a distinctive neo-Byzantine, stripy-stone style. The cathedral is crowned by a large golden Virgin, framed against a perfect indigo sky. It sits on top of its hill looking quite splendid (and more than worth the six-euro cab ride).

But it is the view that gets us. I hadn't known quite what to expect with Marseilles. Other than vague preconceptions that the city was a bit rough around the edges – perhaps based on watching *The French Connection*, the 1971 film about narcotics smuggling, and perhaps on what I'd heard about problems involving immigrant integration – I just wasn't sure. Would it be a bit of a slum? Should we have headed to the more obvious tourist delights of Nice? Would France's second-biggest city be a flop?

Absolutely not. Down below us, back towards the hotel, we see an expanse of higgledy-piggledy stone buildings spreading into the hazy distance, stopping at a craggy, inhospitable-looking mountain range. Beyond the yachts in the old harbour and the domes of Cathédrale de la Nouvelle Major, there are insect-like cranes above cargo ships and a dramatic sweep of coast. Looking directly out to sea, we can see the rocky Frioul archipelago, jagging out of the white-capped sea. In the foreground, the little island of If stands alone with the circular tower of the Château d'If visible. This chateau was first built in the early sixteenth century after Francis I came to Marseilles on an unusual mission to see a rhinoceros that the Portuguese court had been sending to Pope Leo X in Rome. The ship with the rhino had been wrecked on If, and the king wanted to witness the unusual creature.

The chateau is also famous for being the prison setting in Alexandre Dumas's *The Count of Monte Cristo*, in which an innocent man, Edmond Dantes, is sent by enemies to rot in a dungeon, escapes and seeks revenge on those who wrongly jailed him (and soon wish they hadn't).

The mistral whips across the hilltop. It's beautiful scenery, unlike that of any other city I can think of in Europe. I sing the praises of Marseilles to E, not noticing she's shivering away.

It *is* freezing. So we go inside the cathedral, where it's warmer and a baptism is taking place. We enter a glorious golden space with religious icons, small models of sailing boats hanging from vaulted ceilings, and a man with a sign that says: 'AUCUNE VISITE PENDANT LES OFFICES: SILENCE' ('No visits during services'). But you are allowed to stay at the very back of the cathedral, where E and I stand by wooden pews on a mosaic floor with a rose-red pattern made up of thousands of tiny stars. Tourists near us are slightly noisy and the man with the sign rattles it. He also shakes his head and glares at another visitor wearing a cap – which is swiftly removed.

E whispers a translation of the service taking place not far in front of us; it's quite a compact cathedral.

'It is so cold outside that today is a day to come inside and warm up people's faith,' E says, relaying the words of a priest in a white cassock.

'He's right about that,' she adds.

'You are being accepted into the family of the church in front of your parents. Welcome to the kingdom of the church,' E continues.

There is silence and I look over at medals from World War One proudly displayed in glass frames on a wall by the door. There are also rows of crooked oil paintings depicting tall ships at sea; many sailors in days gone by came here to pray for safe passage.

'That little baby resting in the arms of the Virgin Mary,' says E, still translating and explaining to me that the priest is referring to a statue of the Virgin Mary above the altar. 'That little baby is there so that parents can always come here to rejoice in the beauty of their child. The innocence of children is how we open our minds to the heart of God. The whole being is simple, and through Christ we can live in this simplicity, this honesty of the child.'

We watch on for a few minutes more, the coloured light of the stained-glass windows pouring down on us and the handful of other tourists.

'How lucky are we? Coming just before Christmas and seeing a beautiful ceremony like that?' asks E.

'Very lucky,' I respond. Although I'm not in the slightest bit religious, it was a touching service.

We take stairs down beneath the cathedral – there's also a lift – and pass a little canteen with a couple of soft drink machines (I buy E a holy Diet Coke) on one floor, before reaching the bottom, where we find a religious bric-a-brac store run by monks in brown cassocks. Pots of fig jam and packets of biscuits are for sale amid pictures of the Pope (just fifty cents). It's particularly warm here, so we take our time looking through golden framed pictures of various saints.

Then we set off down the hill towards the centre of the harbour, at the other end from our hotel. The mistral is still blowing. The sky is still indigo blue. And the hill is still extremely steep. But at least we're going down.

'I can feel the wind whistling round my feet: that's how cold it is,' says E as we descend. Like me, she's wearing trainers: but the wind is so strong it seems to get through them.

We keep on walking and walking, passing along shuttered streets and little alleys and down steep steps. We're just finding our way, using our sense of direction – something that's easy in Marseilles as you either have a view downwards to where you need to go, or a view upwards to your destination.

At the bottom of a particularly steep set of steps, we find ourselves on Boulevard Notre-Dame. The mistral, or perhaps

it's the altitude, seems to have gone to E's head. We pass a pretty
florist on a corner and E starts (loudly) singing a tune I've never
heard before. 'You don't buy me flowers any more!' she intones
across the streets of Marseilles. I look at her and she starts giggling,
before launching into an even louder: 'YOU DON'T BUY ME
FLOWERS ANY MORE!' At this a dog across the street – a
really mean-looking Rottweiler Mastiff, or something like that
– begins to howl. She's only messing about. I think the mistral,
perhaps combined with the madly-long journey yesterday, may
be getting to her.

Anyway, in a romantic fast-train gesture (and to keep her
quiet), I pick up some pink carnations. E stops singing and smiles
– 'darling, they're luuurrrvvvvly', she says – and the dog calms
down. We continue arm in arm – quietly – to the harbour.

The waterfront is peaceful. This is, after all, the off season. There
are no ferries out to If. There are no boats moving in the water at
all; just yachts moored for the winter. A row of restaurants, half
of which appear closed, runs along the south side of the harbour,
while on the north there's an Irish bar showing Sky football
matches, close to a cinema. There's a nice sense of having the
place to ourselves and we stroll inland to a Christmas market
on Place du Général de Gaulle. A few more folk are knocking
about here, but not that many, even though it's a Saturday with
just a couple of weekends to go before the big day. Wooden stalls
that look like cheap garden sheds sell delicately painted nativity
figures lined on shelves. Each shed offers almost exactly the same
stock, and it's difficult to know how you'd choose between them.
We walk along Rue Paradis, which comes off the corner of the
square, not really knowing where we're heading. This street is
lined with shops selling expensive watches, designer clothes and
perfume. On a side street we enter a nondescript cafe with the
unpromising name of La Globule.

Inside, it's actually more like a bar. A barman with a distant look in his eye is polishing wine glasses while tinny pop music drones in the background. There are rugby shirts on the wall, chipped Formica tables and seats with red plastic coverings. It couldn't be more French. E goes to the loo and comes back appearing slightly horrified. In the meantime, the barman has brought thick black espressos. He offers us olives with these – all part of the service at La Globule, it would appear. We politely decline the espresso-olive combination.

A couple of customers arrive. 'They're ordering pastis,' E points out. So they are, from little glasses filled with the milky-looking drink. It looks rather tempting... but perhaps it's a little early in the day to be hitting 45 per cent proof French aniseed-flavoured liqueurs.

A man enters, and before he can say a word, a glass of red wine is poured and placed by the bar.

It's a funny, sleepy sort of spot. The barman smiles broadly and almost salutes as we depart, perhaps hoping we'll be back for something a bit stronger later. We walk back towards de Gaulle's square, pass the Christmas stall and a woman shopping while carrying just about the tiniest dog I've ever seen in a tartan blanket, its alien-like head poking out, and on to the Lafayette shopping centre, on the side of which we find the Musée d'Histoire de Marseille.

This museum opened in 1983, coinciding with the inauguration of the high-speed line from Marseilles to Paris. A pamphlet on the counter says the museum displays important Greek and Roman finds. We are, we discover, in the oldest city in France, founded in 600 BC by the Greeks.

E goes to the toilets to see if they are any better than the ones in the cafe, while I check out a few displays by the entrance that consist of old carts, weighing scales and trolleys. There are some cracked pots from the Massalia period, the name the Greeks gave to the port. Apart from an elderly man in a crinkled blue shirt at the ticket desk, there is no one else about. I go up to him.

'*Je voudrais deux billets, s'il vous plait,*' I say in my finest GCSE French.

He doesn't appear to hear me right and gives me a single ticket.

'*Deux euros,*' he says.

'*Deux billets,*' I reply, perhaps a little gruffly, trying to sort out the confusion... not very well.

'*Deux billets?*' he responds, sounding incredulous. It doesn't seem as though that many tourists make it to the Musée d'Histoire de Marseille. Perhaps this will go down as the 'sale of the month' and end up being written about in the museum newsletter or something. As if just to make sure, he repeats: '*Deux billets?*'

'*S'il vous plait,*' I say.

He hands over two tickets and I pay four euros. Just after I do so, E arrives and looks at the two of us, sensing the air of linguistic confusion. She arches an eyebrow. She says something charmingly polite to the elderly man, who smiles charmingly back.

Perhaps we're a bit tired from yesterday and not full of the necessary powers of museum concentration, but it's not exactly a stunner. We walk around the stone remains on our own. Between these remains, which include an old Roman wreck and a pair of shoes dating from the third century, there are poems written in French. 'They're kind of existential. This is the weirdest place,' declares E.

'It's not a thrill a minute,' I agree, examining more third-century stones in feeble light by a dusty counter.

We continue round more dimly lit display cabinets in silence.

Then E pipes up. 'I really do think this might be the most tragic museum I have ever entered in my life,' she says, seemingly having made up her mind. I think she means 'tragic' in the sense of 'not so good', rather than 'highly dramatic'. There is nothing particularly dramatic about the Musée d'Histoire de Marseille, which is so dull and worthy (and incomprehensible in places) it's actually quite funny.

'I'm overwhelmed. Speechless!' E continues, hamming it up; she's not being serious… just going off on one.

'It cost us four euros,' I say.

'You actually paid for this!' she says, chortling; she obviously hadn't seen any cash change hands earlier and assumed entrance was free.

'Yes,' I reply.

'Ha! You got done!' She grins broadly as though it's not such a bad place after all. 'Ha! Daylight robbery!'

She has another giggle. I think the mistral may be getting to her again.

We head out into the streets of Marseilles, realising we've rather enjoyed the Musée d'Histoire de Marseille, after all. We go for a walk round the quiet south side of the harbour, a former ghetto during World War Two that was blown up by the Nazis in 1943, with 20,000 inhabitants, including many members of the Resistance and Jews, forced to leave after being given a day's notice. Most were deported to camps.

Now there are all sorts of restaurants: Italian, sushi bars, Chinese, burger joints, 'Le Mistral' fish restaurant, pizzerias. All closed. We find a tiny sandwich shop that's actually open – Le Dauphin (The Dolphin) – where we're the only customers. We order ham and cheese baguettes from a tiny oriental woman who is sitting on a stool next to a green Buddha. We sit at a table with fake yellow daffodils and eat our baguettes, looking across to the harbour where a sleek catamaran with the name *Song Saigon* is bobbing close to a double-masted yacht that looks as though it could handle an Atlantic crossing. On the promenade a couple of guys in diving gear are messing about next to a skip filled with rusty salvage, apparently collected from the harbour basin: old bikes, shopping trolleys. Up on the hill beyond the harbour, the golden Virgin on the top of Notre-Dame de la Garde gleams in the sunshine, and the cathedral looks down majestically on proceedings below.

We walk on past the imposing stone walls of the fort of St Jean, built in the seventeenth century to quell local uprisings, drop into Cathédrale de la Nouvelle Major (big and airy and empty), and look down on the port. It was from here in 1792 that many volunteers marched to Paris to join proceedings during the French Revolution. The most famous consisted of a group of 500 hearty republicans, who enjoyed a bit of a sing-song along the way. One of their favourite ditties had a catchy tune and included strident lyrics declaring that '*l'étendard sanglant est levé*' ('the bloody banner is raised') and calling on people to rise up against *la tyrannie* in the form of *traîtres, rois conjurés* and *cohortes étrangères* ('traitors, conjured kings and foreign cohorts'). Thus was born *La Marseillaise*, named after the marchers and soon to become the French national anthem.

Then we walk round charming old lanes lined with little houses with peeling lilac and lemon shutters. A couple of kids are booting around a football with their father, there are little squares with twisted plane trees, and a sense of being in a hidden part of the city. There's a building with an 'Egyptian Collection' close to one of the squares. E gives me a look that says 'not after the last one!' I give her a look back that says

'I agree!' And we walk down some steps, passing a belligerent wino in a beret, and go back round the harbour to the hotel.

Somehow the day has disappeared. We're worn out again; maybe it was yesterday's travel... or maybe the miles we've walked today. We have a splash in an odd basement hot tub surrounded by pebbles, and some food and a drink at a bar with 'frozen jellyfish' decorations amid more flashing plastic Christmas trees. We look out across the orange sodium lights of the harbour. The mistral whistles against the windows, while a chanteuse by a piano sings 'Silent Night'. 'I do like it here,' says E.

But even so, we both agree, Marseilles is a surreal place to go at Christmas.

Having gone in an almost straight line south from London to Marseilles (about 620 miles) on our crazy trip not much more than a day ago, E is now heading back in an almost straight line north. She's got to be in the office on Monday. We say goodbye at the grand station amid officers in camouflage and jackboots, guns and batons at their sides. Security seems pretty tight. The snow conditions have improved over the past day and E's journey should be OK. She waves from the window and seems to be saying something along the lines of 'Enjoy the history museum!' (or perhaps it was more romantic) as the long grey double-decker moves away up Europe's original high-speed track, disappearing into the *banlieue*.

I have a day to discover the remaining delights of France's second city, solo. I also have nowhere to stay; we'd only booked two nights at the Sofitel. I'd planned to wing it for the third.

I walk along a street leading back to the harbour, dragging my roll-along case, looking for a place to stay. There are hotels round here that cost €28 a night. There are also one-euro clothes shops and winos and a woman sitting on dirty apartment steps with a scrubby piece of cardboard scrawled with: 'J'AI FAIM.' She's huddled in a yellow headscarf and a bedraggled old coat from which poke filthy Adidas trainers that look several sizes too big. I drop a euro in a can and she looks up brightly for a split second, before returning to her huddled posture. It's bitterly cold; too cold for smiles. Near a Marché Plus mini-market, three men are also begging, with cans of beer in their hands. I don't give them a euro. Instead I turn into Rue Sénac de Meilhan, where I stumble upon a hotel called Le Ryad in a tall cream-stone terrace. I knock on the door. A short man with a skinhead and a moustache answers and shows me a room with North African-style lamps, archways and unlit candles. He tells me that the room is *'très agréable et gentile'*. It will be €80 with breakfast, after I talk down the price from €90. There appear to be no other guests. It is gloomy and all the lights are off. I leave my bag and head back into the streets.

The neighbourhood here, just off La Canebière, a main street leading to the harbour, is unlike anything we saw yesterday. I turn into another side street and find a flea market consisting of old blankets and sheets laid out haphazardly. It begins to rain heavily, and everything is soon dripping wet: pairs of shoes with curling soles, battered kitchen mixers, tiny upside-down TVs (seemingly just dropped that way), kettles without plugs, plugs without kettles, faded DVDs, heaps of clothes, stained crockery, yellowing books. But no one seems to care in this narrow lane. Almost all the faces look North African, almost certainly mostly Algerian from the days of 1960s immigration. People sift through the junk looking hopeless. It is a miserable sight.

From this squalor, I walk to the end of the lane, where there's a small fruit and veg market with wooden stalls. Garlic, pears, apples, bananas, lettuces and cabbages lead through to a couple of cramped shops built into the terrace selling fresh fish, octopus, shark, mussels and shrimp. People push past and there is a sense of clutter and urgency. This feels like another continent, let alone another city. Beyond the bowls of mussels, there are trestle tables under parasols that once belonged to cafes. On these tables, manned by stallholders of black African descent, all sorts of odds and sods are for sale: cheap plastic belts, shower units, clumps of socks, boxes of rat poison, 'NON POISONOUS GLUE' designed to finish off cockroaches, underwear and 'designer' watches. Realising I'm getting as soaked as everything else seems to be round here, I point at an umbrella. A man with a glint in his eye says: '*Cinq euros.*' This seems OK, so I hand over a note, which disappears in a flash into the pocket of a hoodie. I keep going and look inside a long, thin shop with baskets heaped delicately with spices, raisins, dried apricots, prunes, cashew nuts, pecans, almonds, chickpeas, rice and various types of couscous. The smell of cumin and coriander fills the air. This really could be North Africa, or somewhere in the Middle East.

At the end of the lane I come to a junction where a man is slumped in a doorway selling bottles of water. There's another fruit stall, tumbling with tangerines and bananas. A couple of characters in puffa jackets are smoking under the blue awning of Gare de la Marée. Further on, there are rubbish bins, where people (perhaps charities) appear to have dumped unwanted goods. More hunched figures are here, picking up sodden Le Coq Sportif trainers, broken picture frames, vacuum cleaners with parts missing, dented computer keyboards and whatever else is strewn across the pavement. A man stands on a corner selling umbrellas. I haven't used mine yet as the lanes are so crowded.

'*Deux euros,*' he says, offering me exactly the same type I bought earlier.

I wave my umbrella and explain, as best I can, how much I paid earlier.

'Ha ha ha!' he chuckles good-naturedly, beaming a broad smile.

I'm not sure I'd be quite as cheerful if I were a two-euro-umbrella salesmen standing on the corner on a wet Sunday in December on the backstreets of Marseilles.

I leave this 'other world' and again walk towards the harbour. From here, I take to public transport to see two tourist sights.

The first is an apartment block known as *Unité d'Habitation*, designed by the Swiss architect Le Corbusier in 1952. I catch a bus along Rue de Rome and find myself in a northern suburb surrounded by all sorts of residential towers. Corbusier's tower, frankly, does not look a whole lot different from the rest – but this is for a reason. When he constructed this seventeen-storey block it was a first of its kind: a series of spacious apartments with balconies and a rooftop terrace with a small pool that was considered a template by many for a modern way of living. As I approach, I'm reminded of estates in the grimmer parts of inner London. The tower looks deeply depressing. I pass a small five-a-side pitch that's empty apart from two seagulls in the process of tearing apart a dead pigeon.

Not the nicest of images. I take a lift to the roof where I see the small empty splash pool and a concrete jogging track around the edge of the thin rectangular building. Thin rectangular towers just like this one are all about, standing like totem poles to 'progress' (as it was known back in the 1950s and 1960s). I take a look at the reception of the small hotel on one of the middle floors; the rooms are all occupied, according to the receptionist. Next to this is a totally empty

1950s-era cafe, with shapely black chairs and curving wooden panels that will no doubt interest lovers of old interior design... though I don't particularly wish to linger.

I catch the lift down and leave the joys of Corbusier behind. Half an hour later, via buses and metros, I arrive at L'Estaque.

This little port is just to the north-west of Marseilles and during a period roughly stretching from 1860 to 1920 it attracted painters of the calibre of Cézanne, Braque, Derain, Dufy and Renoir, among many others. The painters were inspired by the sea and the rugged inland mountains, with a railway viaduct at one end particularly catching their artistic eyes. The viaduct is still visible (not looking particularly high-speed train friendly as it curls round some cliffs) close to a beach. There's a short row of shops and restaurants. As I wander about, I'm not surprised to discover I am the only tourist. It's almost an existential feeling, walking down to the waterfront with not a soul about, with just the sounds of waves breaking on the shore.

I stop by a gallery run by local artists known as the Association des Peintres de l'Estaque. Inside, there are pictures of the port, the cliffs and the viaduct, as well as Notre-Dame de la Garde. Prices range from around €100 up to €700. I have one of my most hopeless conversations in French to date.

'Est-ce qu'il y a une bon restaurant près d'ici?' I ask a woman who seems to run the place.

'Le Littoral,' she replies, though a friend who's keeping her company cuts in.

A heated discussion begins between them about whether the restaurant is open or not.

She turns to me. It seems that restaurants are no longer a topic of conversation. 'Cézanne, Braque!' she says in broken English. 'The first painters of zee Cubism was here!'

In a mad mixture of French and English, I ask if you can visit where they lived.

She looks at me totally blankly, and begins to tell me that her daughter lives in Cambridge and her husband is a doctor. At least that's what I think she's saying.

I say '*merci beaucoup*' and hotfoot it to the bus stop.

Back in Marseilles, I eat the local dish of *bouillabaisse* (a lovely fish, mussels, octopus and vegetable soup), while watching the local football team play on TV screens at a restaurant by the harbour. Then I return to my North African abode, where candles have been lit everywhere and I still appear to be the only guest. Even though it's dark as I walk back, there is no hint of 'trouble', of which I'd read much before coming; no muggers or gangs hanging about, just dark wet streets. And after a sound sleep – and one of the strangest weekends of my life – I'm heading northwards through snowy France the next morning... 160 mph plus all the way.

CHAPTER TEN

BRUGES: 'DOWN BY THE LAKE OF LOVE'

A fortnight on and Britain is even colder. It's freezing at 6 a.m. at my bus stop in south-west London. There is, I am not particularly surprised to discover, no sign of a bus. There's just a guy in a fluorescent jacket who appears to be a cleaner of some sort. He's parked his white van next to the bus drivers' tea room, and is attending to matters while commentary blares from his car radio. England are playing Australia at cricket in Perth. To pass the time of day, I ask him the score.

'159 for six,' he replies, looking pleased that England's batters have collapsed.

'Not good,' I say.

'No, not good at all,' he comments, grinning, and then adds: 'Ha!'

I pace up and down, listening to Jonathan Agnew's dulcet tones crackling on the other side of the globe. A bus arrives twenty minutes late. It continues slowly across the icy streets and I wait for a Tube that creeps across the city. At St Pancras I buy a Bruges and Ghent guidebook from Foyles bookshop from an assistant who says 'This one flies off the shelf. Bruges is meant to be lovely', and meet E at the Marks & Spencer across the way; her flat is a short cycle ride away (our 'moving in together' plans are still at the planning stage). We've been worrying that Eurostar will have seized up again, but it hasn't. We're soon on board and been told that there will only be a fifteen-minute delay on our train to Brussels, from where we're catching a connection to Bruges. There's a high pale-blue sky and the English countryside looks stark and peaceful in its coating of white. E attempts to pay an electricity bill using her mobile phone but tunnels keep cutting reception. She gives up and starts reading the paper. 'Did you know that more than 300 million people live along the Yangtze River?' she asks me apropos of nothing. There's a story on China.

'I can't say that I did,' I answer.

'That's one in eight of the world's population. That's more than in America.'

We fall back into silence. Then a woman in the row in front begins talking to a companion, a little loudly, about the Roman Empire.

'The Roman matrons were very powerful,' she says. 'They went into business and were successful – very much like in our society. But life was really much different back then,' she pauses and points out a snow-covered windmill to her companion. 'Oh yes, much much different. People lived cheek by jowl in very close proximity back in those days. Nothing like all the comforts we have now.'

She continues in this slightly maddening vein all the way through the Channel Tunnel. I'm learning all sorts of things I never thought I'd learn this morning on the 8.27 a.m. to Brussels.

Through the Channel Tunnel, Europe gets snowier and snowier. We hurtle on through the crisp white landscape. In the far distance, big powder-puff clouds are gathered, looking like a magnificent new mountain range that's mysteriously risen out of the snowy lowlands. I read from the *Rough Guide* that Bruges is a very romantic city in which 'you can't help but be amazed by the number of couples wandering its canals hand-in-hand, cheek-to-cheek'. But it's not so romantic at Brussels station, where we have a fifteen-minute wait for our connecting train.

'Oh yes, I remember this ropey platform,' says E, as we wait for our express-train north.

'So do I.' Brussels station is no St Pancras: there are no glorious Barlow train sheds or neo-Gothic beauties by George Gilbert Scott here. The platform is cold and cheerless, with old wooden benches.

We enter a freezing waiting room. 'Don't close the door!' says E. 'People sleep and do other things in here.'

There *is* a bit of an eau de tramp. 'This is proper cold,' says E. 'It must be minus three or something like that.'

As if to confirm this, a train with icicles hanging from the roof arrives. We board and the carriage pulls away, moving down the very line that George Stephenson helped design back in the 1830s when he supplied the first locomotives for Leopold I, the first king of Belgium. Steam billows from a power station in the suburbs. Derelict lots and old scrap heaps are covered in snow. 'Normally it's pretty grim round here,' says E. We're becoming very familiar with the train tracks of Europe. 'Now it looks like a winter wonderland.' We show our tickets to a jolly Belgian Railways conductor wearing a grey cap with an orange band – who later sits at a table nearby, happily eating little chocolate cakes. All the Belgian conductors seem a cheerful lot.

We continue on across snowlands, passing through Ghent, where spires poke up and the train pauses briefly. And before we know it, just three and a half hours after leaving London, we've arrived in 'romantic Bruges'.

It is snowing and extremely cold as we step out of the station. Shivering, we crunch across an icy forecourt where a 'Snow and Ice Sculpture Festival' is being held in temporary tents. Inside these, according to a pamphlet we pick up at the entrance, 'international artists' have sculpted versions of UNESCO World Heritage Sites such as the Leaning Tower of Pisa, the Taj Mahal and the Coliseum in Rome. It looks rather good, if a bit odd. We're tempted to go in but then check out the price. The Snow and Ice Sculpture Festival would set us back €22, so we rein in our newborn curiosity in frozen art in the shape of heritage sites.

'There's a recession on, it's no time to be shelling out euros to see lumps of ice,' I say.

'I couldn't agree more,' says E, who seems secretly relieved.

We stride on purposefully across a road and enter a park with a long path heading towards a lake just south of the city centre. I'm pulling my roll-along case, which develops a routine in which snow seems to build up underneath until it feels as though I'm dragging a sack of coal, amusing E. This build-up of snow reaches a tipping point and then breaks off, freeing the wheels so they run smoothly again, with the bag feeling the weight it should, until the snow starts to mount again. I explain this process to E, who perhaps does not seem as fascinated by the mechanics of roll-along cases in the snow as I had expected. She has her stuff in a neat little rucksack.

We reach the lake. This is not just any old lake. It is Minnewater: the 'Lake of Love'. I know this as it says so in the guidebook. The lake does look exceptionally beautiful in the bright afternoon sunshine with sheet ice on the surface and willow trees around the edge. Ducks are swimming in a little section where the ice has been broken. Old stone buildings rear up at the far side. Already, we can see that this is a charming city. We walk along a path by the lake with my case doing its sack of coal thing. Apart from the dragging sound, it's very peaceful. Hardly anyone else is about. At a wall at the end, I take out my camera and with one hand stretched, take a picture of us overlooking the icy lake.

'Hurry up, it's freezing!' says E, as I mess about trying to sort out the right angle and lens width. Romance is all very well, but not when it's several degrees below zero with a wind whipping off the Lake of Love.

'I'm doing my best, darling,' I say, with the camera, a quite heavy SLR, wobbling in my hand in the nippy air as I struggle to press the button without dropping the damn thing in the snow. I take a couple of snaps, with only a small part of my arm snaking up out of the corner.

Then we wheel onwards to a narrow cobbled lane – even more awkward with the bag now bouncing up and down and seeming not to have lighter moments any more – where there are cosy looking tea rooms and shops selling lace.

The city is not short of tourists here: they're everywhere, many of them hand-in-hand, some of them cheek-to-cheek. They mill about peering into windows of tea rooms and chocolate shops. We stop by one of these to look at liqueur truffles, *sneeuwballen* (circular chocolates sprinkled with icing sugar), *cerisettes* (chocolate-covered cherries) and various 'Christmas Collection' offerings in the shape of snowmen and reindeer. Another shop has a series of 'chocolate breasts', complete with prominently protruding nipples and a notice saying: 'A NICE PRESENT FOR YOUR FATHER OR FRIEND.' A lot of the signage is in English. Further along, a shop has a giant chocolate turkey resting on a bed of chocolate carrots and peas and roast potatoes, with a chocolate Santa poised to carve with a chocolate carving knife.

Folk are heading to a Christmas market on a square – which looks a lot livelier than the one back in Marseilles. We continue along old streets lined with medieval buildings and fine churches, turning right at the looming presence of the thirteenth-century Church of Our Lady. We walk along a canal full of cracked ice reflecting the tall, elegant red-brick buildings on either side. Many of these have A-shaped roofs with steps built into the edges. The roofs remind me of Aztec temples; a strange thing to think of in sub-zero temperatures in the north of Europe in December, I can't help reflecting. There are oval shaped windows and doors with curved archways. A few houses are whitewashed. All about there are spires, towers, gables and turrets.

It's no wonder that this is one of the first 'tourist cities' in Europe, and indeed the world. The place is stunningly beautiful; almost unbelievably so. When the Victorians came here, starting the city's 'tourism', they found a sparsely-populated medieval centre full of canals and little rivers – earning it the nickname 'Venice of the North' (which, as clichéd as it sounds, feels as though it's true in Bruges). They fell head over heels for the city; both for its beauty and its rich history.

Bruges had had its heyday way back in medieval times when it was an important trading port for Flemish cloth, grain and spices. Its stock exchange, founded in 1309, is believed to be the oldest in the world. Philip the Good of Burgundy (him again) made the city one of his courts in the fifteenth century and at around this time art and culture flourished. William Caxton printed the first book in English in Bruges in 1473, the *Recuyell of the Historyes of Troye*, which he quickly followed when he moved back to Westminster in 1476 with Chaucer's *Canterbury Tales*. The painters Hans Memling and the Van

Eyck brothers were creating masterpiece after masterpiece. In short, it was doing very well indeed.

But then it went into a tailspin of decline when the Zwin channel connecting the city to the North Sea began to silt up, preventing ships gaining access. This coincided with fierce competition from Antwerp, where the waters were clear and business was booming. The result was catastrophic. The population fell from around 200,000 during its peak to 50,000 by the end of the 1800s, prompting the Belgian novelist Georges Rodenbach to go as far as to write a book entitled *Bruges-la-Morte* in 1892, depicting a city seemingly in terminal decay.

Bad times for Bruges. But it still *looked beautiful* with a delightfully empty sense of faded grandeur that nineteenth-century tourists loved. William Wordsworth, who visited in 1820, said that there was 'a deeper peace than in heavens found'.

In short, it appealed to the British love of all things medieval. At a time when medieval was 'cool' and à la mode – which was why Scott's Gothic hotel at St Pancras was such a hit with just about everyone (barring the prime minister Lord Palmerston) – Bruges was the place to go.

It still is, if the crowds are anything to go by. E and I amble along the canal with the bag bouncing along on the cobbles. We see a sign that says 'Romantik Pand Hotel' and follow onwards around a corner, where we come to a distinguished eighteenth-century building on a side road. There are box hedges in window boxes and an oil lantern hanging from the wall. We enter our romantik hotel, where there are chandeliers, mahogany antiques, chesterfield armchairs, an open fireplace and no receptionist. After waiting a few minutes and finally collecting our key, we go upstairs in a miniscule lift, stopping at a floor with hallways decorated with tartan wallpaper. We drop our bags in a tiny room with a tiny bathroom. First impressions: 'Perhaps not so romantik'. Then we walk back along the tartan hall, where we notice a fold-down ironing board connected to a wall; something neither of us can remember at a hotel before.

Unsure of what to make of our digs we head back into the streets of Bruges, where it's begun to snow. Gentle flakes are floating down as we retrace our steps and go to a spot that caught our eyes earlier: De Proeverie Tea-Room. In a city full of twee tea rooms, this one had struck us as being perhaps the most twee. Why not go for the jugular and take on the tea drinking experience of Bruges in full chintz style?

This is how we find ourselves sitting by a window in a room covered with pictures of Labradors wearing military uniforms while playing billiards and cards. The curtains are covered in pink roses and the walls are apple green. There are Santa Claus-shaped tea lights. There are also elderly Belgian customers (a good sign) and tourists like us. Waitresses with frilly lace-embroidered dresses flit to and fro. While E is in the bathroom, one comes over and I order coffees and cupcakes. As she walks away I read the menu more closely. Coffee and cupcakes will come to €19. I almost call her back and bring an abrupt end to the 'Bruges tea room experience', but don't, figuring that we're still living on borrowed Snow and Ice Sculpture funds.

E returns and we soon have before us a feast. It consists of our coffees and two enormous cupcakes with green icing shaped like grass with little icing snowmen on top. The snowmen smile and have carrot-shaped noses. The icing is piled almost as high as the cakes beneath them. Next to these we've each been given china bowls filled with little round pieces of milk chocolate, dark chocolate and white chocolate. There are also two separate bowls with large swirls of cream, and two jugs of milk. The coffee is excellent and comes with an extra little wrapped chocolate in the saucer – just in case you're still hungry. The table is covered in calories.

'What did you order?' asks E, her eyes widening.

I explain and say: 'I thought that was the Belgian tea house way of doing things.'

E looks at the spread, chuckling a bit. 'They look great,' she says after a pause, while dismantling one of the Santas. 'Delicious, love.'

They are good. Under the gaze of the snooker-playing Labradors, we silently but steadily settle into the task of demolishing piles of Belgian chocolates and icing – hanging out like true Bruges tourists amid charming chintz and chatter.

Afterwards we step out into the snowy street, quite content after our little afternoon snack. Across the way, through throngs of tourists, we enter the Church of Our Lady. It's quiet inside with high ceilings and a cold Gothic gloom. Empty pews are lined neatly next to an elaborate wooden pulpit. To one side, candles flicker on racks. The smell of wax and incense lingers in the chilly chamber, with a faint murmur of intonations coming from somewhere close by.

We walk to an altar in an aisle. Here we find what is believed to be the only work by Michelangelo to have left Italy during his lifetime. It was originally bought by a wealthy Bruges family, who donated the work to the church in the early sixteenth century during the height of the city's boom years; a sign of just how well-to-do and arty locals were back then. The white marble *Madonna and Child* sits in an alcove surrounded by columns, the Madonna looking serenely to one side and her child resting happily on her knee. Though only a few feet high, the details of the folds in her gown and the expressions on their faces are exquisite and you can tell you are in the presence of a masterpiece. A sign says: 'One is struck by the contemplative Virgin. The expressive work never fails to move and impress the beholder.' It's spot on.

At the back of the church there's a kiosk where an elderly man is surprised into action by our arrival. 'Is this the way to Charles the Bold?' I ask. Most people seem to speak English in Bruges.

'Ah!' he replies keenly. 'Yes! Yes!' He blusters a bit, seeming to be waking up. 'Yes! Charles the Bold! Indeed! Five euros sir!'

He seems, we gather, more than a little delighted that tourists have come to see the mausoleum of Charles the Bold. After our visit to Dijon back in August, we are making a pilgrimage to the resting place of the last of the golden era Burgundy dukes; the one who brought about their downfall. Although he died in battle during the siege of Nancy in 1477, his remains, or what are believed to be his remains, were much later brought to the Belgian city to be laid next to those of his daughter Mary of Burgundy. When Mary died in a riding accident at the age of twenty-five in 1482, all the territories of Flanders passed to her husband Maximilian, a Hapsburg prince.

The mausoleums are in a chancel with a black and white tiled floor. We are their only visitors. Both tombs are topped by shiny golden figures resting with hands held together in prayer. Long unruly hair spills from the crown of Charles the Bold, while Mary wears netting over her hair and has puffy cheeks.

E has been a little sceptical about this pilgrimage, remembering my 'obsession' (her description) with the dukes back in Dijon. But she's taken by the tombs. 'Look, this is really quite amazing,' says E, pointing to a glass floor at the far side. Through this we can see into recesses underneath Charles and Mary, where even more ancient burial places are hidden. Pictures of Christ on the cross and figures wearing halos are etched on to the walls, which are decorated in little red flowers. It's strange to think of tourists, including Wordsworth and all the eminent Victorian travellers of the nineteenth century, coming to this very place and witnessing the same scenes.

The attendant is on the ball, no chance of catching him snoozing on the way out. 'Very good! Charles the Bold! Yes! Yes!' he says as we depart, almost waving us through.

And we head back into the frozen city.

We may not have had a thirteen-hour travelling day. No Marseilles snow disaster this time. No transport meltdown. But fast trains, even on a short trip like this, can take it out of you; especially if you've been up since the crack of dawn waiting at bus-less depots in south-west London. I'm sure it would have been worse if we'd flown, though. And we wouldn't have seen the frozen flatlands in all their wintry splendour. We'd have been stuck in airport lounges waiting to be marched through security and into cramped seats. Tetchy cabin crews bored of doing short European hops would probably have snapped at us. We would probably have snapped back.

Even so, we're pretty tired. With snow falling heavily now, we wind our way back to the hotel, crossing a cute stone bridge and following the cobbled streets. There's an inch of fresh snow and Bruges is quiet as tourists head inside. The city looks more medieval and beautiful than ever, if that is possible.

Our room at the Pand Hotel has not magically expanded in our absence. It's still tiny and looking like a shoebox. E sits on a little chair jammed by the bed and peruses a magazine article about the hotel reproduced from the Belgian version of *Elle Decoration*. She reads a passage. 'The bathrooms' interiors,' it says here, 'harmonise perfectly with the tonality of the bedrooms.'

E looks up. 'I don't think our room particularly harmonises with anything,' she says, waving the article at me as though it's an incriminating object.

She looks into the small bathroom, where she'd earlier had to catch her washbag from falling off a little shelf. 'I don't see much tonality in there,' she says, warming to her theme. 'There wasn't much tonality when my washbag took a nosedive for the toilet.'

She's only joking... but it is a very small room.

Bruges is even lovelier in the morning – it's almost too good to be true. We rise to find the city blanketed in even more powder. Pointy roofs are covered in snow and one side of the Belfort, a tall, thin, slightly crooked belfry tower connected to the former city treasury, has turned white. The writer G. K. Chesterton, another of the early tourists, once described this tower as 'an unnaturally long-necked animal, like a giraffe' – and you can see what he was driving at. The cracked ice of the canal has refrozen overnight. The city is restful and calm, with the sound of silence that you only seem to get when you wake to overnight snow.

E and I walk through a square known as the Burg, where we pass the ornate medieval façade of the town hall and a charming twelfth-century basilica. Everything looks gorgeous in the soft morning light. We continue on to another square, known as the Markt. Here we find the Belfort and a monument in the centre of the square depicting two famous locals. The statue is in honour of the leaders of a successful uprising against the

French on 18 May 1302, known as the Bruges Matins. At dawn on that chilling day, Pieter de Coninck and Jan Breydel attacked the French garrison controlling the city, killing any of their number who could not correctly pronounce the Flemish saying *schild en vriend* – which translates as 'shield and friend'. Medieval buildings loom all around the statue; gaunt, Gothic and rather fine.

Everything looks gorgeous in the soft morning light here, too. Bruges is – quite simply – a ridiculously gorgeous place.

Not far on, we stop at Tea-Room Laurent. It's much more modern than yesterday's affair and we are the only customers. Hip hop music is playing and enormous pink baubles hang from the ceiling: Christmas decorations. We order giant waffles covered in castor sugar… our first waffles in two trips to Belgium, Antwerp included. We read a copy of *The Sunday Times*, which we picked up earlier from a newsagent. It has an article on Belgium. Since June, when there was an inconclusive general election, there has been no government in the country. The right-wing Flemish nationalists of the north – where we are – can't form an understanding with the French-speaking socialists of the south. There's a stand-off. The country is rapidly heading towards a dubious record – that of achieving 'the longest period of a democratic nation without a proper government since the Second World War'. There is no one in charge of Belgium, apart from a 'zombie government' that has no authority.

We look around Tea-Room Laurent. It doesn't seem to make a jot of difference here. Everything seems calm and quite relaxed. The music has switched to a pleasant song with the refrain: 'You smile, I smile.' We eat our excellent waffles. On the basis of our two fast-train experiences to the country so far, Belgium has been an oasis of efficiency and order.

'Maybe zombie governments are the way forward,' I suggest to E.

She nods in agreement. 'I adore Bruges,' she says.

And, with that, we order more waffles in peaceful, zombie-land Belgium: the perfect country for a fast-train break.

Outside, stallholders have set up the Christmas market. Customers are busily examining cut-price fleeces, electronic Santas, Venetian-style masks, 'quality watches', earrings, carved wooden camels, piles of chocolates, woollen scarves, sculptures of hippos, colourful boiled sweets, pots of honey, tissue-holders in the shape of puckered lips, and snazzy digital radios. Anything and everything... and lots of it.

The set up is so different from Marseilles, with its garden sheds full of nativity figures in Place du Général de Gaulle in the area most tourists visit, and its flea market sprawl and North African shops offering couscous in the backstreets. We walk past a stall selling hippy beads and ethnic clothing that wouldn't look out of place in Africa. The trumpets of an oompah band break out over speakers near a beer bar on a corner, where a group of Germans, by the look of them, is in a happy state; big guys gripping beers that look too tiny to make much of a difference to them. There's a stall with huge wheels of cheese and pots of olives. Beyond, we come to a kiosk smelling of *braadworst* and *glühwein* – a heady combination that seems to suck in passers-by. Not far along people are queuing for waffles covered in caramel, Nutella and banana puree.

Snow flurries rake across the square. We walk past a stall offering slabs of marzipan the size of high-speed railway buffers. A couple stops us and asks directions in French for Minnewater, and E tells them the way to the Lake of Love. And off they go hand-in-hand, cheek-to-cheek. Then we turn a corner by the Church of Our Lady, where people with paper napkin bibs round their necks are already seated for lunch at a busy restaurant – the napkins have holes in the centre for your head, and it looks as though you fit them on as though you are putting on some sort of cape.

E stops and goggles for a while at the scenes of paper napkin dining inside. She seems astonished. With great formality, as though they are at a three-Michelin-star restaurant of the highest repute, the cape-wearing diners are tucking into delicious-looking broths and sloshing it all down with dignified abandon. They look like a room full of people about to have their teeth checked by dentists, except they're not: they're eating their lunches. They seem completely content and at peace with the world. No worries about making a mess with those paper bibs. It's an arresting scene: the gourmet dining setting and rarefied ambience mixed with the crazy bibs. I look at the menu: reasonable prices. An idea regarding dinner begins to form.

'How about we go here later?' I ask.

E raises an eyebrow and adds nothing further.

'I mean it's not too pricey and we can try out the bibs,' I continue, not catching the eyebrow vibe.

I get the eyebrow again.

'I could pop in and book a table for later,' I plough on, realising I may be fighting a losing battle on this one.

The eyebrow shoots up once more.

We continue along the snow-covered cobbled streets (no reservation for a paper bib dinner made).

We pause by a canal covered in broken ice and take pictures of jagged turrets of old buildings. We stop at a picturesque bridge near a weeping willow and take more snaps. We get a little lost in tiny lanes lined with A-shaped houses. It begins to snow heavily, but in a beautifully heavy way. We find ourselves on a long open space, not far from the railway station.

Here we bump into the tourist information office, which is in a modern building connected to a concert hall. Reasoning that we might as well go in, seeing as it's in front of us and getting cold, we enter through automatic doors.

Inside, we soon discover, everything is not so gorgeous, happy and generally all-round perfect and charmingly pretty and medieval in Bruges. We move into a big, ugly modern room with a row of kiosks, dim lighting and a ticket system. Before us we find a machine that seems to be the starting point of this ticket system. A screen asks us to choose from 'MAP' or 'INFO'. We select 'INFO'. Then, feeling a little as though we're about to be called at a Post Office or for an order at Argos, we wait and wait – and wonder what is going on, while at the same time thinking: 'At least it's warm in here.'

There aren't that many people about and there are several assistants apparently doing nothing whatsoever (just like in Post Offices back home).

Eventually, our number, 26, flashes. We head for our allotted booth, but find the space taken by a couple deep in discussion with a tourist information officer. We lurk with our ticket, sensing that we've broken some sort of important rule, though we're not sure what rule exactly. As we stand there, feeling a bit gormless, a woman in a booth next to ours looks up.

'I should not,' she says, slowly and somewhat wearily. 'But can I help you?'

Her booth has number 312 above it.

'Yes please...' I begin tentatively.

She cuts me off: 'I am sorry. Number 312 has arrived.'

We turn to discover couple number 312 is indeed before us... how the numbers have jumped quite so far onwards from 26, we are uncertain.

'I'm sorry. But I must take number 312,' says the assistant, sounding grave. Why we had not received this 'priority treatment' back at our original booth, we are also uncertain.

We step to one side as number 312 takes our place.

We stand by a cordon watching the numbers flick up, deciding to stick this out and see what happens. After some time, another assistant calls us over. She seems to have taken pity on us.

We go to yet another booth. The tourist information officer smiles grimly as I ask for some tourist information: a map or a brochure perhaps. We've been in here so long we've almost forgotten why we came. No numbers flash up as we talk to her, and we are soon the proud owners of another map and a small publication entitled *Love Bruges: The Official City Guide*.

We step once more into the streets of Bruges, clutching our hard-earned guide. There's a blizzard outside. We head in the direction of the hotel passing a strange row of what look like abominable snowmen, or perhaps floating ghosts. The peculiar creatures slide out of the snow towards us. On closer inspection, they turn out to be tourists on battery-powered Segway personal transporters. We've seen these before – and I tried one a long time ago, feeling as though I was standing at some kind of moving pulpit. But these ones look very weird indeed.

Amazingly, and quite eerily, they slide across the road in front of us with a leader yelling something about 'monumental Gothic portals' and 'Romanesque French style'. Each of the tourists is almost blanketed in white. They appear quite content, lined up on their electronic contraptions. They pause for a moment, and then head down a side street, a ghostly voice explaining that they are entering a 'typical medieval working-class neighbourhood' where there were once many bars: 'Drinking was the favourite pastime after a hard day...' The spooky commentary trails off into the whiteout.

We follow in their direction, getting a little lost, despite our new map, and reading about the origin of the name Bruges in our new guide. It comes from the Old Norse *bryggja* or jetty. We learn that the Zwin waterway linking Bruges with the North Sea had been in danger of silting up in the twelfth century, before the golden age of the city began. This caused a 'period of anxiety', but then the great days of trade began 'and soon the city developed a magnet-like radius'.

We read on and wander on. The guide makes much of the city being 'mysterious'. Not only is it a 'somewhat sleepy, yet extremely mysterious place', it also has a 'mysterious intimacy' and is also 'mysteriously medieval' with an 'elegant mysteriousness'. Never has a city, it would seem, been quite so proudly mysterious. Meanwhile, we read, Bruges is 'unashamedly Burgundian' and 'poetic', as well as being 'easy and inexpensive' with 'bargain prices!'

Wondering if this is quite true of the coffees and waffles, we walk onwards and turn into the Groeninge Museum. This is the 'most famous museum in Bruges', according to *Love Bruges*, and it contains one of the world's finest collections of early Flemish art. The entrance is near the cute stone bridge we crossed yesterday. We go down a path to a nondescript building with a long queue for tickets and soon find ourselves, €16 lighter (not too bad), heading through a doorway... about to learn all about early Flemish art.

There is, it seems, a lot to learn about early Flemish art, judging by all the information panels. And it's a very popular pursuit in these parts: the museum is jam-packed.

We enter the throng. An early display panel begins: 'This exhibition invites you to observe the dissemination of early Flemish romanticism…' Another discusses the 'all but unilateral' qualities of the brush strokes. People peer at the displays, appearing either to take it all in, or look very puzzled. We join the latter group.

'It's all art-speak to me,' says E. 'Really: what does all this stuff actually mean?'

'Don't ask me,' I reply, unable to make head or tail of half of it.

Instead, we decide just to look at the pictures.

They are, we soon realise, absolutely marvellous. The first rooms are full of fifteenth-century depictions of Baby Jesus with Mary. What strikes us is both the brilliance of the colours – the fine blues, sharp reds, crisp greens and delicate pinks – and the superbly individual expressions of the faces. So often in galleries stuffed with art depicting scenes from the Bible canvases take on a melodramatic air: classic moments seem as though they were painted to be viewed through 'historical glasses', deliberately portrayed in an epic way. But the early Flemish artists weren't like that. The works are full of peculiar expressions: long curious faces, some grinning, others looking slightly perplexed, others a little tired at the way the world has been treating them, some appearing frankly hacked off with things.

In short, they're *fun*. One Baby Jesus has a craggy, old man's face. Another looks as though he may have been hitting the port. One has mad ginger curls that seem to have been exaggerated by the painter for comic effect. The cast of characters are all slightly odd, but it is precisely this unusual quality that makes them feel real, as though they were based on people who actually existed in medieval Bruges. It's almost as if we're walking through a gallery of ghosts.

The sense of humour leaps out at every turn. We walk through into another busy room with people crowded round a peculiar picture of a woman wearing a white headdress over amazing red hair that seems to stick out like horns from either side of her head. She appears almost ridiculous on first inspection, though her gaze falls calmly to one side as though quite in control of her thoughts and hoping the artist will just get on with it. The painting is by Jan van Eyck (1385–1441), who lived in Bruges for eleven years until his death, during the city's great artistic heyday. He signed the work, a picture of his wife, with his customary *'als ich can'* ('it's the best I can do').

Almost every painting has a sense of realism. They may be medieval faces, but they are faces that seem uncannily similar to those in the room right now. We stop by a *Portrait of a Man* from 1480. He's holding a piece of paper and has a twinkle in his eyes and the type of bulbous nose that suggests taverns were not unfamiliar with his tatty beret and unruly curls. Then we come to a painting of Adam and Eve from 1535 in which Adam is portrayed as a devilish rake.

'Eve's offering him an apple. But he's got other ideas,' says E.

'There's no doubting that,' I reply – Adam is leering at his Eve and the painter makes no mistake as to why he's leering (in a charmingly raffish way). Bruges is after all the city of romance that will 'capture your heart' and 'stir all your senses', according to our guide. Perhaps this picture should be taken up as some sort of city symbol.

The gallery seems to prompt wry comments and almost all the visitors seem to be at it: pointing, joking and occasionally snickering. Near the end of the rooms – packed with so many works by such greats as Rogier van der Weyden, Hans Memling and Hieronymus Bosch that you could spend hours peering at the unusual medieval characters – we come to the painting *Death and the Miser* by Jan Provoost (1465–1529), who settled in Bruges in 1494. It depicts a merchant who has lived a life of enormous wealth and is facing a manic, grinning skeleton, appearing as though he might be attempting to pass on a payment of some sort. He looks chubby, slightly harassed, and distinctly like the former prime minister Ted Heath. The skeleton shuffles coins on a desk with one hand and considers the promissory note he's been given with a look that says: 'That won't do you much good where you're going.'

The picture seems as though it's a time capsule representing the city's better times, before Bruges 'died', before the population fell by a quarter, before the Victorian tourists revelled in its empty streets, and before its reinvention and days of romantic weekend breaks, waffle houses and cosy tea rooms with seven-euro coffees. Back when Bruges was a thriving place of commerce and the river had not yet silted, there was so much money people were trying to buy their immortality. Or so the picture seems to imply. The eerie scene seals the ghostliness that the gallery captures. And it is also *funny*. It's poking fun at the fat cats of the time, with a delightfully wicked sense of humour.

What a terrific place. Afterwards we walk for miles, getting lost in the snow. Through the white blur we see a windmill on a little hill where children are sledding, shrieking and generally having a ball. We pass the old Bourse, a tall thin building dating from medieval times that is considered by some to be the home of the world's first stock exchange: where traders met to do business in the 1300s. The word *bourse* either comes from the Latin *bursa* (bag) or from the surname of one of the city's merchants at the time. Now it has taken on the meaning of 'stock exchange' in many countries – and this is where it all began, not far off Burg square. We continue along lanes with chocolate and comic-book shops. We avoid a dull-looking diamond museum. We skirt a fish market. And then we do as medieval working-class Bruggians do after a long day: we find a cosy bar.

The EST Winjbar, just round the corner from our hotel, is in a tiny old building on two levels, with exposed wood beams, wood tables, terracotta tiles, fake fires, candles and a lovely feeling of steamy warmth after the blizzard. We push through a thick purple curtain by the door and find a seat near the packed bar. We order large glasses of white wine. An older couple, who appear to have been in here escaping the cold for some time, totters out, cheerfully nodding and smiling as they pass. Twangy blues music plays. Our wine appears, served by a man who looks like a younger version of the actor Gérard Depardieu. A waitress with red hair and a stripy pinafore brings a small plate of star-shaped crackers. And we take it easy. We couldn't have found a better place to warm up.

As we do, characters begin to enter – completely covered in snow.

'They look as though they've just scaled the heights of K2,' says E. The blizzard seems to have intensified. 'They've got snowflakes hanging off their noses.'

'So they do,' I answer, swigging down the wine a little quickly at our table by one of the fires.

'He looks like a proper Shackleton,' E whispers as one chap with a snow-covered beard shuffles past. Bruges appears to have stepped into the Arctic Circle.

'So he does,' I reply, taking a thoughtful swig. Belgium may be best known for its beer, but its wine bars are pretty good too, if this place is anything to go by.

We pass an hour or so in EST Winjbar. Then we retire to the Pand Hotel. In our absence, after asking if there was another room free this morning, we've been moved to a bigger one in the attic. It's much nicer, with a view across the snowy rooftops of the dark city, blue-and-white wallpaper with a floral pattern, and a small metal four-poster.

We go to bed quite early... and then we realise something. The room may be nice looking, but the walls seem paper thin. From the next door room we hear a gurgle and a growl. The gurgle and growl subsides for a moment. And there is silence in this little garret in the heart of medieval Bruges. Then the gurgle and growl, complete with a wheeze, a rattle and a grunt, picks up again. The frame of our bed begins to vibrate in tune with the sounds from next door. A man is snoring loudly, so loudly that *our bed is shaking*.

This is a new one to us. It's almost impossible to get to sleep. Wordsworth's 'deeper peace than in heavens found' is not to be found in this room at the Pand Hotel. We consider calling downstairs, but wonder what good that would do (what are they going to do, wake him up and give him a nose clip or something?). Anyway, after asking to move from the last room, we're not sure we're in any position to moan about rooms again. This is our lot. We consider what to do. We shift the pillows to the other end of the bed – so we're not right next to the paper thin walls. E drapes a towel over her head.

'It's not even a joke how loud it is,' she mutters from beneath the towel. 'Why doesn't his wife hold his nose or something?'

She pauses. The snoring steadily continues; as it does throughout the night. 'Pand Hotel... more like Pandemonium,' continues the voice from under the towel at some point in the early hours.

It's a long night.

We're exhausted as we walk through the wonderful snow-covered streets, past the Lake of Love, to the station; my case rolling along, collecting snow and feeling like a bag of bricks this time. The train takes us through white tunnels of landscape along George Stephenson's old line. We change at Brussels and zoom onwards, suspiciously stopping at Calais ('ladies and gentlemen, we are waiting for approval to continue our journey'), before heading into whiteout Britain, and arriving to find complete mayhem at St Pancras.

Queues snake for hundreds of yards through the station, running this way and that around hastily constructed lines made out of red-and-white plastic tape. A trolley is providing free cups of tea and coffee to those desperately waiting. Boards announce cancelled trains. People are tetchy; as well you might expect. Wheelie bag rage breaks out as people try to squeeze across the concourse. Thank God we've missed all of this.

But poor them. Everything seemed perfectly calm on the Continent, yet it's completely unravelled here. We've just missed, by one train, one of the worst snow delays of the winter.

Feeling very lucky (who cares about snorers in attics now?) we head home. It's been an amazing weekend. We're with the Victorians: Bruges is lovely. Soon we're off to another fast-train city, and it's got a lot to live up to.

CHAPTER ELEVEN

TOURS: 'FINE WINES, FAVOURITE LADIES AND KING EDWARD VIII'

Christmas and New Year's Day have been and gone amid flurries of snow and festivities: family feed-ups, office knees-up, pubs, long restorative walks, more pubs and hangovers aplenty.

It's three weeks since our last high-speed adventure and it feels a very long time ago. But our journey south to Tours has progressed smoothly – no snow-on-the-line chaos in early January – and we're enjoying the sense of being on the move once more. We arrive in the chief city of the Loire Valley in almost precisely four and a half hours, where we pick up a hire car. Then we drive through confusing ring roads, cross a bridge over the lazy-looking, olive expanse of the River Loire, and arrive at a place that is not marked on our *AA Road Atlas of France*. It's not mentioned in our *Rough Guide to France* either. It's on the outskirts of a small town called Monts, just to the south of Tours. And it's where one of the greatest British royal scandals of the twentieth century was, eventually, played out.

We park our natty silver Golf in a field with two other vehicles. There is no one else around. A wind whips across a row of plane trees and under a sunny, pale blue sky we walk down a gravel path feeling as though we've landed in the middle of the French countryside, just five hours since leaving St Pancras. We persevere along a lane, wondering if we've got the right place, while enjoying the solitude and the utter quiet of our new surroundings. There is something blissful about being hidden away in this rolling landscape without a soul in sight.

After a while, we come to what we're looking for: a tall, damp, grey Gothic building with a circular tower, turrets and a slate roof. This is Château de Candé, dating from the sixteenth century, though much changed over the years. It sits on a grass bank on the top of a hill. We walk along the empty gravel path and find a gift shop without any customers. We enter and glance at the postcards and tea towels. A serious-looking man in a black T-shirt says '*bonjour*' and returns to the book he's reading. Perhaps it's by Honoré de Balzac, the hermit-like writer who lived in Tours for many years, describing many local sights in his fiction.

We don't interrupt to ask – he looks too engrossed. Instead we continue on to the chateau, which overlooks a peaceful valley with an elegant railway viaduct dating from the 1840s. Trains: we can't get away from them! It was across viaducts such as this fine example that the world's first express services ran; the French created the term 'express', using it to refer to faster trains that did not stop at every station. The average speed of trains in France was already above an impressive 50 mph on its expresses at around the time the tall brick arches of the viaduct below were completed.

E and I huddle on a wooden bench eating late-lunch baguettes picked up earlier during a pit stop at a giant Carrefour supermarket, contemplating our new surroundings. Down the grass bank of the steep hill, past delicate lines of cypress trees, the river Indre moves slowly by, turning under the viaduct and disappearing towards Tours.

Everything is so silent – so far removed from London, peaceful and calm.

But the chateau appears to be closed. While the front door of the Gothic tower is open and we're able to walk up and down a stone spiral staircase inside, all the interior doors are locked. There is no ticket kiosk, and nothing at all in the way of information apart from a poster for a local fête. We walk back to the gift shop. The Balzac-reader in the black T-shirt is still there, and he's been joined by a colleague, also in a black T-shirt. They look up as we enter.

'*Parlez-vous anglais?*' I enquire expertly.

'Yes, of course,' the woman replies brightly, seeming astonished at our presence.

'Is the chateau open?' I ask.

'Yes,' she replies brightly.

'May we go in?' I ask.

'No,' she responds, wide eyed and upbeat.

'Why?' I enquire.

'You have just missed the tour – by a few minutes,' the woman replies happily. She's extremely cheerful, even if her news is not so great.

'Oh,' I say. 'I hadn't realised there were only tours of the chateau at appointed times.'

'Yes, that is the way,' she says breezily, waving a brochure at us. 'The next one, see,' she points at a paragraph. 'The next one is later this afternoon.'

She beams at us. The Balzac-reader puts his book to one side, raises an eyebrow and fixes us with a steady stare.

'Oh,' I reply.

There's a pause. 'Are there many people on the tour right now?' I ask. There hadn't seemed to be anyone about.

'No,' she replies matter-of-factly, grinning broadly now. 'No one.'

'Oh,' I say. 'Do you think we might have a tour now? We could go round a little faster than usual, finish it on the usual time?'

She considers this, and glances at Balzac-man. Not a flicker of expression passes across his features. She turns back to us.

'Absolutely,' she says, wide eyes twinkling. 'Why not!'

We retrace our footsteps to the Gothic tower in the company of Melanie Manceau, who begins very cheerily to tell us about some unusual houseguests who visited the chateau in 1937: namely, Wallis Simpson, the twice-divorced American socialite from Baltimore, and the Duke of Windsor, who had been King Edward VIII until he abdicated on 11 December 1936 so he could marry her. It's this history that caught our eye about Château de Candé when we were looking up places to visit over the weekend. Tours is in the centre of what is known as 'Chateaux Country' in France: there are dozens from which to choose... and this one looked especially intriguing.

'Wallis came here in 1937, in the month of March,' Melanie explains. 'She came to escape from all the journalists, to a place where they would not find her. Since the previous December, journalists had been on her back. She was really sick of them: really, really sick of them.'

We step into a small room with pistachio-coloured walls. We have entered one of the world's first, and surely one of the best-preserved, gyms. The owner of the chateau in the 1930s was a rich American industrialist, Charles Bedaux, whose wife Fern was friends with Wallis. Lovers of the finer things in life and in touch with the latest trends, they had adapted the interior of the chateau to make it one of the fanciest in the whole of France, with this gym (which once contained rowing machines that looked like full-sized rowing boats), more than eighty telephones hidden in boxes in walls, secluded rooftop sunbathing terraces, and en suite tiled bathrooms of the sort that might have been expected only at the suites of the plushest five-star hotels in Paris.

In front of us we see shiny old exercise bikes with tough leather seats connected to an amusingly big circular display, about a metre in diameter, crudely showing the number of metres travelled (though not calories consumed or heart rate or CNN news). There's a leather saddle on an extraordinary mechanical horse-riding contraption. This, on closer inspection, could be set to 'trot' or 'gallop'. There's also a very odd-looking massage machine. Leather golf bags full of wooden clubs are stacked in a corner, next to a set of weights.

'Oh yes, Wallis used these,' says Melanie, pointing at the bikes, before striding on purposefully.

We pass along a long corridor hung with a highly unusual picture of Wallis and Edward, dressed smartly while leaping upwards together. The arresting snap is entitled '*Jumpology*' and was taken in 1956 by Philippe Halsman, a Latvian-born American photographer, who explains in a caption: '*Il ne peut plus contrôler ses expressions, ses gestes faciaux et les muscles de ses membres. La masque tombe, la vraie personne se fait visible.*' Which I take to mean: you capture their real faces and feelings when they jump in the air.

Wallis, who seems to have been an active type (in love affairs and in general), looks as though she's having a ball. Meanwhile, the former king appears bewildered and more than slightly terrified; confirming the received wisdom that Wallis wore the trousers in their strange partnership. The camera on this occasion, it seems, didn't lie. It's rumoured that Wallis had several affairs while she was with the former king, including an attachment with a Nazi foreign minister and with the playboy grandson of F. W. Woolworth, twenty years her junior. According to Philip Ziegler, Edward's official biographer: 'There must have been some sort of sadomasochistic relationship. He relished the contempt and bullying she bestowed on him.'

It feels as though we're walking into the epicentre of a very odd coupling. Upstairs there's the bedroom where the duke slept. A cabinet contains a pipe, a top hat, a tartan tie, a gold cigarette lighter and a badger-hair shaving brush, all purported to have belonged to him. There are also a couple of pairs of sunglasses said to have been Wallis's. We check out the swish, all-mod-cons tiled bathroom and the telephone box in a panel in a corner of the bedroom.

'They had a phone in every room. They didn't go "Oh, where's my mobile?" or run to pick it up down the hall. They just opened a panel wherever they happened to be,' says Melanie. 'They had a woman at the chateau to make the connection.'

Melanie strides on once more. Along another corridor we come to the library. This is covered in traditional oak panelling – no doubt with many a phone lurking inside – and it looks very grand indeed. It was here on 3 June 1937 that the civil ceremony was held for the marriage of Wallis and Edward. After declaring their everlasting love, the couple carved their names in the panelling near a fireplace, as though to prove they were here, marking in the date as 6/3/37, using the American month-day date system in line with how Wallis would have wanted it, of course. The marks are still clearly there. She was aged forty-two and he was forty-four. So was sealed the biggest romantic scandal of the age; in this quiet countryside setting by a bend of the river Indre near Tours.

There are yellowing cuttings from newspapers in glass cabinets. 'AYANT RENONCE A L'EMPIRE, LE DUC DE WINDSOR A EPOUSE, A CANDE, "LA FEMME QU'IL AIME"', says the headline in *L'Intransigeant*. 'LE DUC DE WINDSOR A REALISE HIER LE REVE D'EDUOARD VIII: SON MARIAGE A ETE CELEBRE A 11H 45 AU CHATEAU DE CANDE,' runs the front page of the *Excelsior*. Meanwhile the *Daily Mirror* back in the UK took a different approach: 'THE KING AND QUEEN PHONE 'BE HAPPY' TO DUKE' as well as 'BBC ANNOUNCES DUKE'S WEDDING IN FIFTY-FIVE WORDS' – the phone boxes scattered in each room at the chateau coming in handy for the important call that day.

The coverage seems quaint compared to what you'd expect now. 'There were very few journalists for the wedding,' says Melanie, leading us through the library into a side room with a mahogany piano. It was in this room that the religious marriage ceremony was conducted. 'Randolph Churchill, the son of Winston, was here – as was the photographer Cecil Beaton. So there were a few press here. But not many.'

E asks if Madonna, who is in the middle of producing a film about Wallis Simpson, has visited the chateau.

'Not yet,' replies Melanie, grinning again. 'We don't know if she'll come or not.'

'You'd have thought she'd bother,' I say.

'Yes, but we haven't heard a thing,' Melanie replies, showing us into another room with expensive jewellery and dresses belonging to Wallis as well as a book in a cabinet entitled *La Scandaleuse Duchesse de Windsor* with a picture of a roaring leopard on the front cover.

We say goodbye to our effervescent guide. We've learnt a whole lot more than we ever expected about the scandalous duchess and her scandalous sidekick king. That's one of the great things, as we keep on finding, about these breaks. You're shot into Europe at 186 mph and you stumble upon stuff you probably never would have known if you lived to be 186 years old: so many old secrets and stories just waiting to be discovered, at the end of these relatively new high-speed tracks.

E and I walk across the field to the car – essential for chateaux-hopping in these parts – and drive into the centre of Tours. This does not turn out to be the prettiest or the simplest or the least painful journey of our lives.

In fact, it's a nightmare.

To start with, we quickly lose ourselves in a complicated one-way system on the edge of town. We pass superstores and ugly residential tower blocks overlooking ring roads. We circle round, thinking we have found our way, but then appear to be in the same place again. E curses the satnav system I bought cheaply back in the UK. I curse the satnav system I bought cheaply back in the UK. It doesn't seem to understand this city at all. We drive through infuriating, grid-like streets dating from the 1950s and 1960s, many built to replace damage caused by the Germans during World War Two. For four days Tours was the seat of the French government in 1940, before it moved to Bordeaux.

But that knowledge isn't helping us get anywhere. We drive on. We pass the big Carrefour where we bought our baguettes – for the third or possibly the fourth time. It starts to darken. Rain pours down, at first steadily, then heavily. All the streets seem to look the same. But then we locate the River Loire and, using the tall Gothic towers of Cathédrale St Gatien as a landmark, begin to make progress, threading our way towards Rue de la Rotisserie. As we do, I check the satnav for divine inspiration; perhaps it will suddenly snap into life and magically lead the way. It doesn't. There are too many one-way systems in Tours for satnavs. We begin to lose ourselves again.

'It doesn't work. It's hopeless,' says E, referring to the satnav.

'Yes, I know that. We agree about that,' I say through gritted teeth.

'Where did you get this thing?' E continues.

I mention a well-known high street shop with a ticket system for collecting your purchases.

'Is it a good one?'

'I'm not sure,' I reply dishonestly (E has no idea that I went for the cheapest one).

'Why can't people read maps any more?' E comments rhetorically, sounding as though she's about to launch some kind of 'demise of understanding/reliance on technology' spiel.

'I have no idea,' I answer a little unhelpfully.

We drive onwards. I sense E looking at me. 'There should be a map at the back of the AA atlas,' I suggest.

'They're never any good,' E responds decisively.

Friday night thunder crackles above as we almost feel our way forwards, craning for landmarks and stopping every now and then as I compare old churches, grand theatres, *jardins* and government institutions to the tiny map in the *Rough Guide*. It's slow progress. Rain is bucketing down as we eventually find our *rue*. This turns out to be an alleyway we cannot drive along. We park at a pay-and-display, and fish out euros to stick in the machine. We're on a cobbled street several hundred yards from our hotel, next to a dreary takeaway called 'Mangez Moi' offering five-euro cheeseburgers. There's another place called 'Restauration Rapide Chez Sam' serving similar delicacies. Rain pelts down even harder. Police have turned up at a bar on the corner. Officers rush inside and come out with two diffident-looking fellows. Some sort of bust appears to be in progress. We walk through filthy puddles amid the downpour, soaking wet thanks to the umbrella I bought in Marseilles, which has almost totally collapsed.

Up the alley, we find the narrow entrance to Hotel L'Adresse. We're dripping wet. The receptionist in the bright minimalist lobby smiles and gives us a key to a room on the top floor. We ascend a long steep staircase, and find ourselves in a tiny space looking across to the other side of the alley. Opposite, there appear to be student flats. Groceries and bottles of milk and wine have been left on window shelves to keep cool. Curtains seem to consist of old sheets. Meanwhile, inside here there's not much more space in the room than the bed itself, which for some reason has tiny pillows. E writes on a piece of paper: '*Excusez-moi, Madame, est-ce que vous avez deux autres oreillers?*' And I go downstairs to repeat this, asking for extra pillows.

I read out the message and the receptionist replies: 'Sure.'

She disappears into a backroom and returns: 'Here you go.'

'Thanks.'

'No problem.'

There's been much talk about English going global of late, and that's definitely true on the evidence of just about everywhere we've gone on these fast-train trips.

We head out into the city; population about 300,000. There's little evidence of any of the 300,000 right now. Perhaps that's because it's raining so hard that there's a small river down the centre of the lane. I've had a go at repairing the Marseilles umbrella, so at least we have some cover. We dive into a bar in our alley called Kandy's Bar à Vodka. There are red leather chairs crammed into a small space with a low ceiling and no other customers. The barman turns off a little TV he's been watching and switches on some pop music to create 'atmosphere'. We examine the drinks menu, searching for a nice glass of white wine – the Loire Valley being famous for its great whites (and reds). There is no wine on the menu. I go up to the bar, squeezing past the red leather seats. I ask the barman for the wine list.

'There is no wine,' he says gruffly.

'No wine?'

'That's right.'

'This is a bar in France and it does not serve wine?'

He just looks at me.

I get the impression he doesn't particularly like my line of inquiry. Anyway, I suppose if it says it's a vodka bar, it's a vodka bar.

We head back out into the rain, the pop music ending abruptly before we have left; the TV back on again.

We sidestep the stream, heading deeper along cobbled lanes into the old quarter of Tours. We're just round the corner from Place Plumereau; nicknamed Place Plum by locals, who are referred to as *Tourangeau* (if male) or *Tourangelle* (if female). This is at the heart of the oldest part of the city. Medieval houses with criss-cross wooden support beams and red-brick walls loom upwards crookedly and damply. There are plane trees and washed-out green plastic tables and chairs. We enter a bar on the square named Le Vieux Mûrier, which translates as 'the old mulberry'; there's a mulberry tree outside the front door.

Inside, locals and tourists are steamily drinking glasses of Vouvray Sec or pints of lager, sitting at beaten-up wooden tables. There's a burgundy carpet and the walls are covered in gilded mirrors and pictures of 'traditional scenes': folk in top hats and floppy caps. We sit at the back and order Vouvray Sec, feeling as though we're in a bit of a tourist trap.

As if to prove it, we hear: 'Hi, Tom!'

I look up. It's Andy, a fellow travel journalist who works on *The Guardian*, a rival paper to mine.

He's with his family, who are crammed into seats at a table by the door, on a driving trip south to stay near friends in Bordeaux. Tonight he's booked into a Novotel on the edge of town; a stop-off to break the journey. Like us, they've headed into the old quarter and have found Le Vieux Mûrier, which seems somehow to draw you in, especially when it's pouring.

'Are you doing a story?' I ask.

'I can't tell him that – not the opposition,' he replies jokily, turning to E.

'What are you up to?' he asks me.

'I can't tell him that – not the opposition,' I answer jokily too, turning to E – who appears rather mystified by our conversation (as well she might).

We chat a bit about Tours, and moan about the weather.

'It doesn't look so good,' says Andy.

This is a bit of an understatement. Through the windows we can see rain lashing across the green plastic furniture very optimistically placed out in Plum Square. Channels have formed from the streams of earlier, running in torrents across the cobbles, like new tributaries heading downwards to the Loire.

The three of us pause to take in the rainy scenes. Plum Square may be the most ancient and picturesque of neighbourhoods in Tours (the *Rough Guide* calls it the 'epicentre of social life') but it's pretty dismal when it's pouring.

'Oh well,' I say, as the door to the bar is opened by new customers, letting in the sound of plastic furniture taking a pounding.

'Could be worse,' says Andy, as wind whips through the mulberry tree.

Then he cheerily returns to his family, with a parting: 'Have a good time in Tours.'

Which we are, in a funny way: despite the conditions outside seeming to indicate a flash flood alert.

Small world. 'Seems like a nice chap,' says E.

We settle into our mulberry tree bar, drinking our Vouvray Sec, produced in a winery a few miles from where we're sitting. We order more glasses – as you're meant to when it's raining cats and dogs in an old city in the middle of France. It's a cosy, romantic place to be really, holed up in Plum Square, as the heavens open up over the Loire.

On Saturday we go chateaux-hunting. The weather has cleared and it's a brighter, but still overcast, morning in medieval Tours. We look out of the window of our garret, across to the groceries and bottles of the student flats – no sign of life there yet, though the wine bottles have disappeared overnight, and now only the milk remains. After packing our bags, putting them in the back of the natty silver Golf, checking whether we need to update the pay-and-display ticket and sitting down to a good croissant and coffee breakfast in the minimalist lobby of the hotel (which doubles as the breakfast room), we're ready to head forth into the much-hyped Chateaux Country.

We're staying tonight in a different hotel to the east of town, close to some of the most famous chateaux. But before we head off, we wander over to Rue Descartes, a short walk from Hotel L'Adresse, not far from the bar we saw yesterday in the middle of a police raid. The streets are almost completely empty, and there are no cafes open on our route to Basilique Saint-Martin; the city is dead on Sunday morning. Other than the odd dog walker, there isn't anyone else about.

As we walk up to the basilica we can see grey circles on the street marking the places of the columns of the former church devoted to St Martin, a fourth-century bishop of Tours, who gained fame for tearing his coat in half to share with a freezing beggar. The old church was destroyed in 1793 during the French Revolution – the clergy being seen as oppressors of the poor during the uprising. But a new basilica was built in the 1880s after remains from St Martin's tomb were discovered. As it has been for many centuries, the site is a place of religious pilgrimage for Catholics, and it is at the heart of the history of the city. Since medieval times, the church has been a major stopping off point on the route of those making pilgrimages to Santiago de Compostela in Spain.

Inside we find rows of grey marble columns leading to a crypt with a mausoleum dedicated to St Martin. We are the only visitors. A notice board shows pictures of Pope John Paul II's visit in 1996. We enter the mausoleum, which is lit by red candles in a room with a low domed ceiling. Images of Christ shine down through unusual stained-glass windows that we've learnt from a brochure are made from 'layered stained glass, a style invented in Tours'; the effect is a bit blurred and abstract. There's a smell of wax and the sound of silence. It's a very peaceful place.

But we've got chateaux to explore. We make our way back to the car, feeling (if we have to be totally honest) a little let down by the centre of Tours. Yes, we enjoyed the basilica and Plum Square, but it felt as though the city was a place to use as a springboard to go elsewhere. The *Rough Guide to France* says as much, warning 'don't expect too many culinary fireworks', and mentioning a 'slightly depressing absence of bars and pubs with really individual character'. Maybe we were missing something... though we're not so sure we did.

We drive east towards Amboise and our first very famous chateau, glad to be on the move. The one-way systems of the city seem much easier with no traffic about; the satnav long relegated to the boot, we're now using a tourist map from the hotel. We follow a long curve of the Loire under a white luminous sky. The river moves slowly but surely, looking a little like a French version of the Mississippi and making me think of Tom Sawyer and Huckleberry Finn. Thick trees and areas of wilderness line the banks, in which you could just imagine Sawyer or Finn camping out. There are sandy beaches, muddy escarpments and a sense of untamed grandeur; the water flowing along at just the pace it wants to flow, no matter what else is happening in the world around.

We keep on driving and find ourselves crossing a thin, grey stone bridge. The river on either side stretches into an olive distance. Ahead, there are cream-coloured buildings with slate roofs and the grisly-grey ramparts of the old castle on the hill. Beyond those sits the Château d'Amboise, with its rocket-turret and tall thin windows; through which kings of France once looked out enjoying the majestic views of the Loire from medieval times until the days of the Revolution.

It's breathtaking from below. We find ourselves parking some distance from the fortifications, and following a long path next to the river, passing icecream kiosks and colourful stalls selling cheap slices of quiche and pizza. We turn into a side street and then up stone steps to the foot of the castle. After handing over twenty euros, we go to the jagged ramparts and gaze down at the wonderfully languid Loire as Charles VIII and Louis XII must have so long ago. Charles VIII was responsible for transforming the old castle into a grand palace in the fifteenth century as well as for successful campaigns in Italy, taking Florence and Naples by force, though he unfortunately died after banging his head on a doorframe while playing *jeu de paume* (real tennis) and collapsing into a coma in his dream creation; which seems a sad story for such a splendid spot.

The river is even more captivating from up top. Here we are on the traditional dividing line between the north and the south of France, looking down from its most famous vantage point. The countryside spreads out seemingly forever under the milky sky; green, abundant and flat. There's not a train track in sight. And standing here on the ramparts of Château d'Amboise it's strange to think of how difficult it must have been getting around this enormous territory in the days of the royalty, before the locomotives came and conquered the landscape. Back in the time of Louis and Charles, you had to be pretty damn wealthy to travel across the land: part of the aristocracy, with teams of horses, coaches and servants.

When railways finally came in the 1840s, they opened up the country we see spread out before us, fitting in with the still very fresh notions of *liberté, fraternité* and *egalité*. Without wishing to overstate the effect, it was an important turning point. The masses were mobile! Long marches up and down the country – as the dockers from Marseilles had undertaken to join in the Revolution in Paris, singing *La Marseillaise* along the way – were no longer necessary. Just as in the new country of Belgium, trains acted as a unifying force.

Standing here, it all seems to click into place. Perhaps that was why the French invented the 'express'. Perhaps that's why France, with its extensive network of TGV lines, feels as though it's at the forefront of the high-speed train revolution in Europe. Maybe I'm just imagining this, but somehow fast trains just seem to fit into the French national psyche.

It's a short stroll from here, past a cafe filled with bikers, their Harley-Davidsons parked outside, to Chateau Number Three.

Up a hill we come to Château du Clos Lucé, a much smaller building tucked away on the side of a hill, also dating from medieval times. It was here that Charles VIII sent his wife Queen Anne to reside. His fourteen-year-old bride had been reluctant about the arranged marriage (showing this by rather dramatically arriving at the ceremony with two beds) and Charles VIII wasn't best pleased with the way things had panned out either. So Anne went to this little chateau, with rolling parkland leading quietly down a slope in the shadow of Château d'Amboise.

But it was a more famous visitor that sealed the fame of the chateau. As the ideas of the Renaissance in Italy spread around Europe in the fifteenth and sixteenth centuries, so did many of the Italians themselves. Amboise, not long after Charles and Anne's unusual domestic arrangements, was fortunate to attract one of the greats.

Leonardo da Vinci lived at Château du Clos Lucé for the last three years of his life, from 1516 to 1519, after being invited to France by François I, who had appointed him 'First painter, architect and engineer of the King'. It wasn't a bad arrangement for the sixty-four-year-old, who was provided with a pension of 700 gold ecus (by all accounts, extremely generous) and extra gold ecus for any works he created that caught his master's eye. His only requirement was to engage in regular chats with Francois, who enjoyed listening to him and who arranged that he popped by Château d'Amboise on most days.

So came Leonardo to France, crossing the Alps on the back of a mule and bringing with him three paintings in leather saddlebags. One of these was a picture of 'a Florentine lady painted from life on the orders of the late Giuliano de' Medici'. Thus arrived the *Mona Lisa*, later to become the country's number one tourist attraction.

The chateau is a mixed affair. There's a huge amount on Leonardo: his drawing techniques and how he studied human and animal anatomy to perfect the realism of his works, as well as his engineering inventions such as pictures of the first tanks, cars, paddleboats, flying machines, helicopters and parachutes. He did not, we learn, create any of his greatest works during his last three years. Rooms are decorated as they might have been in his time, with tapestries, tables, flamboyant velvet curtains and four-poster beds, but it's not entirely clear how Leonardo would have recognised things now. 'THE CHATEAU IS LOOKING FOR WALL-THINGS RELATED TO LEONARDO DA VINCI'S PERIOD. THANK YOU FOR YOUR UNDERSTANDING,' says a prominent sign.

'So how much of the chateau is really as it was?' asks E, who takes against this touting for antiques.

'I'm not sure,' I answer.

'So how can we trust what we see?'

'Hmmm,' I reply. 'I don't know.'

'And as for these!' E is pointing at a series of seemingly random sayings that are dotted about on the walls of the chateau. 'What do they all mean? *"The desire for death is stronger than the desire for eternity."* What's all that about?'

'I'm not sure,' I respond, scratching my head.

We proceed through the rooms reading the odd sayings – '*la passion intellectuelle met en fuite la sensualité... la service de l'art est l'art de la service*' – and reach a chamber with models of Leonardo's helicopters, water turbines, catapults and swing bridges. Beside this, there's a large gift shop with posters, books and mini models of some of da Vinci's inventions ('Step away from the cashpoint!' says E, when she sees me eyeing a model water turbine). We take a walk around the garden, which has large-scale versions of da Vinci's dreams including his amazingly futurist early-sixteenth-century helicopter.

Then we wander back down the hill to the car – and drive on to Chateau Number Four.

'Another chateau?' asks E.

'Yes, another chateau,' I reply.

'Really?' she asks.

'It's a good one,' I answer.

E gives me a searching look.

'We are in Chateaux Country, so we should see the chateaux,' I add, hoping that we're heading in the right direction now that the satnav days are over.

'OK,' says E, with a sense of resignation. Chateaux fatigue seems to be setting in – they are quite big and take a bit of walking around.

'It'll be wonderful,' I say, trying to talk up the next one, as I take a wrong turn and loop back at a roundabout. 'It's the most visited chateau in France, if you don't count Versailles. It's got to be good.'

And so we arrive at Chateau Number Four. We park in a madly busy car park with picnic tables lining the edges and French folk determinedly eating baguettes and drinking steamy cups of hot drinks. I hand over another €22, blanching a little at the cost of this chateau business; it doesn't come cheap. Feeling a bit as though we have entered some sort of Disneyland, we head along a corridor of trees, pass a stunning walled garden with decorative box hedges and fountains, and enter a building covered in scaffolding.

This is Château de Chenonceau, about twenty-five miles east of Tours on the River Cher. It is almost ridiculously busy inside. Tourists are walking about in every direction, through rooms with parquet floors dating from the fifteenth century, decorated with fading tapestries and fine old oil paintings. There seems to be little order whatsoever, though at least the brochure we're given as part of our €22 shows clearly which rooms are which, explaining some of the history. As we amble through the packed bedrooms, drawing rooms and chapels, we discover that the palace was for many years the home of mistresses of kings, queens of France and kings' widows; hence the nickname of The Ladies' Chateau.

We pause by the blue velvet bed of Diane de Poitiers, Henry II's mistress or 'favourite lady', as the brochure puts it, back in the sixteenth century. Diane liked her accommodation, but preferred better access to the other side of the river: so she ordered a bridge to be built to the opposite bank. This was duly constructed. However, when Henry II died, his widow Catherine de' Medici, the regent, understandably gave Diane her marching orders. Catherine then proceeded, as if in the spirit of one-upmanship, to build a continuation of the chateau on top of Diane's bridge, in the form of a 60-metre long gallery with a black and white checked floor. The result is a remarkable chateau stretching in a series of arches across the calm green water of the River Cher; one of the most famous structures in the country.

Walking up to the scaffolding at the front, it was hard to get a sense of its scale, but inside we do.

E's mutterings of 'This is the number one chateau in France?' cease as we look out across the river in the lovely gallery.

'Wouldn't this make the most wonderful flat,' is her verdict as we walk along to the opposite bank.

'Quite a big and unusual one,' I reply.

'You could do a lot with this,' E says, seeming to size up how she would re-do the place, rather like Catherine de' Medici.

We read the brochure, learning that the chateau was saved from destruction during the Revolution as the revolutionaries found crossing the bridge quite useful. During World War Two, the river was at the line of demarcation between the occupied

Nazi zone to the north and the (supposedly) free zone run by the Vichy government to the south. The Resistance often passed by this way and 'throughout the war, a German artillery unit was kept at the ready to destroy Chenonceau'.

We are officially shattered – totally chateaux-ed out. E has confiscated all tourist information; there's no way we're going to another chateau. It's late afternoon and dark as we drive back, following the Loire. Near our new hotel, we stop at the commune of Vouvray, just outside Tours. This is home to the wine we were drinking last night, so we stop in the gravel drive of a building with 'DOMAINE RECOLTANT' on its façade. An old barrel in the drive says *Bienvenue: Ouvert*.

We may have put away a fair few glasses of *vin* on these fast-train adventures – one of the great joys of speeding around France along its high-speed tracks – but we have yet to visit a winery, we reason, as we pull in. Maybe a drop of Vouvray will liven us up.

We enter a room lined with displays full of bottles, where a wizened fellow with a ponytail and a goatee is soon whipping out bottles from the local vineyards, pouring glasses and declaring: 'Ah, I think you will like zis one: sparkling, dry, light! It is made with zee Chenin Blanc.'

We try the bubbly Chenin Blanc, which has a picture of a frog on its label. It is very good.

'*Très bien*!' says the wizened fellow. 'It is made with zee same methods as champagne. But it is not zee champagne: no, no! It is zee same, but not zee same! Ha ha ha!'

He pauses. 'Ah, I think also,' he continues. 'Also, zis one! It is zee Chinon Rouge.'

We try the Chinon Rouge. It is also very good. E says so in French.

He is delighted. 'Ah, you speak zee excellent French!'

He whips out another bottle. We are given a lesson in 'zee physical explanation of zee vin rouge' showing how the flavour of red wine changes when it is aired; losing us a bit.

'With or without zee air, ha ha!' he proclaims. 'Vinegar or not zee vinegar! For twenty-four hours! It depends on whether you wait a little now! Yesterday for zee tomorrow!'

He beams at us. We have absolutely no idea what he is trying to say. But he's full of enthusiasm for the wines of the commune of Vouvray. We mark down a handful of bottles on a buyer's list.

'*Très bien*!' he booms, then adds conspiratorially: 'Are you driving?'

I explain our hotel is a few hundred yards down the road.

'Ah ha!' he says, touching his nose and revealing two more bottles.

We leave with a full box of the wines of the commune of Vouvray – wondering slightly how we're going to get them all back on Eurostar.

Our hotel is indeed close by... in a cave. We go up a drive and see a series of windows built into a sandstone cliff overlooking a sleepy bend of the Loire. This is Les Hautes Roches, a hotel created out of caves formerly belonging to the monastery of Marmoutier Abbey, which was founded by St Martin in the fourth century. The abundant soft stone cliffs in the Loire Valley have meant that many people over the centuries have dwelt in caves. It's such a popular thing that cave-dwelling has become a tourist attraction of sorts and you can buy postcards marked 'TROGLODYTES' showing various caves serving as homes, some still occupied.

We check in and walk up steep steps to our cave. It isn't at all gloomy, though. Actually, it's rather spacious and airy and plush, with big windows looking across the darkened river. There's an enormous bed set in a corner with acres of thick red carpet. The walls have been straightened and covered in stone cladding on one side and red-tulip wallpaper on the other. There are white orchids in a vase, and two champagne flutes on a side table, next to a minibar with a half-bottle of the Vouvray bubbly Chenin Blanc.

We order room service, crack open the bottle and take it easy in our cave by the Loire, watching a DVD on my laptop: *Mad Men*, the box set.

Perhaps not the way fourth-century monks would have done it. But it's not the fourth century and we're not monks. We're tourists in Tours, and we're tired.

We sleep very well (you don't have to worry about the sound of snorers through walls in cave hotels). And we head off fairly early on the road along the Loire.

Gare de Tours, a ten-minute drive away, is a beautiful edifice with a grand curved façade and figures atop columns guarding the entrance. It was built in the 1890s by Victor Laloux, the same architect behind the Basilique Saint-Martin. We arrive in the mid-morning and admire the lovely tiled panels capturing destinations down the line. A bridge leading to a castle depicts Chinon, while a stone archway with a narrow medieval street shows the centre of Fontarabie, and an elegant woman dressed in a flowing white dress accompanied by her smart husband in a straw hat is walking along the beach in Biarritz.

The whole station feels like a very well-preserved work of art: yet another indication of how important trains seem to be, and have long been, in France.

Carrying the box of Vouvray wine, we board a train with purple seats to Paris Austerlitz station, catch a cab across the

French capital with a semi-sane driver playing jazz music on his car stereo, board our high-speed train home and zoom northwards. One minute dwelling in a cave by the River Loire, the next (or so it seems) passing the shiny triangular tower of Canary Wharf.

We've been to one of the most beautiful regions, if not the prettiest of cities, in France. And we've got a box of bubbly to prove it.

As we pull into St Pancras, I ask E what she enjoyed most about Tours.

'Château de Candé,' she replies automatically. 'It felt like a secret place.'

The doors open into a cold January Sunday. 'And the cave hotel,' she says; where we were having breakfast just a few hours back, looking across the magnificent Loire. 'I adored the cave hotel.'

I thought it was pretty good, too. We drop down the escalator into the depths of the station, as I think ahead to the next high-speed adventure.

E's opted out this time, as it's not quite her thing: namely, a beer-drinking weekend in Cologne. It's an idea my old university pal Danny came up with after hearing about all these fast-train trips a few weeks back.

We'd been discussing them in the pub after work. 'Hmmm,' he'd said, in a thoughtful manner. 'Hmmm.' And he'd rubbed his chin.

'Cologne!' he'd said all of a sudden. 'Let's go to Cologne! I'll ask Claire,' his wife, with whom he has two young children. 'I'm sure she won't mind.'

His eyes lit up as he warmed to the idea. 'Definitely, Cologne!' He paused, letting the idea sink in. 'Yes: let's get wasted! Drink lots of beer! Ha ha ha!'

My penultimate fast-train weekend was decided.

CHAPTER TWELVE

COLOGNE: 'FEAR AND LOATHING BY THE RHINE'

There are, happily, a few handy benefits to leaving at the crack of dawn to catch an early Eurostar train for a weekend break: (1) You make the most of your trip by maximising the time at your destination; (2) You avoid the commuter rush on the way to St Pancras; (3) You almost always find a seat on the way; (4) You quite often find that buses and trains run on time that early as you make your way across London.

But there are quite a considerable number of drawbacks, too: (1) You find that 'rule' number four above can be very shaky, particularly when it comes to buses; (2) You're knackered; (3) You run the risk of forgetting things in a rush to leave – sometimes important things like passports and ticket references; (4) It's cold early in the morning; (5) Bankers.

There seems to be a remarkably large number of bankers travelling on London Transport between the hours of 5.30 a.m. and 6.30 a.m. on the handful of occasions I have made it up that early to get anywhere (perhaps it's the only time they feel truly safe). It's just gone 6.20 a.m. on a Friday morning in late January and I'm listening to a man in a pinstripe suit with a squash racket poking out of a briefcase talking to another man dressed almost identically.

'Equity is not high enough, money is low,' says one, loudly.

The other nods sagely. 'Yes, yes. There's a big hole,' he agrees at equal decibel levels.

'But who is going to fill it?' the first pinstripe responds.

'I don't know,' says the other. 'There's a hole, it's a problem.'

'Hmmm,' says the first pinstripe.

'Hmmm,' echoes the second.

There's a pause. 'How often does the government issue its budget update?' says the first.

'Quarterly,' says the second.

'Hmmm.'

'Hmmm.'

'It's not enough!' says the first, sounding outraged.

'You're right, it's not,' says the second.

'It's a disgrace!' exclaims the first, suddenly and decisively unfurling a copy of the *FT* and patting the pages into place.

They return to their papers. I watch them perusing share prices in their pinstripes, wondering how much they earn in bonuses. Is Britain, as we're told so often, really relying on these gentlemen to return us to the good times?

If so, we'd all better be jumping on fast trains heading out of the country soon.

I meet Danny outside Foyles bookshop. He looks exhausted. He's been up watching England seal victory against Australia in the Ashes cricket last night, as I have been (maybe it was fatigue that prompted the banker rant).

'I had to see the final wicket,' he says, clutching a coffee. 'Up until 1 a.m. But it was worth it.'

'Definitely,' I agree, even though it's meant about four hours' sleep.

'Very good to see,' says Danny.

'Excellent,' I concur.

'You look terrible, mate,' he adds.

'Thanks,' I say. 'So do you.'

'Cheers,' he replies.

Civilities over, we proceed to the security check. Danny attempts, quite calmly, to carry his coffee through the X-ray machine. A guard stops him and wags a finger. He dumps the coffee in a bin.

'Great, just great,' he mutters. 'That's £1.60 wasted.'

But we're soon on the train, with no delays, no bankers, no further security breaches, and with fresh coffees from the queue-less Caffè Nero, as we pass out of an East End shrouded in a thick Dickensian mist. Apart from an unexpected stop at Ebbsfleet, everything goes smoothly and as we move through the tunnel Danny turns to the matter at hand: Cologne and what to do in the city on the western tip of Germany.

'This may sound like the pot calling the kettle black – or the blind leading the blind,' he begins. 'But I think we've got to remember that we're not twenty-five any more.'

He's referring to drinking. I tell him about my new year's resolution: not to drink Sunday to Thursday; which I've kept so far. Admittedly we are only halfway through January, and I did fairly well with the Vouvray on Friday and Saturday in Tours.

'Moderation,' I agree. 'No need to go crazy.'

'Absolutely,' he says, as though that's decided. We're going to Cologne to drink beer and see the sights, but we will not drink too much beer, as we're not twenty-five any more. We're both getting on for forty. These facts having been established, we doze off for a while.

We awake feeling well rested as the train pulls into Brussels. The journey to Cologne would have taken 4 hrs 9 min. if we'd booked the perfect connections. But unfortunately we haven't. We've got a two-hour wait in Brussels, before our 1 hr 45 min. train to our destination. We exit down an escalator into the chilly depths of Brussels station and look out into the wet, unappealing streets with damp uninteresting buildings, wheelie bins and a taxi rank with a single vehicle.

As we do so, Danny, who works for a TV current affairs programme, takes a call from a political spin doctor who's annoyed about a minor aspect of coverage from the day before; about who got the 'last word' in an interview. As he gesticulates defending his programme's handling of the interview (boy, can politicians be touchy), I enquire about the price of a cab to the centre of town: €18, which seems a bit steep and I get the sense that the sole taxi driver knows he's cornered the market. But we catch it to the Grand Place, passing through dreary, dirty streets with cheap fast-food restaurants and 'EROTIC STUFF' and 'HOT STORE' sex shops. The area around the station looks tacky and dismal.

'I've never liked Brussels,' says Danny. 'I've been a few times for press conferences: never liked it.'

The taxi stops in a few minutes on the edge of the Grand-Place, and we walk into the central square of the city; which I've been to before and always found quite beautiful. The square is surrounded by splendid, looming guildhouses dating from the seventeenth century. They glitter with gold decorations; gables, columns, tall windows and statues of horses and ancient dignitaries all around. On one side, there's the elaborate façade of the Hôtel de Ville, with its pointed spire reaching almost 100 metres, not far from a narrow building where Karl Marx used to meet Engels in 1848 when they were writing *The Communist*

Manifesto. Dozens of tourists are milling about on the ancient, glistening cobblestones in the centre, some heading for the cafes and bars at the bottom of the old guildhouses.

Danny stares about, open-mouthed. 'Wow,' he says. 'I think I've been to Brussels three times and I've never come here.'

'It's the main attraction in the city,' I point out.

'It's amazing. How did I manage to come to Brussels and not see this?' he asks, looking almost perplexed. 'If I did come,' he continues. 'I certainly don't remember.'

He pauses, as we stand right in the centre of the square, taking in the fine buildings. The Grand-Place feels like an oasis of grandeur amid the dull, downtrodden streets with boring photocopier shops and grimy XXX-rated corner bars we were driven down from the station. 'Anyway,' Danny says, a couple of hours after his 'blind leading the blind' address, 'I think it's time for our first beverage.'

'Why not,' I reply. 'It's gone midday. We're not overdoing it.'

'Just the one,' says Danny, striding forwards. 'Just the one.'

And we make our way to La Brouette, a tavern with hanging baskets of purple flowers outside and a cosy interior with tables made out of old barrels, fake wood fires, exposed beams and waiters in black waistcoats who swiftly take our orders. We soon have before us bottles of Tripel Karmeliet (Danny) and Mort Subite Gueuze (me). We look at the labels. 'Bloody hell, this is eight point four per cent,' says Danny. Mine is four point five per cent. 'Why don't they have the percentages on the list?'

We take our first sips of beer, which come in little bottles and onion-shaped glasses. It's glorious stuff; a kind of connoisseur's brew, with subtle, warm tastes of hops and barley and whatever else went in. *Mort subite*, the waiter has told us, means 'sudden death'. Jazz plays quietly in the background. Solitary folk in black, some with beers and others with coffees, read crumpled

copies of *Le Soir* newspaper under harlequin-shaped glass
chandeliers. There are posters for Museum of Modern Art
exhibitions in New York City dating from years ago. It's a very
cool spot to spend an hour. Danny regales me with a few of
the old stories he covered, switching from when he visited New
York soon after 9/11 – 'we drove down from Canada, it was like
a ghost town, the only way to get around Manhattan was to
walk, we talked to a woman whose husband had been a trader
and had left a final message on the family answering machine: it
was extraordinary' – to when he spent four weeks in Baghdad.
'It was just before they started to kidnap journalists, we used
to go and have lunch and stuff in normal restaurants,' he says,
taking another sip of his thick brown beer.

We finish our drinks, walk through the Grand-Place, catch a
taxi close to the birthplace of *The Communist Manifesto*, and
are soon on a Thalys train listening to rain pelting on the roof
of the carriage, sounding like peas being dropped into a bucket.
The patter is quite relaxing, and we doze off once more. I awake
to find that we're in Aachen station. My mobile phone pings to
tell me we have arrived in Germany, our fourth country of the
day. I'd considered coming to Aachen for one of these weekends;
just because it sounded so unusual. When I read up about the
town I'd found that it was once home to Charlemagne, the
powerful ruler of the Holy Roman Empire who moved to live
here in 768. It was also the birthplace of Ludwig Mies van der
Rohe, one of the great modern architects, born in 1886. There
are some of the hottest springs in Europe, with natural waters
bubbling up at 74°C. For this reason, the town qualifies for the
prefix 'Bad', which means 'spa' in German. But apparently this
prefix was shunned as the town would no longer appear first
on alphabetical lists. Perhaps not strong enough reasons to visit
the place.

A few spires poke up in the distance over terrace rooftops. The rain clatters down. And we move on through an empty brown landscape. I fall asleep again. I wake to find the landscape has turned white, looking like some kind of Siberian tundra; it's much snowier near Cologne, as though the region has an Arctic microclimate. I watch the frozen landscape pass. Danny soon awakes, too, and before we know it we've arrived at Cologne station.

'Are we there yet?' he asks, blinking and looking directly at a sign that says 'KÖLN'.

'Yes,' I reply.

We disembark, and so begins the tricky business of finding our hotel. It is pouring in Cologne. We walk out of the station and into a courtyard with the giant cathedral looming up, looking very solid, damp and big. Across the square we see a tourist office. We enter through automatic doors and I go to a kiosk, where there is no ticket system (or wait).

'Do you speak English, please?' I ask a youngish assistant, trying to be polite and not assume that everyone speaks English.

'I try from time to time,' he replies, with an unmistakeable note of sarcasm.

'We're trying to find the Marriott Hotel,' I explain.

He looks at me totally blankly.

'The Marriott Hotel?' I repeat. It's quite a big one and I know it's somewhere nearby; we just can't see it.

He looks at me totally blankly.

'Perhaps you could show me on a map... the Marriott?' I blunder on.

'Oh, that place is very close to here,' he says, almost dismissively, before pulling out a map with what seems like reluctance (I don't like this guy at all). He points to a place behind a museum down by the River Rhine. 'It is behind a construction site. You will see a sign.'

I say thank you and take the map.

He shoots me a fierce look. 'That will be twenty cents,' he snaps. I pay twenty cents; very reasonable really. The tourist information 'welcomer' snatches the coin and says nothing.

Going in the direction we've been told, we cross a square full of puddles. We find the construction work. But there is no Marriott Hotel. I step into a small hotel and ask a receptionist. He explains that the hotel is on the other side of the station, quite a long way away, and he has no idea why we have been sent here. We retrace our steps and arrive at the tall Marriott Hotel; there's a stylish bar on one side of the reception with red velvet padding on the walls and dance music playing. We collect the keys to our rooms, which are on an 'executive floor'. The strategy of leaving early to make the most of the day has backfired – perhaps it was staying up late to watch the Ashes or the beer in Brussels. Despite sleeping at 186 mph most of the way across the Low Countries, we're shattered. We agree to reconvene later after a rest in the 'executive lounge', to which our rooms allow access. We've already checked it out and there appears to be free food and drink, plus computers; all in all, well worth the room upgrade. Just after university, Danny and I drove across America staying along the way at $20 motels of the sort in which murders are committed and cockroaches come free. The days of slumming it, we'd decided before this trip, are behind us.

I have a lie down and call E, who inquires about our plans for the evening. I explain the 'we're not twenty-five anymore' stuff but fail to mention the lunchtime beer. E says: 'Have fun... Don't stay out too late!' And then I check out the executive lounge. Danny is already there, wrestling with one of the computers.

'I mean what is this: pre-Internet?' he says, struggling to send an email. 'This should be in some sort of museum. I don't regard myself as a great technical person, but bloody hell. What's this symbol: is it for some secret society or something?'

He's struggling to find the '@' symbol and getting strange hieroglyphics instead. 'I've been all over the globe but I've never come across this before.'

An assistant in a red jacket comes over. She can't find the '@' symbol either. It's impossible, it seems, to send an email. The woman calls another assistant, as I try to log on at the neighbouring computer on which a notice comes up saying: 'Purchase a voucher from reception.'

The second assistant in a red jacket arrives. She tells me my computer should not be asking for vouchers, and plugs in a code so it works. Then she turns her attention to Danny's problem. 'I don't have a keyboard like this at home,' she says, looking nonplussed. The original assistant says: 'Yes, it is very strange.'

Eventually, the computers both spring to life. But in the midst of this, a manager named Hubert has arrived, to whom I've explained the fast-trains adventure in passing. He looks a little like a middle-aged version of Tintin and he's offered to show me round the hotel, which he declares with aplomb is 'very fashionable... Heidi Klum stayed the other day, she had her after-show party here: oh yes!' The supermodel was raised in Bergisch Gladbach, a city not far from here, he tells me, and I find myself racing to keep up as he paces in a super-energetic manner along a corridor in the direction of the penthouse suite, where Klum and other notables have stayed. It's very big, plush and slightly bland in an international hotel chain sort of way. From the windows we can see the damp cathedral and the city's Media Tower and TV Tower. 'Cologne is the media capital of Germany: there are fifty PR companies in there. Oh yes!'

He paces onwards in his super-energetic manner, telling me over his shoulder that 'to be honest, I prefer the train, I always catch the Thalys to Paris'. He stops in an empty conference hall, which he wants to show me for some reason. He tells me that there are 3,400 Marriotts in the world and that every single bed in every one is exactly the same so that 'you always feel at home wherever you are'.

Then he says, apropos of nothing: 'There's a carnival tonight.'

'A carnival? Where?' I ask, wondering what he's referring to.

'In this hotel: a carnival.'

'Here?' I ask. I haven't seen any sign of carnivals.

'Yes, tonight: when a man gets dressed as a woman,' he replies. 'It's that kind of festival.'

I take this in. 'You mean a transvestite festival... er, carnival?'

'Oh yes!' he replies. 'There will be five hundred to six hundred people,' he continues. 'You can join in if you like. It would look better if you wore a dress, but you don't have to.' He pauses, seeming to enjoy his shock tactic style of information release. 'You can fake it until you make it,' he says, mysteriously, and then he paces onwards once more.

We arrive in another hall with a disco ball and a man with three-day-old stubble wearing a gold ball dress and smoking a cigarette; he's fixing tape onto a microphone on a stage. There are pink tables on which canapés and light sticks are waiting to be twirled on the dance floor. The man in the gold ball dress says '*Tag*' gruffly. We walk up some steps that lead to the reception, as a 200 lb man in a black dress sweeps by holding a guest list.

'Oh, yes!' says Hubert. 'This is also a very good outfit he is wearing: like my grandmother. Or Mrs Thatcher.'

He stops in the reception, where there are no 200 lb men dressed as women. 'This is why I like Cologne!' he says. 'It is not a typical German city. Oh no! People think Germany is full of perfect Bavarians: very strict and distant. But that is not really Germany. That is not Cologne. People are very different here.'

I thank Hubert for the tour. 'Maybe see you later!' he says, as he disappears in a flash in the direction of the bar.

I return to the 'executive lounge', where Danny has ceased cursing the computer. I tell him about the transvestite party with 500 to 600 transvestites at the hotel tonight. 'Good lord,' he replies. 'Really?'

'Yes, really,' I say, explaining that we have just been invited.

'Good lord,' he says once again.

We go to the free bar and take out two bottles of the pale, slightly fizzy local Kölsch beer. They go down very well. And we fetch two more. As we drink and check out the city map, very large American tourists pass, their plates piled with sausages, hashed potatoes and crisps – grabbing handfuls of jelly sweets from a row of jars. The plates are small, so they have to return time after time, grabbing yet more sweets, which they seem to somehow be eating alongside their savoury food. It is bamboozling to witness, in the course of two swiftly consumed bottles of Kölsch, the sheer extent of their eating.

We depart into the Cologne night, about to test the sheer extent of our drinking capacities. We head for the Alter Markt, a big square down by the Rhine that is said to be the place to go for Kölsch beer. We enter a cacophonous bar called Gilden im Zims, where a sign in German translated into English says: 'HOME OF COLOGNE HEROES.' We sit at a rough wooden table near a romantically-engaged couple, the *Fräulein* resting on her boyfriend's knee and whispering sweet nothings into his ear. Then we order two beers from a barman, who swiftly delivers two thin glasses and writes '11' on a beer mat on the table.

'Christ, these are expensive,' I remark.

Danny looks at the menu. 'I think he just means two,' he replies.

We finish our beers very quickly. They are tiny, about a third of the size of a usual pint. Apparently, the point of serving them so small is so they are always fresh and at the right temperature. Just as we are beginning to bemoan the system and say how useless it is, the barman returns as if reading our minds and says: '*Zwei*?' Danny replies: '*Bitte*.' And we have two more beers in little glasses, with '1111' marked on the beer mat. We swiftly reverse our opinion of earlier, discussing how nice it is to be drinking very fresh beer like this. Then Danny begins to debate dinner.

'I mean, shall we go for traditional German fare or should we just go for a curry?' he asks, sounding as though this is a serious matter indeed.

'Definitely traditional fare,' I reply.

'Not a curry?' he asks, as though we could be about to make a big mistake.

'Definitely not a curry,' I say, as I ask for the bill, which comes to six euros and forty cents. It's my round. As I have six euros and sixty cents or else a fifty-euro note, I put the former amount on the beer mat marked '1111'.

'What an ambassador for your country,' remarks Danny. 'A twenty-cent tip.'

We cross the square and enter a beer hall that doubles as a restaurant named Pfaffen-Brauerei. Inside, we find a room with a high wooden ceiling, exposed wooden walls, wooden tables and wooden chairs, all with decorative floral carvings. A window near the entrance is filled with stained-glass panes depicting devilish characters wearing sunglasses. It's an odd sort of place and only a few of the tables are full, though they appear to be German locals.

'Two beers?' says the waiter, who has a bit of English and is wearing Michael Caine-style dark-framed glasses.

'*Ja bitte*,' says Danny.

'What would you like to eat?'

We look at the heavily meat-based menu: bacon, liver sausages, black pudding, pork, 'rumpsteak', saddle of wild boar, venison, goulash, *Wiener schnitzels*. The waiter pipes up: 'How about leg of pork.' He pats his leg. 'With mashed potato and sauerkraut?'

We both say yes, the menu's too much to take in.

'That was very easy,' he responds, pleased.

Our beers arrive and we drink our beers. Danny has suddenly, and vehemently, taken against Kölsch beer. 'I want a dark beer!' he declares. 'I don't want to drink this ****. It's like drinking nothing; like maid's water.'

He nevertheless finishes it and orders a dark beer.

Our food comes: two giant cuts of meat, with large sections of crackling on top of a mound of potatoes with sauerkraut on the side. Our knives are presented sticking out of the crackling as though they have been plunged downwards in some kind of death-stab.

'Gluttony at its best,' is Danny's verdict, and mine too, as we work our way through the pile of German food under the gaze of the devilish figures wearing sunglasses.

We order more beers, Danny switching back to Kölsch as he now realises he prefers it to dark beer.

And then we take a cab to an area the waiter recommended, Friesenplatz, just off the city centre. Memories of this period of the evening are sketchy. We go to a bar called Brauerei Päffgen (vague recollection: older clientele, lanterns and long wooden tables), and then a bar called Stuck (vague recollection: younger clientele, neon lights, cocktails, pop music). We return to the hotel. There is confusion over my room key, which I'm guessing has been wiped out as it's been in my pocket next to my mobile phone, and the magnet from the phone usually wipes out hotel cards. A passport or driving licence is required to prove my identity, but I don't have these as they are in my room. Meanwhile, as these negotiations go on, Danny goes to the bar and orders *two more Kölsch beers*. There are no signs of '500 to 600 transvestites', they all appear to be down in the conference room, from which dance music thuds. My key is fixed. We drink our final beers of the evening, as if for luck. And head back to the executive floor. It has been a very long *Tag*.

It's got the makings of quite a long *Morgen* the next day, too. We reconvene in the executive lounge, which is beginning to feel like home in Cologne, where breakfast is served. There is a pale blue sky above the media and television towers of the city.

'I'm in desperate need of some paracetamol,' says Danny. 'Maybe we should lay off a bit tonight. Start later. What time did we get back?'

'I'm not sure,' I reply, feeling edgy. 'After midnight, I know that much.'

'Yes, it was late,' says Danny.

'Very,' I say shakily.

We go to the breakfast bar and collect scrambled eggs and bacon and sausages and toast and beans and hash browns and fried tomatoes and little rolls and croissants; just like our fellow guests. We eat these. Danny goes for more and begins to perk up remarkably. 'Don't worry about paracetamol!' he says, out of the blue. 'I'm fine. Fine!'

But I'm not, and am astonished at this sudden and unexpected burst of exuberance.

'I felt like an observer,' Danny continues, turning ruminative. 'Yes, an observer.' He appears to be referring to last night. 'Sometimes as a tourist you feel as though you are seeing a constructed reality.'

I look at him in frank amazement at what I'm hearing.

'Yes, the tourist sees the constructed reality. But I feel that we were in the middle of it all. Observers. Yes, observers! Like social anthropologists!'

He seems on top form and it's only 10 a.m. I finish the last of my scrambled eggs.

Then we go downstairs, where a man with a goatee, a grey hoodie and a ski jacket is waiting to meet us. Andre Fischer is a guide who works for the local tourist board. We don't tell him about the fellow who sent us in the wrong direction yesterday. Instead we step forth into sunny Cologne, heading for the cathedral, and crossing the modern station. It's a bracing, bright day, the kind of morning that wakes you up and clears your head, and I soon realise I'm not feeling too bad at all. Remarkable really, after all those Kölschs: nothing short of a miracle. It's got to be a temporary 'feel good' lull.

As we progress out of the station and onwards, Andre is telling us that there will be a direct link on German-owned ICE trains to London from 2013. The journey time to the city is to be reduced to less than four hours on slick new trains with top speeds of 200 mph; a clear example of the steady high-speed train revolution in Europe. Given that our journey took about six hours with the long, though enjoyable, wait in Brussels, I get the feeling that a whole lot more Britons, and travellers in general, will be coming this way soon.

Andre is an enthusiast for All Things Cologne... and he's soon telling us an intriguing history of which we knew absolutely nothing. Cologne was, he tells us, an important Roman settlement that grew up around 50 BC when Julius Caesar was conquering Europe and when the city had the official name Colonia Claudia Ara Agrippinensium – which was perhaps why the shortened version eventually prevailed. It was a Roman city until the middle of the fifth century, when it was taken by the Franks. But for many years it was the north-eastern border of Roman civilisation. 'The barbarians were over there,' says Andre, waving in the direction of the other side of the Rhine. 'Just like they are today. We still make that joke. Over here there was always wine and Latin. Over there they were illiterate, without any nations – just wandering through the woods. Like on the other side of Hadrian's Wall.'

'Scottish savages,' mutters Danny.

'Yes,' says Andre. 'But it was safer here: nobody could throw a spear or shoot an arrow across the river.'

He begins to rattle off a few stats. Cologne is the fourth biggest city in Germany after Berlin, Hamburg and Munich. The river across to the current-day barbarians is 350 metres wide. The cathedral is the third church on its site. Construction of the cathedral began in 1248 and lasted 632 years (pretty good going even by British builder standards). For nine years from 1880, it was the tallest building in the world. More than 60 per cent of the local population is Catholic, and people from 183 countries live in the city. 'We are very cosmopolitan,' Andre declares, in a determined manner. The population is almost exactly one million. The local football club, FC Köln, won the German title three times in the 1980s, though it is third bottom in the table during our visit.

Then he asks us for a stat of our own: 'In the last World Cup, can you tell me the score between Germany and England?'

A funny fellow, this Andre.

We enter the Römisch-Germanisches Museum. This is in an ugly grey building on the square by the cathedral that Danny and I had vowed to give a miss after seeing it when trudging hopelessly lost in search of the hotel yesterday. It just goes to show that appearances can be very deceptive. Inside, there is a wonderful collection of mosaics, busts, columns and old relics from the Roman period. We ascend a staircase that overlooks the most beautiful mosaic I've ever seen: mallards, peacocks, parrots and leopards are depicted in striking colours, with Dionysus holding court in the middle, the God of wine seeming to be enjoying himself immensely, while leaning on a satyr and surrounded by nymphs. All around stand grand Roman columns.

'To see anything on this scale you will have to go to Italy,' says Andre proudly. 'This would have been the floor of a Roman house. Dionysus is leaning on the satyr because he is drunk. You see he is tickling a nymph: they are about to go somewhere more private. There have been some very nice parties on these tiles over the years, you can be sure of that.'

We enter a virtual reality room. Danny and I glance at each other in an 'oh no' kind of way; the very look of the room gives me a sudden Kölsch hangover twinge. I've always dodged this kind of place in museums, for fear of not understanding how to make the computers work or suddenly pressing a button and finding myself watching a fifteen-minute film about working-class conditions in the 1930s. But we don't learn about pre-war working-class life in Cologne, as interesting as that may be. Instead, Andre is pressing a few simple switches that transform the city from how it looks now into how it would have in

Roman times, with the modern outline faintly below. You can zoom in and out and can see where the outer defence wall once was – we'd ventured beyond this last night to Friesenplatz in search of beers.

In a few minutes, we get an incredibly strong sense of city; one that's impossible to grasp amid the higgledy-piggledy streets with all the usual high-street shops in 1950s buildings and beer halls in structures rebuilt after World War Two, during which the twin spires of the cathedral are said to have been used as a sighter by Allied bombers. Much of Cologne was rebuilt in the 1950s and 1960s (though nowhere near as much as Rotterdam).

'The museum is not so very beautiful from the outside, but inside it is super-interesting,' says Andre.

He begins to wax lyrical about the city. 'We Cologners are very proud of our culture,' he says. 'First we are Cologners, then we are Europeans, then we are Germans. Over the years we have been part of the Roman Empire, then a city state, then part of France, and then Germany. When Germany was founded by Bismarck in 1871... we became part. But only then!'

He pauses. 'We are Cologners first!' he says, almost pounding his chest. 'Cologners! Cologners!'

Once Andre has this out of his system, we continue down to the river. He tells us about the original eau de Cologne – invented in the eighteenth century by Giovanni Maria Farina, an Italian perfumer in the city who aimed to recreate a scent to remind himself of 'an Italian spring morning, of mountain daffodils and orange blossoms after the rain'. Although Andre, who is becoming franker and franker, says: 'I hate the stuff, it smells horrible.' He assures us that 'the old town is not old, don't be misled, many of the buildings are new'. He waves to a female friend in the distance. 'She is a lesbian,' he informs us. 'She is not alone. About 10 per cent of the population is estimated to drive on the other side of the road. Cologne is famous for its homosexual subculture.'

I mention the transvestite festival in our hotel last night.

'Quite normal, oh yes!' he responds, sounding a little like Hubert the hotel manager.

We reach a green metal train bridge over the Rhine, which E and I crossed on the way to Frankfurt. On our journey east, we'd noticed a statue of a figure on a horse, which we're coming up to now.

'Who is that?' I ask.

'Wilhelm II, the last German emperor. A complete idiot! A total moron!'

He moves onwards, reaching an extraordinary fence covered in thousands of locked padlocks, running alongside a footpath. 'It was a craze that began two years ago. Nobody knows why. People lock a padlock and throw the key in the water, so that the love will last – like the lock.' He pauses and adds: 'I personally enjoy a combination lock. I mean what if you get divorced? Are you going to go fishing?'

He paces ahead once more as an extraordinary siren breaks out across the city, echoing over the river. I ask what this is; I haven't heard anything like it anywhere else before. The wailing noise is, says Andre, an annual siren test 'in case of catastrophes'. It's more than a little disconcerting. Here we are in the centre of a German city that we've just been told took a pounding during the war, with emergency sirens echoing eerily across the rooftops as though Cologne is under attack; bombers on the way.

Almost inevitably, we get talking about the war. 'When my mother refers to that time, she just talks about "the war", not about the Nazis or the Third Reich,' he says, the sirens still sounding. 'It made people very, very ashamed... what we did to Jewish people.

He looks down the Rhine, in the direction of the river's source in Switzerland. 'But then in the 1960s we had the first "innocent generation",' he continues, referring to the first generation of adults who were born after the war. 'And since then we have been dealing with that part of our past. There were the "68ers", who created a new state of mind. They accused the older generation, asking them: "What have you done?" All of this ended with the reunification of the country.' He pauses again. 'Yes, that was the end. The reunification created a whole new Germany. It is different now.'

ICE trains, Romans, barbarians, cathedrals, perfumes, lesbians, padlock lovers' declarations of devotion, and, of course, the difficult matter of 'the war': Andre has been brilliantly offbeat and candid. After the bridge, Danny and I say goodbye. I know that some people believe that tourist guides give you a superficial and hackneyed view of a place. But not all do. And when you're a bit hungover in an unfamiliar city on the western edge of Germany, they can be very helpful for setting you right on a few matters.

As if to reward ourselves for Valiant Acts of Tourism Not Involving Beer Halls, we turn down a lane and enter Peters Brauhaus, just off Alter Markt. Admittedly, this is a beer hall, but we're only going in for lunch. And so, amid wooden tables and with a waitress dressed in some kind of traditional costume with flowers and frills, we launch into a modest little meal starting with 'a soup of corn with thin threats [sic] of chilli' for me, and potatoes with herrings for Danny. 'They're virtually alive,' he comments, of the herrings. First courses come with thick slabs of bread, plus a glass of apple juice for me (the waitress eyes me as though I am off my rocker) and a non-alcoholic beer for Danny, against my advice.

'It's undrinkable. Horrible,' he says.

'I did tell you,' I reply.

'Yes you did,' he says. 'It's like treacle.'

This sparkling conversation takes us into our main courses. Danny has opted for a bucket-sized bowl of steaming mussels, while I've gone for 'green cabbage with smoked pork and sausages'. We plough through this substantial fare in contented silence. And when we finish Danny says: 'This is a very pleasant way to spend a Saturday, isn't it?'

'Absolutely,' I agree.

'You've got to have some apple strudel in Germany,' he adds.

'Absolutely,' I agree once more.

He waves over the waitress, and we finish off this snack-on-the-run lunch with thick slabs of strudel covered with cream.

Superb. We highly recommend Peters Brauhaus.

Feeling at peace with the world, we tuck in another tourist attraction: the Wallraf-Richartz Museum, just round the corner. This contains contemporary art including a photography exhibition on our visit featuring naked pregnant women, old men sitting down to Dunkin' Donuts meals while watching porno films, moody boxers, and a man posing as Jesus Christ wearing Y-fronts. 'Let's do this at walking pace,' says Danny, who is not impressed. Upstairs, though, there are beautiful pictures by greats including Rembrandt, Rubens, Monet, Dürer, Van Gogh and Munch: masterpiece after masterpiece. 'I'm enjoying this a lot more,' says Danny, a little grudgingly in the face of some of the world's finest paintings.

Then we tackle the cathedral. While visiting a beautiful cathedral that has taken 632 years to build may sound like a pleasurable thing to do, it's not when you decide to climb to the top fairly soon after putting away lunches at Peters Brauhaus. It takes us several minutes to find the tucked-away entrance to the fabled South Tower, with its 509 steps to a viewing platform way above. We pay a few euros, and then begin the ascent.

'It's like a recurring nightmare... Jesus please... Oh God, lord, there's more,' Danny says, speaking for us both as we make our way up the steep spiral staircase and, thinking we've reached the upper platform, come to a huge atrium-like space with another staircase in a metal cage heading straight up. 'There's more? Why are we doing this? Jesus... Oh lord... I don²t know why they haven't got a lift... Jesus... Jesus,' runs Danny's commentary. I suppose he's in the right place to be asking for assistance from the Almighty.

But it's worth the climb. We gaze across the city, seeing the sweep of the mighty, muddy Rhine, the loops of the green bridge with its padlocks, the modern shopping district, the media towers, and the spires of the city's many Romanesque churches, reconstructed after the war. Wind whistles past as tourists crowd round taking pictures. It's a smaller, more compact city than Frankfurt, nowhere near as spread out and green as the financial capital of Germany.

We descend. We walk through the enormous main hall of the church, passing an area with a sign that says: 'ENTRANCE FOR CONFESSION ONLY,' where Danny, who was brought up Catholic, stops and comments: 'You have to confess to all your sins in there... We'd be in for hours.' He looks nostalgically towards the confessional boxes as though remembering more innocent days: 'When I was a kid, we used to go in and make things up: "I didn't help an old lady cross the road, Father," things like that.' We stand looking past the sign at the boxes, and a man in a red tunic gives us a look that suggests: 'Please move along now.' So we do, along to the hotel – for a break before our second assault on Cologne at night.

This time we're off for a Turkish meal. As a result of the policy of *Gastarbeiter* ('guest workers') in Germany that was at its height in the 1960s and 1970s, many immigrants came to the country to take up jobs left unfilled in West Germany's booming economy. Now about 6 per cent of the city's population is of Turkish origin. Earlier, Andre had recommended that we try a place called Öz Harran Doy Doy, not far from our hotel on the north side of the station.

So after a sharpener in our favourite executive lounge, we head towards a street called Weidengasse, passing a series of kebab fast-food joints and 'YES DISCOUNT!' shops in a district that doesn't feel as though it attracts too many tourists. We locate the unusually-named restaurant, and gather from its menu and from looking through the window that alcohol is not served. We pop across the street for a pre-dinner drink at a poky bar, the only one we can see round here.

There's a fug of smoke and rave music is playing at low volume. A man wearing a ragged coat is sitting on a stool at the bar and making crazy clucking sounds. There are strings of red Christmas tree lights, a couple of Monte Carlo Casino fruit machines, and a black waitress with gold hoop earrings named Jacaita. She's originally from Nairobi, but spent some time living in Harrow and Nottingham as a care worker, she tells us chattily as she delivers Kölsch beers and marks a bar mat '11' on our simple Formica table. The music turns to 'Say You, Say Me' by Lionel Richie and the man at the bar stops clucking, and proceeds to croon to the lyrics.

Danny is getting philosophical. 'Basically, when you get to a certain age, you realise the human condition is tragic,' he says, as he nods to order more beers. 'Our little lives come and go. It's so fleeting isn't it?'

I nod and sip my Kölsch.

'I mean, I'm not being morbid, I'm just aware of mortality. We're only here for a finite period. Yet we worry about trivial things at work. I mean, we'll all be dead in fifty years, so what's the point in worrying?'

I nod again and sip my Kölsch. The man by the bar has begun clucking again. Meanwhile, a companion has begun slurring along to the lyrics of 'No Woman, No Cry' by Bob Marley. We spend half an hour or so discussing the 'human condition'; this bar in this part of Cologne seems to bring that out of you.

Then, after being accosted by the Clucker – 'you don't know if people are going to stab you, pat you on the back or embrace you round here,' says Danny – we cross the street to the Turkish restaurant and eat chicken kebabs with generous piles of rice and salad, accompanied by glasses of iced Coca-Cola; served swiftly in an elegantly decorated room with a ceiling painted sky blue and dotted with gold flowers. The food is fresh, spicy, cheap and very good indeed. Turkish music twangs. Waiters dressed in black scoot about. On the wall near the open kitchen, there's a picture of Mesut Özil, the German-born son of a Turkish immigrant who's now one of the stars of the national football team.

'You come here and you realise how important it must be that Germany's best player is Turkish,' says Danny.

You do, there's clearly a lot of pride. 'He was brilliant in the World Cup,' I say.

'Absolutely fantastic,' says Danny, drinking his Coke. 'I'm sure that his being there made it that much less likely that people round here would support Turkey rather than Germany.'

We finish our kebabs. And, well fed yet again, we head off into the chilly Saturday night. The streets round here are surprisingly empty. We go in the direction of the cathedral. And though we thought we had already achieved this feat, we soon come to a place that has to be The Biggest Dive in Cologne. We venture through a door under a neon sign. Inside, steel band music plays over a stereo and lost souls stagger drunkenly in the company of barfly women with spaced-out eyes.

One of them sidles up and asks in German for a drink. She doesn't seem bothered when we decline, her eyes flickering upwards as though saying: 'Suit yourselves fellas. I got other places to be.' No doubt she does. She totters away, looking as though she's on a completely different planet.

We continue on to our favourite tourist trap: Alter Markt. This is more like it. We resume the noble task of notching up pencil marks on beer mats, like all good beer-drinking weekend breakers. It's another lively night out in the jolly *Brauhäuser*: great atmosphere, quick service, cheap drinks and plenty of ice-cold beer served in funny little glasses.

There's no doubt about it: just as Bruges was the perfect fast-train destination for romance, Cologne is definitely where to go to let your hair down.

In the morning we're feeling shocking. But it's a content shocking: even if small things such as finding train tickets and walking short distances to train stations, where correct trains need to be located and boarded before they depart, induce stabs of deep-down pain somewhere behind the eyes.

'How are you feeling?' I ask Danny.

He looks at me queasily but does not reply. Instead, he goes to buy a Burger King cheeseburger as some sort of top-up breakfast.

Then we catch the correct train west towards Brussels, setting off into countryside bathed in warm orange light.

After a period of silence, just enjoying the view, Danny pipes up. 'Mission accomplished,' he says, polishing off the last of his burger.

I think he's referring to the weekend, not his food.

Another high-speed weekend – and yet more evidence of how Europe is changing thanks to all these faster trains. With the new 200 mph ICE trains coming soon, and with people like Hubert and Andre talking casually about zipping to Paris and Brussels as though it's no big thing, I get the strongest sense yet of the shrinking Continent. In a fortnight's time, I'm going with E on the final trip. It's the furthest distance so far. And a new country and a very different experience lie down a brand new high-speed track.

We're off to the Costa Brava for the weekend.

CHAPTER THIRTEEN

GIRONA AND PARIS: 'SURREAL SEASIDES AND THOUGHTS BY THE SEINE'

There remained one last journey: the longest yet. I wanted to test the future. As the high-speed network explodes – more than 2,200 miles of tracks are under construction in Europe – it will soon be possible to travel for weekend breaks far beyond the comfort zone of nearby Europe. How about, I suggested to E, a last hurrah to the far side of the Pyrenees? It would be over 800 miles and take ten hours, but it would test whether it is now practical to say goodbye to easyJet and Ryanair for fast-train weekend breaks that few would have contemplated even when I was planning this book.

We have three days to play with, and it's likely to prove a slightly mad dash. But wouldn't it be wonderful to arrive in Spain a few hours after our final meeting at the Betjeman statue and that now familiar journey through Kent and northern France? It is still late winter, and we would be leaving the leaden skies of London and waking to the clear blue light of the Costa Brava, a stroll from the fruit markets, the flower stalls, the sparkling Mediterranean. At least, we hope so.

Can we really make a weekend of it? If so, it would prove that high speed is now offering a different dimension. And why not, on our way back, stop for one last nostalgic night in Paris? After all, Paris was the first destination most people enjoyed when the Channel Tunnel opened nearly twenty years ago and made the adventures that E and I have been enjoying totally possible. This last journey would top and tail our fast-train adventures neatly.

Standing on the corner by the M&S amid the forest of columns by the security check at St Pancras, I work out that it is five months and one week since these weekends began. But the sense of adventure is as strong as ever, and the station still feels like a part of London that's not really London: modern, efficient, sparkling clean and generally well-run (not characteristics that spring to mind when I think of the rest of the capital). Staff in charcoal uniforms head to their Eurostar posts. Commuters who have arrived on the new high-speed trains from Kent walk on by to Friday tasks.

Looking around, each place here now has a memory. Le Pain Quotidien cafe is where I sat one chilly morning while a nearby elderly American couple debated the rights and wrongs of giving money to London beggars after a twitchy man had shuffled up cupping his hands: 'I wanted to give them something: but are they just gonna spend it on drugs?' Not long back from Frankfurt, I'd piped up: 'Probably "yes" with that one.' And then felt uncharitable: maybe he was just down on his luck. I've perused the Fat Face clothes shop one idle hour. I've picked up notebooks, novels and guides at Foyles. I've bought wine at this M&S. Just across the way, E had a crisis one morning, when she arrived late on her bike, having realised she'd lost the key for her padlock. She'd cycled to a nearby shop and bought another and we'd only just made the train.

A woman whose face I recognise, wearing a camel-coloured coat and carrying a red House of Lords bag, appears looking a little lost: Estelle Morris, the former Secretary of State for Education, now a baroness, who resigned from her post after admitting 'I just don't think I'm good at it'. If only more politicians could be as honest. She shuffles in the direction of the bookshop. And moments later E arrives, no padlock emergency this time. We go up to the level of the platform and a man in a khaki cap kindly takes a picture of the two of us by the Betjeman statue. 'Just think: this is the last one, the last time,' says E, as we make our way down to the check-in gates. We clear security. We board our final train from St Pancras. We pass the derelict lots of the East End and the motorways of Kent under a mottled grey sky. At Calais we stop 'to pick up passengers from a train with a technical problem: please do not leave the train here'. Fast trains, as we've discovered, are not always fast. Rain patters on the carriage roof as we make our way through the lowlands. In Paris, we catch an underground RER train to Gare de Lyon, competing for space with commuters. 'That guy looked like he wanted to kill you,' says E, as we squeeze onto an escalator. We board our TGV, sitting on purple seats. We move very slowly, then quickly out of Paris. I buy bottles of water from the buffet car: they're three euros each. '*Très cher*,' I comment, handing over the cash. '*Oui*,' replies the no-nonsense buffet man. A soft copper sun sets slowly to the west, turning the sky pink and orange, against a background of cobalt blue. 'Wow, it's amazing,' says E. And the train rolls onwards, southwards – past village steeples, farmers on tractors and vineyards funnelling in neat rows into the distance, bathed in delicious golden light.

This trip from London to Girona is roughly 870 miles. Our train from St Pancras departed at 10.20 a.m. This train left Paris at 3.20 p.m. and is due to arrive in Figueres in Spain at 8.48 p.m., when there's a short connecting service to Girona arriving at 9.33 p.m. Total journey time: 10 hrs 13 min. This works out at an average of 85 mph over the entire trip. Is this madness or is this fun, I'm thinking? Why not take a plane for this one?

Because you wouldn't see the world go by. Rugged mountains with wispy clouds on snow-tipped peaks stretch westwards. Lazy rivers twist slowly into open plains. Bumpy fields populated by horses and cattle roll into valleys beyond. Wild hedgerows ramble and crumbling stone walls crumble.

The sun drops away in the direction of the Atlantic. It grows dark. We arrive at the yellow lights of Nîmes in Languedoc-Roussillon at 6.20 p.m. We look across the city known for its Roman ruins and for being the birthplace of the world's most popular material: *de Nîmes* fabric, originally made for slaves in the US Deep South in the nineteenth century, before becoming denim jeans (which we're both wearing now). A whistle blows. The doors close. The train continues onwards through the quiet darkness of the South of France.

The train pulls in at Montpellier, one of the most vibrant cities in the south, said to have an average age of twenty-five; so says our *Rough Guide*. Lots of people get off. No one gets on. And E wistfully says: 'I've always wanted to go to Montpellier.'

Next comes Agde, another Roman town, originally Greek like Marseilles, on the coast of the Med. But we can't see the water; it's too dark for that. More passengers disembark. No one embarks. And E says: 'I wonder what it's like in Agde?'

Narbonne is even darker, and grimly industrial-looking. There are football floodlights and neon signs advertising 'DISCOTHEQUE' on the edge of Perpignan, where the last passengers in our carriage depart, leaving a solitary man sleeping with his coat over his head at the far end.

'We really are the final survivors!' declares E, sounding dramatic, as though the toil of travel is taking its toll.

'This is true,' I agree, eyeing the snoring lump in the corner.

'The dregs of the dregs!' she says. 'The survivors of a nuclear fallout! It's like a party when everyone's gone home,' she continues, warming to her theme and glancing at the snorer. 'A bad party! It's 3 a.m. and we're wandering round the rooms…'

She tails off, looks thoughtful, and says: 'Last night, my sister said: "You do know that easyJet goes to Barcelona?"' She pauses, as if for effect. 'I said to her: "Yes, I know: we're weird."'

'We are a bit,' I concede, as the TGV sinks into a tunnel through the Pyrenees. It is 8.50 p.m., nine and a half hours since we left St Pancras.

E says nothing. She begins filing her nails. We shoot out of the tunnel, and our mobiles bleep into action for Spain. There's an announcement that we'll be arriving shortly in Figueres.

'Perhaps they should re-do that one and say: "If anyone is still alive, we're about to arrive in Figueres. You will be awarded a medal on disembarkation",' says E, enjoying a good rant. 'I mean, seriously, look at that guy,' she continues.

I look at the man with the coat over his head in the corner, who is being poked by a guard.

'I mean, he could be dead or alive right now.'

We haven't heard him snoring for a while.

But the lump comes alive. Everyone gets off at Figueres and most of us cross the platform to a train for Barcelona that has been held waiting for ours. Classical music is playing in wide carriages lit with neon bulbs; it looks as though we've entered a moving hospital ward. A xylophone sounds and there's a rapid announcement in Spanish in which we catch something that sounds like *destinacio Girona, Barcelona Sants*. And then we're

off. Bizet's *Carmen* starts up. The music echoes round the almost
empty pale-green carriages. A digital display says the train is
going at 120 kph (75 mph). I buy one-euro sodas from a machine.
The moving hospital playing Bizet arrives in Girona at 9.33 p.m.

We disembark with a handful of others into a deserted,
fluorescent station. There's a Café Gratis shop selling cheap
sandwiches and nothing much else. I buy two sandwiches for dinner
(no German pork crackling, sausages and sauerkraut gluttonous
feasts tonight). Then a cab takes us through quiet streets, passing
a bank that says it is 8°C; the temperature back home had been
just above zero. Tall ochre buildings line the cobbled roads. Over
a bridge we see the beautiful lit-up cathedral: a giant cube on a
hilltop, dominating the little city below (population 95,000).

Hotel Llegendes is in a narrow street. The taxi driver and I have
an altercation over paying with a fifty-euro note; completing a fine
set of cab disputes which now covers most destinations reachable
by high-speed rail in Europe. We enter a lobby with classical
figures, daybeds (in case you feel like a snooze in the reception,
or so it would seem), and golden lights shaped like eyes hanging
from the ceiling. We collect a key to a room across the street,
cross the cobbles and find ourselves in a cold, dimly-lit abode
with temporary radiators dotted about. There's a mini kitchen
with water that seems to be supplied by a garden hose that snakes
through a hole in a window. The bathroom comes complete with
a prominently displayed bucket and mop. A portrait of a dour
Catalan couple hangs on a wall next to a dusty grandfather clock
telling the wrong time. We can hear trains rumbling by and youths
cackling and singing in the street below the bedroom window.

'At least the noise is cultured noise,' says E, as another group
clatters past.

'I'm sorry,' I say. It was my choice to go for this place; it had
looked so good on the website.

'At least they're not going 'arrrrrggh' like they do back in Britain or in Belgium,' she says, remembering our Antwerp night. 'It's almost sophisticated. At least when they're drunk they sing proper songs,' she continues, putting a pillow over her head.

Another group passes our windows, bellowing a tune.

'I'm sorry,' I say again, feeling a little guilty that I've dragged E 870 miles across Europe in a series of fast trains to spend the weekend in a chilly side street next to a run of bars in a small city in north-east Spain.

Silence reigns under the pillow.

This is a whistle-stop weekend. We've got two nights in Girona before a morning train to Paris. This gives us one full day in Spain, for which I've hired a car so we can see as much as possible. In particular, we want to go to Cadaqués, the tiny port and old artist colony on the Costa Brava that attracted the likes of Picasso, Man Ray, Thomas Mann and Salvador Dali, who settled nearby with his wife Gala. We also want to go to the Dali museum in Figueres, the town where the great surrealist was born in 1904.

In the morning I go down to the lobby across the street, where a receptionist named Laura wearing a black polo neck kindly lets us change from the apartment to a much-smarter room in the much-smarter main hotel (I feel as though we've switched quite a few hotel bedrooms on these trips).

Laura is all smiles, telling me the hotel has been open two years and attracts a fair number of British visitors as well as professional cyclists from around the world; who come for the rugged landscape and high altitude. 'The US Postal Service Team and other pros have stayed,' she says, after showing me the other room, which is really nice and extremely stylish (in other words:

very E friendly). Many of the best cyclists ever have lived in the city, she adds, including Lance Armstrong.

What are they like, I ask?

'They train hard and they have loads of massages,' she says, reaching into a cabinet.

From this, she hands me a leaflet about the Girona Cycle Centre, which arranges trips along 'some of the best twisty mountain roads in the world: test your fitness on challenging climbs and your bike handling on the downhill', it says, making me wish we'd organised this in advance. Then she passes over another leaflet, this one belonging to the hotel. It's entitled *The Eros Sofa Manual*.

'What's this?' I ask.

'It is an erotic,' she replies.

'Oh,' I say.

'It is an erotic,' she repeats. 'We have three of them.'

It transpires that the hotel has three rooms with 'Eros Sofas' designed for 'practising tantric sex, an oriental tradition which has developed an infinite variety of sexual techniques'. The leaflet has headings saying 'make your room a temple of love', 'let rhythmic breathing take control' and 'the kiss of desire'. It ends by advising guests to follow the steps shown (there are drawings showing positions) to achieve 'the tantric orgasm, an experience which goes much further than the mere genital pleasure we obtain in our Western tradition… opening up an enormous number of options to bring you new sensations you had never dreamed of!'

What a place. There is not, however, a love sofa in our new room. Laura goes behind the reception and brings out a pack containing strawberry-scented oils. 'We include these in our love packages,' she says straightforwardly, as though she's telling me how the shower works.

I return to the chilly apartment armed with two coffees, a basket of croissants and an *Eros Sofa Manual*, which E grabs and says: 'Ah I see! You were off getting Spanish lessons from erotic sofa ladies!'

She peruses the document. 'Oh my lord,' she mutters, reading the 'temple of love' section, in which guests are recommended to lower the ringtones of their mobile phones 'or disconnect it completely, thus ensuring you will not be interrupted... and after two or three hours of tantric caresses...'

'It's really funny, this,' she says sipping her coffee. 'I thought you were taking a while... off getting your erotic Spanish dancing lessons.'

E is silent as she reads. 'It says here it's all for your "spiritual development",' she says, putting the leaflet down, raising an eyebrow, appearing highly sceptical about the spiritual motivation of the *Eros Sofa Manual,* and saying: 'Pfffph!'

On the streets, Girona is quiet and beautiful. It's a perfect morning, with a pale-blue sky and sunlight splashing brightly against the terracotta rooftops of the tall pastel-coloured terraces near the very unusual Hotel Llegendes.

We walk down a lane and stop in front of the church of Sant Feliu. This is a gorgeous church overlooking a little square with expensive bicycles chained to a public bike rack. There's an inviting restaurant serving two-course meals with a beer or a glass of wine included for €11 (of which I make a mental note... very cheap). Not really knowing where we're going, we walk up well-worn steps behind the church and find ourselves outside the Arab Baths. We go in. Here we learn that the Moors controlled Girona for around seventy years during the eighth century until it was conquered by Charlemagne in 785. These baths, however, were built subsequently, in the twelfth century, as Arab-style bathing was apparently all the rage around then.

Yet again, we are the only tourists. 'I reckon we're the only ones in the whole of Girona,' whispers E. And she could well be right. It's a nice sensation walking through the empty, old stone rooms – there's not exactly an enormous amount to see in Girona's Arab Baths – and stopping on the roof terrace, where pigeons are cooing and the pale-blue sky looks perfect.

The city, we soon find, is a lovely place to wander around. We go down narrow lanes in the direction that feels like the centre, enjoying the peacefulness of this charming medieval place: we're already glad we came. Soon, we reach the cathedral. We ascend its eighty-six steps to the enormous façade, which is decorated with recesses in which austere figures clasp swords, mighty tomes and giant keys that look as though they belong to city gates. We look down to the River Onyar, almost totally hidden by tightly-packed buildings connected by labyrinthine alleys, and across to spectacular snow-capped mountains.

We enter. We've been to a fair few cathedrals on these fast-trains adventures – as E has often wryly noted – but this is perhaps our favourite (along with Notre-Dame de la Garde and its splendid views back in Marseilles). It's the sheer scale of the building, which has a huge space in the middle for pews and altars, yet there are no columns supporting the structure. Instead, there is a quite amazing vaulted ceiling, so far up you can hardly see it – smash a tennis ball with all your might and I don't think it would hit the top – unless you were Spain's Rafael Nadal, perhaps. The cathedral has the widest nave in the world and second tallest, only 3 metres short of St Peter's in Rome. At the time the design was being considered in 1417, many doubted the roof would hold together. But the architect has been proved right for the past 600 years. And you can't help thinking: 'Good on him. Now just hold on for half an hour or so more.'

There are beautiful stained-glass windows casting violet and cranberry light across the flagstone floors. We leave as Gregorian chants begin from somewhere in the direction of the cloisters, and head out into sunlight, passing through the old Jewish quarter, or *call* (ghetto). This is considered to be one of the best preserved Jewish quarters in Europe, where a thriving community lived until the Jews were expelled from Spain in 1492. We soak up the atmosphere of the lanes and little courtyards, passing old-fashioned grocery shops with neatly-stacked shelves of everything and anything from bottles of rum to tins of syrup, vegemite jars, pots of olives and dried sausages. Further down there are fruit and vegetable shops overflowing with fresh produce, as well as retailers selling skis and salopettes; a reminder of how close we are to the Pyrenees. We cross the flat, still river, with its banks of reeds and rows of colourful houses packed on each side, some looking as though they are about to topple into the water. From here we can see the tower and cupola on top of the cathedral; invisible from directly below. The river curls towards our hotel, with a cute, red, metal-framed bridge for pedestrians in the distance.

It's about five minutes to the railway station, where we have the hire car to collect. We cross the empty concourse and find the rental car office. E examines magazines in a newsagent while I produce the documents (E does not have a driver's licence, though she vehemently asserts that she 'knows how to drive').

The rental chap is Nick, from Hayes in Middlesex. He's a nice fellow and seems lonely stuck in his bright, antiseptic rental car office in the north-east of Spain. In the course of checking my licence and taking my credit card details, he tells me he moved here a couple of years ago after falling in love with a local woman. This romance has fallen through, but he still has his job and 'enjoys the area'. All of this I learn before I'm required to sign anything: he seems glad of some English company. It doesn't appear as though many customers, English-speaking or not, have been through of late.

'Where are you off to?' he asks.

I explain about Cadaqués and the Dali museum in Figueres.

'Cadaqués,' he responds with authority, suddenly sounding like a sergeant major briefing his troops. 'Very Mediterranean. White houses and all that. Roads arc twisty on the way. Twisty. Very.'

I study a map he's given me as he continues mysteriously clicking on his computer. I ask about a place on the coast called L'Escala. It looks as though it may be nice.

Nick glances up. 'L'Escala,' he says. 'Famous for its anchovies. Twisty roads. Not so bad. Decent.'

He concentrates once more on his clicking. Then he asks: 'So how did you get here?'

I explain the mammoth train journey.

'Oh yes,' he replies. 'I've heard they widened the track. Wider. Faster. But I had a guy here the other day. English. Said it wasn't as comfortable in Spain. On the tracks. "Coffee on the table was bouncing all over the place." He told me. Bouncing. In Spain.'

E and I collect a natty red SEAT from an underground car park; all hire cars are 'natty' in my view, compared to my old Golf back home. Nick appears to sort out the barrier so we can exit: excellent customer service, for perhaps the only customers of the day.

And we head off into Catalonia. It's a bright day and it's nice to be driving through the sunshine along the A9 to Cadaqués, with the Pyrenees framing the horizon. E cracks open a bottle of Sprite Zero and gives me occasional directions. But halfway along the way to Figueres she announces: 'Look!'

'What at?' I reply.

'Them!' she says. 'Ladies of the night!'

Across the street I catch a glimpse of three young women in miniskirts waiting at a junction by the roadside. One has her leg propped on a metal fence, looking like a ballerina doing a stretch. Another has one hand on a hip while the third holds a cigarette. They all appear extremely cold and bored.

'Prossies. Prostitutes,' says E. 'It's so sad. So sad to see them there.'

I agree. It's midday on a bright but chilly Saturday and the three flimsily dressed young women look as though they expect customers any minute; or else why would they be there? Who are their customers? Truckers? Errant husbands? It's sad and it's also desperate and depressing, too.

'Imagine that on the A40,' comments E as we continue on. 'They'd cause a pile-up and a half.'

We round the ugly, industrial suburbs of Figueres, and scoot along a road notable for a theme park with a giant plastic alligator and elephant, passing onwards through a series of roundabouts with cacti and aloe vera plants. The road to Cadaqués is indeed very twisty, turning this way and that through a rocky landscape covered with low-level shrubs and more cacti. There are fabulous mountain views and, as we continue, the wide expanse of the blue-green sea. We've made it to the Costa Brava.

Past the Maritime Bar and shuttered cafes – it is, obviously, the off season for usual tourism – we arrive at a square where I park illegally and we take in the statue of Salvador Dali. He is sculpted standing flamingo-like with one leg folded across the other and a hand pointing towards the ground, though his gaze is upwards. The dandyish moustache curls on his famous visage.

'Salvador Dali,' I say. 'We've found him.'

We stare at the peculiar statue for a while.

Then, as a policeman lopes in the direction of the red SEAT, we return to the car, crossing a gravel square surrounded by drumstick trees and seafood restaurants that are open with a few folk sitting outside smoking. Around the Cadaqués waterfront, we find an isolated spot with a little pebble beach on which there are upturned rowing boats. A few people are having picnics on the pebbles, and we join them with food we bought at a supermarket on the way.

Leaning against one the boats, we look out to sea. Not far out, an island pokes up in the shape of a shark's fin. The rigging of a super-yacht rattles in the breeze. Waves slap gently on the shore, disturbing the pebbles. I go to test the chilly water. 'It's amazing to think we were in St Pancras yesterday,' says E dreamily. We watch cyclists pedalling along the narrow road around the coast, overlooked by 'white houses and all that' with blue shutters. It's a twenty-minute walk from where we are to Port Lligat, where Dali used to live and where there's a museum that's closed at this time of year. Instead, we amble around the hilly interior of Cadaqués, with its tiny pathways, poky art galleries (most of them closed), and a small church on a hill where elderly women wearing black are nattering on a bench in the sunshine. They pause as we pass and one of them gives us a friendly, toothy grin.

The road to Figueres takes us back through the hills and the roundabouts with cacti to a street with an enormous Restaurant Wok, an equally big Wine Palace and another set of roundabouts. These ones are decorated with abstract art in the shape of huge metal spoons and sculptures of giant zippers and clouds. We pass 'Pacha' nightclub and high-rise concrete apartments. We get lost. We re-find our way and park in a multi-storey car park next to a building with giant golden eggs lining its roof: the Teatre-Museu Dali. The car park, E notes, charges 0.042011 euros a minute: at least that's what it appears to charge. 'Surreal parking rates,' she comments.

We go down some steps next to a sex shop, cross a road and enter a courtyard with a series of works of art consisting of piles of tractor tyres topped by sculptures of the French painter Meissonier (who's resting his head in one hand and looking half asleep). There's a terracotta totem pole in the shape of television sets. A water fountain is decorated with a golden, pillow-like sculpture. This is meant to represent 'the hydrogen atom, a Dalinian iconographic motif'. Near the museum entrance, we also see a 'warrior in armour with a loaf of bread resting on his head'.

It's a good taster for what's to come. Through a reception with a chair made of spoons –rather 'normal' by Dali standards – we come to a circular courtyard in which a sculpture of a busty woman wearing a feathery hat is standing on the bonnet of a shiny black Cadillac next to a column of tyres with a boat that apparently belonged to Dali's wife Gala perched on top. From the hull of the boat, long shapes resembling drops of bulbous blue water hang down. The courtyard is surrounded by golden figurines standing in window recesses, looking a little like the statuettes awarded to Oscar winners, except that the arms are poking out in various jaunty gestures.

'Hmmm,' is all E says.

We enter a room with an atrium and a roof shaped like a giant glass golf ball. One wall is covered by a massive painting of a naked man-woman with a gateway into a dark tunnel in his-her chest; the gender is uncertain. The figure has a bald, drooping head, as though the world has worn him-her down.

'Hmmm,' is all I say.

The museum twists onwards through corridors and side rooms in which you almost feel as though you are stepping into Dali's bizarre mind. There are exquisite paintings of coffee bean clouds, headless cadavers lying on beaches, naked women floating on pulpits and cavorting with swans, and skulls with rams' horns and spoons as tongues – at least that's how I see them. In the Mae West Room there's a sofa resembling a pair of ruby red lips in the centre of the space, and a nose the size of a small car poking out of a wall. Here, you climb some steps to look through a magnifying glass to see that all the various jumbled objects in the room come together to create a face.

Of this, we read, Dali once said in a television interview that 'I have preferred to produce a dream that can be used as a living room. Therefore there is a chimney, and a mouth that is called saliva-sofa, where you can sit very comfortably. For the same price, we have enough space over the nose to place a clock of extremely poor taste, the kitsch of Spanish art, and, of course, on both sides of the nose, the two eyes, which are nebulous impressionist images of the Seine in Paris.'

Of course. I couldn't have described it better. This is a museum that grows on you, and E and I both begin to get into it.

'I love the colours and I love the mood,' says E of a 1921 painting entitled *The Smiling Venus*, in which a naked Venus lies smiling under a tree with a single magpie in the branches and a bottle of half-drunk wine on a table. My favourite is *The Girl of Figueres*, 1926, which shows the back of a young woman working on a piece of embroidery on a balcony overlooking the centre of Figueres, with the Pyrenees jagged and lilac-grey in the background. Dali, who died in 1989, oversaw the building of the museum and the gathering of works. It is on the site of his first exhibition, held in 1919 in a municipal theatre that was destroyed at the end of the Spanish Civil War; and the gallery had its grand opening in 1974, attended by the local boy turned surrealist. He once said: 'I want my museum to be like a single block, a labyrinth, a great surrealist object. The people who come to see it will leave with the sensation of having had a theatrical dream.'

This, we both agree, is exactly how we feel as we depart, pay our surreal car park charge (a happily real, and low, two euros) and return on the road to Girona.

We have a lively penultimate night in the restaurant in Sant Feliu square – drinking cheap glasses of decent plonk and eating tapas – and a restful sleep in our new designer abode. Then we catch the train to Figueres, where we arrive in the wrong place and take a cab for a short journey to where the international services depart. We find ourselves in a station called Figueres-Vilafant, which opened just before Christmas for the first high-speed trains from Paris. We arrive half an hour before the station opens for the day, and there's a security guard at the gate, who won't let us in.

'How weird, a train station that's closed,' says E. We stand by a barbed-wire fence next to a storm drain, and ten minutes later the guard opens the gate. Then we sit in a pristine departure lounge, with a couple of vending machines selling crisps and chocolate bars: 'TASTE OUR HEALTHY PRODUCTS ANY TIME, ANYWHERE,' says a sign, a little optimistically. 'It's a bit hopeless, but at least it's clean,' comments E, referring to Figueres-Vilafant.

I pick up a leaflet that shows two works by Dali: one of the old station in Figueres from 1924, depicting shadowy figures near a platform surrounded by branch-less trees; recognisably where we were half an hour or so ago. The other is of *La Gare de Perpignan* and much more avant-garde, dating from 1965 and showing a train heading down a mad tunnel of light towards a man who appears to have fallen from the sky. I like them both (but I think I prefer Dali's earlier works).

Our train is soon off into the light in the direction of Perpignan. The double-decker train slips along the coast with views across the calm grey sea. Seabirds swoop above the shallows. We come to the industrial edge of Narbonne. 'What a barrel of laughs,' says E, gazing out. A tramp sits down near us and stinks so badly that we move, as do all the other passengers within ten rows: there's no sign of a guard to check the bedraggled fellow's ticket. And so we reverse our journey of two days' earlier. I buy a microwave lasagne from the TGV Buffet, and am stung €8.80 for a lukewarm pot of slush – amusing E, who has a sandwich. I should have known better: the TGV has been one expensive culinary let-down after another.

Farms come and go. Towns, cities, forests, lakes and mountains, too. Silver flashes of express trains pass on the opposite track; sounding, for a split second, like thunder. And somewhere after Montpellier, something dawns on me: 'If I ever have a choice, I will always go across Europe by rail.' And I think I mean it.

The scenery whips by and so does time. We arrive to the usual chaos of crowds at Gare de Lyon, possibly the worst station in Europe, including ones back in Britain. E and I catch an RER train to the Auber stop and walk down to our Hyatt hotel on Boulevard Malesherbes. Our room has long floppy curtains and a chaise longue. It is extremely comfortable and has a view of a photocopy shop and people smoking outside offices on the other side of the boulevard. We go downstairs and check out a bar with black walls and lots of mirrors. Chinese tourists are milling about in the reception. We pass them and walk down Malesherbes. We glance in l'Église de la Madeleine, a superb neoclassical structure with tall columns marking the entrance; originally constructed in 1806 on the orders of Napoleon as a 'temple to the glory of the great army', though it has been converted into a Roman Catholic church. Then we go down Rue Royale to Place de la Concorde, passing Gucci and Villeroy & Boch shops. 'Everyone round here is totally loaded,' says E.. 'Don't you think it's nice?'

'I do,' I reply. It's just a very beautiful place.

We stroll along pavements amid chic Parisians and reach Place de la Concorde with its famous 3,000-year-old obelisk from Luxor. It was here that Louis XVI of France was executed by guillotine in 1793, and where Marie Antoinette met her fate, as did hundreds of others during the Reign of Terror; 1,300 died in a single month in 1794, when the square was named Place de la Révolution.

Then we walk on to the River Seine in the early evening. The water below Pont de la Concorde looks like molten liquorice, with sodium lights reflecting on the gently rippling surface. In the distance the Eiffel Tower stands insect-like, orange and proud. For a few minutes we simply watch the world go by in silence, taking in what has to be one of the finest views in Europe.

If ever there was a time for reflection, it's now – on the Pont de la Concorde as the last light fades across the rooftops of Paris on the final night of our high-speed train adventures.

As the French countryside flashed past earlier, I had worked out a few sums. During these trips, I've covered a total of roughly 10,500 miles, or 16,900 kilometres, on the fast, and sometimes slow, trains of Europe; with E along for most of the way. This is almost, though not quite, the equivalent of halfway round the globe; about the distance, as the crow flies, to Sydney; or the same as a return trip, were there direct tracks, from London to Los Angeles.

While we've been zooming about, enjoying ourselves immensely, we've seen that high-speed train travel appears to be unstoppable in Europe. New lines are being laid across the Continent every day – we've just been on one to Figueres – and more are round the corner between Germany and Britain, with Deutsche Bahn beginning its direct trains from Cologne and Frankfurt to St Pancras soon. Tracks through Spain will cut journey times from London to Madrid from seventeen hours to as little as eight hours by 2012, it is said, while it won't be long until Geneva will be within five hours of St Pancras (not six), Amsterdam four hours away (not four and a half) and Marseilles five hours, rather than six hours forty minutes. While Europe has 3,800 miles of high-speed lines now, there are, as I mentioned earlier, 2,200 miles under construction. A tunnel has just been completed through the Alps, opening up the possibility for a direct link to Italy; although no one seems to be sure exactly what is happening with that.

In short, it's an exciting time for rail travel in Europe. Even in the UK, where there has been so much disgruntlement in the Chilterns and elsewhere over government plans for a £33 billion high-speed link between London and Birmingham, reducing the travelling time by about half an hour to as little as forty-nine minutes, politicians of all colours appear to be in favour of beginning construction in 2015. From Birmingham, the fast trains will eventually (if Britain can afford them) continue to Leeds, Manchester and up to Scotland. The geography of the country will begin to feel different, just as it already does across growing swathes of Europe – as E and I have found on these trips.

When Prince Albert was travelling with Queen Victoria in the days of the 1840s railway mania, he was wont to say 'not quite so fast, Mr Conductor, if you please'. And the message would be passed on to the driver; the royal couple was edgy when the pace picked up, particularly as carriages used to rattle and jolt much more back then. But it's a quaint notion to imagine that anyone would volunteer to go slower now. The Continent has fallen in love with the Japanese bullet train, and it doesn't look as though any fallout is on the way (except in the Netherlands, perhaps, where ticket sales have been slow for some reason).

Nor should there be any fallout. All the 'science' shows that trains are greener than the alternatives of planes or cars. If you want to be 'eco', all the evidence is there: go by train, it's as simple as that. Sure, journeys may be marginally quicker by air. But when you take in all the airport transfers, waits in lounges and by baggage carousels – as I've said before – are they really? And with so many new high-speed routes opening up, even faster journeys lie ahead. It doesn't take much of a crystal ball to see that what we are witnessing now is probably just the start of it all. Soon, we'll be able to go a very long way, very quickly, by train. Travelling in Europe will be greener than ever, with ticket prices that compare favourably with those on planes now that airport taxes have shot up so much.

All good and well, I'm thinking – looking out across the Seine. But that's not the real reason for these travels. Being green has been incidental. The underlying motivation, what set us on our way in the first place, has been the desire to see the Continent from the window of a carriage... and then, of

course, when we get there, to investigate what lies at the end
of the tracks.

From the famous Dukes of Burgundy, to the wonderful
modern architecture of Rotterdam, the harrowing battlefields
of Fromelles, the fairy-tale battlements of Luxembourg and the
sheer splendour of Lake Geneva, these high-speed trips have
opened our eyes and ears to so many stories and places. E and
I have enjoyed every journey. Chateaux belonging to mistresses
in the Loire Valley, love lakes and Victorians in Bruges, the
birthplace of Karl Marx in Trier, the story of Goethe in
Frankfurt, the *Brauhäuser* of Cologne, Dali in Figueres, Rubens
in Antwerp, Cézanne in L'Estaque – it's been quite a journey, so
enjoyable I struggle to think of which place I've liked the best.
Perhaps Lausanne with its lake... beautiful, medieval Bruges...
lazy summer wine in Dijon... the sleepy harbour in Marseilles...
the hideaway cave by Tours.

E and I have become total high-speed converts. And it's not just
been the arrival; it's been the getting there, too. We've both, to
slightly varying degrees perhaps, enjoyed the whole experience
of the journey; not really minding the sharp-elbowed moments
in Gare de Lyon, snow delays in Kent or dodgy lasagnes on
TGVs. You go with the flow on these high-speed adventures
and, yes, it's not nice when there are delays, but they don't come
along all that often.

Not in our experience, anyway. E and I walk across Place de
la Concorde and go for a final evening drink at the Hôtel de
Crillon, a fine stone building overlooking the obelisk and the
site of the old guillotine. We enter a bar with a shiny black
piano and order two glasses of Pouilly-Fumé. A waiter wearing
a black suit and a white tie with a fat knot raises his eyebrows
and says nothing. He comes back and unceremoniously puts

down our glasses, swivelling onwards as he does so. We can't help smiling; it's a classic 'snooty Parisian' routine.

'These drinks cost fifteen euros each, the cheeky *******,' I comment.

'He could have been working down the World's End in Camden, the way he put those down,' says E. 'Anyway, where did they get those outfits? They look like doormen at a nightclub.'

We continue a Hôtel de Crillon waiter rant for a while, as music over a stereo switches from an instrumental version of 'Billy Jean' to 'Jailhouse Rock'. Despite the aloof service, it's surprisingly low-key at the hotel.

E suddenly says: 'I can't believe this is our last trip.'

'Neither can I,' I reply. And I can't. It feels like yesterday that we were first meeting up at the Betjeman statue.

We raise our glasses for a fast-trains toast (it won't be the last trip really, we'll be off along the high-speed tracks again, no doubt quite soon), and drink our superb wine to our superb time over the past five months.

Our final train leaves punctually in the morning. We're out of Paris in a shot, through the corridor of graffiti and the housing estates. As we go, I try to put my finger on what makes fast-train travel – and train travel in general – so appealing to me. Because there is something about going by rail that *just feels right*.

As I do so, my mind goes back to something I read a long time ago in a book by the travel writer Bruce Chatwin. He said that the sensation of motion is intrinsic to the human make up, as we were all once nomadic and moved from pasture to pasture in search of food. This instinct, he believed, is still with us; a strain that has stayed in our veins through the many centuries. Hence the desire to travel – and to *feel as though we are travelling*.

Maybe, I'm thinking as we pace towards the Channel Tunnel... maybe he's right. Maybe there is a bit of that going on. Maybe it is that sense of movement; that sense of feeling the carriages rattle and seeing the landscape zooming past. Maybe that's why the fast trains seem so right, to me at least. Maybe that's why they're such a better, more satisfying, experience than flying.

Or perhaps I'm just firing off random thoughts on a train heading north out of France. But whatever the reason, it does seem as though a new golden age of train travel is arriving; not just here in Europe, but all over the globe. There are plans for high-speed links to be built on just about every continent – from China (where an 825-mile line is shortly to open between Beijing and Shanghai) to America (where President Obama, no less, has announced he's a fast-trains fan). Whether we'll all be able to afford to build them all is another matter. But it certainly seems as though people want to give it a try.

We drop through the Channel Tunnel for the umpteenth time; all those fish up there above – it still feels strange. We cross Kent and arrive at St Pancras, where new signs are up saying that George Gilbert Scott's splendid Gothic hotel is going to re-open in a few weeks' time.

You *can* go for a weekend by rail to Spain: it *does* work. E and I say goodbye at the corner by the M&S, near the departure gates. She's cycling back to her flat in Shoreditch and I'm catching the Tube and then the bus to south-west London.

It feels sad, very sad, that it's all over... but it's been a fun (and speedy) ride while it lasted.

ACKNOWLEDGEMENTS

During these whirlwind trips, many people very kindly offered their time and assistance. Although I wanted the journeys to have the slightly random feeling of not quite knowing what was coming next (part of what made them so enjoyable), I researched each destination in advance and I am especially indebted to Vanessa Treney of France Tourism Development Agency, Samuel Buchwalder of Touraine Loire Valley, Els David and Anita Rampall of Tourism Flanders, Bruno Cappelle of Lille Tourist Office, Jean-Claude Conter of Office National du Tourisme in Luxembourg, Franziska Heuer and Jeanette Schuchmann of the German National Tourist Office, Roland Minder of Switzerland Tourism, Vicky Norman of Neilson Active Holidays, Evelina Hederer of Visit Holland, Kim Heinen of Rotterdam Marketing, Eddie Everard of ZFL PRCo, Brigitte Obel of the Cologne Tourist Board, Jenny Mathieson of Nylon Communications and St Pancras Renaissance Hotel, Alice Johnstone of 77 PR and Holiday Autos, Amanda Monroe of Rail Europe, Karen Carpenter of Travel PR and Kirker Holidays, and Aude Criqui and Jeremy Duck of Eurostar. My colleagues at *The Times* have been terrifically supportive, especially Jane Knight and Kate Quill. My parents Robert and Christine Chesshyre have offered excellent advice, as has Lucy Luck, my agent. Jennifer Barclay at Summersdale has been incredibly encouraging and a superb editor, supported by the sharp editing of Chris Turton and Ray Hamilton. And E has been (extremely) patient, an inspiration – and great company along the way.

APPENDIX

Quickest journey times, where to change, and latest best prices:

1) Dijon: 4 hrs 40 min., via Gare de Lyon in Paris (£89)
2) Antwerp: 2 hrs 53 min., via Brussels (£80)
3) Lille: 1 hr 20 min., direct (£65)
4) Luxembourg: 4 hrs 38 min., via Brussels (£148)
5) Frankfurt: 5 hrs 56 min., via Brussels (£131)
6) Lausanne: 6 hrs 42 min., via Gare de Lyon in Paris (£114)
7) Rotterdam: 3 hrs 34 min., via Brussels (£115)
8) Marseilles: 5 hrs 31 min., via Lille (£119)
9) Bruges: 3 hrs 25 min., via Brussels (£80)
10) Tours: 4 hrs 33 min., via Paris Austerlitz (£89)
11) Cologne: 4 hrs 9 min., via Brussels (£96)
12) Brussels: 1 hr 55 min., direct (£69)
13) Girona: 9 hrs 25 min., via Gare de Lyon in Paris and Figueres in Spain (£191)
14) Paris: 2 hrs 15 min., direct (£69)

Sources: eurostar.com, raileurope.co.uk. All prices quoted are correct as of April 2011.

TO HULL AND BACK
ON HOLIDAY IN UNSUNG BRITAIN

Tom Chesshyre

ISBN: 978-1-84024-060-6   Paperback   £8.99

'*Tom Chesshyre celebrates the UK… discovering pleasure in the unregarded wonders of the "unfashionable underbelly" of Britain*'
                                        THE MAIL ON SUNDAY

'*You warm to Chesshyre, whose cultural references intelligently inform his postcards from locations less travelled*'   THE TIMES

As staff travel writer on *The Times*, Tom Chesshyre had visited over 80 countries on assignment, but wondered how much he really knew about the country on his doorstep. Were there destinations still to discover close to home?

In a series of mad adventures that took him from Hull to Hell (actually a rather nice holiday location in the Isles of Scilly) and back again, Tom visited secret spots of Unsung Britain. He explored *Blade Runner* Britain in Port Talbot, learned that everything's quite green in Milton Keynes, came to his Wit's End (a quirky guesthouse) in Slough, met a real-life superhero and watched a football match with celebrity chef Delia Smith in Norwich. Tom embraces the unfashionable bits of Britain, and finds plenty to write home about.

TO PRUSSIA WITH LOVE
MISADVENTURES IN RURAL EAST GERMANY

Roger Boyes

ISBN: 978-1-84953-125-2   Paperback   £8.99

'Roger Boyes' thigh-slapping account of a Brit's attempt to make it in rural Germany will leave you choking with laughter on your bratwurst'
Ben Hatch

'Boyes went to East Germany so no-one else has to. Danke!'
Henning Wehn

In a desperate attempt to save his relationship with girlfriend Lena and take a break from the world of journalism, Roger Boyes agrees to make a great escape from the easy urban lifestyle of Berlin and decamp to the countryside. He has hopes for Italy, but Lena has inherited a run-down old schloss in deepest, darkest Brandenburg.

Needing a form of income, they decide to set up a B & B with a British theme. Enter unhelpful Harry and his Trinidadian chef cousin, an unhinged Scot to advise them on re-branding Brandenburg, some suicidal frogs and a posse of mad tourists. It all culminates, naturally, in a cricket match between the Brits and the Germans on an old Russian minefield. Farce meets romance in this hilarious romp through East Germany's very own version of *Fawlty Towers*.

Have you enjoyed this book?

If so, why not write a review on your favourite website?
Thanks very much for buying this Summersdale book.

www.summersdale.com